BS
540
.F7

Brengle Memorial Library
The Salvation Army

DISCARD
3m, N.Y.

.8-491

10649474

BS 540 .F7
Frazier, Claude Albee, 1920-
Through the Bible with a
  physician,

DISCARD

Brengle Memorial Library
The Salvation Army
School for Officer Training
Suffern, N.Y.

THROUGH THE BIBLE
WITH A PHYSICIAN

By

CLAUDE A. FRAZIER, M.D.

Deacon and Sunday School Teacher
First Baptist Church
Asheville, North Carolina
Chief of Allergy
Memorial Mission Hospital
Asheville, North Carolina

With Forewords by

Mrs. Billy Graham

Dr. Woodrow Clark

and

Dr. Cecil E. Sherman

CHARLES C THOMAS • PUBLISHER
Springfield • Illinois • U.S.A.

Published and Distributed Throughout the World by

CHARLES C THOMAS • PUBLISHER

BANNERSTONE HOUSE

301–327 East Lawrence Avenue, Springfield, Illinois, U.S.A.

NATCHEZ PLANTATION HOUSE

735 North Atlantic Boulevard, Fort Lauderdale, Florida, U.S.A.

This book is protected by copyright. No
part of it may be reproduced in any manner
without written permission from the publisher.

© *1971, by* CHARLES C THOMAS • PUBLISHER

Library of Congress Catalog Card Number: 76–149183

With THOMAS BOOKS *careful attention is given to all details of
manufacturing and design. It is the Publisher's desire to present books
that are satisfactory as to their physical qualities and artistic possibilities
and appropriate for their particular use.* THOMAS BOOKS *will be true
to those laws of quality that assure a good name and good will.*

Printed in the United States of America

BB-14

Dedication

This book is lovingly dedicated to my wife, Kay, whose simple faith has been an inspiration to me. Her patient sacrifice has made possible my attainment of a small measure of knowledge of the Great Book.

Foreword

Claude Frazier's interests are legion. Whether it is allergies, tennis, current social problems, fountains for beautifying cities, public speaking, writing, or his charming wife Kay, he approaches that interest with a keen inquiring mind, humor, and an enthusiasm that is contagious.

Because of his deep personal relationship with Christ and his broad interests, Claude Frazier has brought to this series of studies a freshness and an insight that are stimulating and inspiring as well as enlightening.

It is a pleasure to recommend this book because I know you will get pleasure from reading it.

RUTH GRAHAM
(Mrs. Billy Graham)

Foreword

Many things have come out of the West Virginia hills other than coal, oil, gas and lumber. Among the finer products have been her sons and daughters many of whom have gone out to other states to make a fine contribution to our society. Among these people is Dr. Claude A. Frazier. He comes from good stock being the son of a physician of many years who is also a practicing Christian and has served on the Board of Deacons in Baptist churches a great portion of his lifetime.

Dr. Frazier has been singularly honored by the West Virginia Institute of Technology as "Alumnus of the Year 1970."

He is a man of unusual industry, skill and accomplishments. His books in the medical field, particularly in allergy, have made very significant contributions to the health and comfort of many people. It is good to see a man of his stature in the world of science and medicine take pen in hand to write in behalf of religion and in leading people in a greater understanding of the Bible. In this age of doubt and agnosticism we need more men of his breed.

WOODROW W. CLARK*

* Dr. W.W. Clark is Minister, Fifth Avenue Baptist Church, Huntington, West Virginia

Foreword

The strength of the faith lies not in great institutions or churches, though these are impressive. The best spokesmen for the faith are not the clever words of theologians. Both the strength and the spokesmen are found in the Christian layman. It is he who has given life to the great institutions and churches; it is he who has given credibility and persuasiveness to the great ideas and ideals. When our Lord wanted to make an impact upon the world, he chose a few highly dedicated, though obviously human, laymen. From Jesus to the present the Christian religion has moved well and comfortably when in the hands of laymen.

Claude Frazier is one of the disciple type. His work is medicine, but he is curious about and deeply committed to the Christian faith. Medicine is a ministry in itself, but Dr. Frazier was not content. He has chosen more direct ways to communicate his deep commitments to Christ. He teaches a Sunday School class of young men. He writes a Sunday School lesson for The *Asheville Citizen* and *The Asheville Times*. Each week he becomes the "Sunday School teacher" for thousands of people in Western North Carolina. Several other and creative approaches he has taken to the popularizing of his faith commitment. He is a layman who made for himself a ministry and a witness.

This book is another of the ways Claude Frazier has found to say his faith. It is thoughtful; carefully done. There is not the jargon of the minister, but there is the careful work of a serious Bible student. I believe in this man and his work, and it is with deep satisfaction that I recommend his work to you.

CECIL E. SHERMAN*

* Dr. Cecil E. Sherman is the Minister of First Baptist Church, Asheville, NC

Acknowledgements

It is with much gratitude that I express my appreciation to my wife, Kay, for her assiduous editing of this manuscript. She has served as an indispensable aid to me in this work.

To the Thomas Company I express my appreciation for their excellent presentation of the material.

A special thank you is extended to Mr. Luther Thigpen, Executive Editor, ASHEVILLE CITIZEN-TIMES for his permission and cooperation in allowing this work to be republished.

Brengle Memorial Library
The Salvation Army
School for Officer Training
Suffern, N.Y.

Contents

THROUGH THE BIBLE
WITH A PHYSICIAN

The Bible: Written Record of Revelation

As an introduction to a survey of the Bible, we should understand its nature. The Bible was given to man by God through men. God reveals Himself in the Bible. God has revealed Himself in many different ways. In Jesus Christ, we have God's greatest revelation to man.

Old Testament Revelation

Hebrews 1:1

"In many and various ways, God spoke of old to our fathers by the prophets." (Verse 1)

When Hebrews was first written, it was written by a scholar for scholars. Hebrews is not an easy book to read. There is, however, no book more worth the effort to understand. It gives a glorious picture of Jesus Christ. The author found Christ to be the one who could take him into the presence of God. One important point stressed by him was, "Let us draw near."

The basic idea of this whole letter is that Jesus Christ alone brings to men the full revelation of God.

Our first passage affirms an important fact—that God has spoken. If God has spoken, then we had better hear. The prophets declared God's word.

The prophets were "spokesmen for God." A recurring refrain was, "Thus saith the Lord."

God revealed Himself to the prophets in many ways, such as by dreams, visions and mighty acts. He has spoken through creation and nature. The prophets used different methods, such as speech and dramatic action.

NOTE: Biblical quotations in this book are taken from the Revised Standard Version of the Bible.

New Testament Revelation

"But in these last days he has spoken to us by a Son, whom he appointed the heir of all things, through whom also he created the world." (Verse 2)

In the fullness of time, God revealed Himself to man in the person of His Son. If you want God's clearest word, study Jesus Christ. This is the Gospel and heart of the Christian message. The Son is the Supreme Revealer of God. The revelation God gave in His Son was not merely in what the Son said, but also all that He is, says, and does.

In Jesus Christ we have God's final, full revelation of Himself. He was not part of the truth; He was the whole truth. The prophets had a fragment of the will of God to share with mankind, but in Jesus we have the final, full revelation of Himself. Jesus revealed God by being Himself. He is heir because He is Son. The New Testament witness never doubted the ultimate triumph of Jesus. In the end, the kingdoms of the world would be the kingdoms of the Lord and of Christ.

"He reflects the glory of God and bears the very stamp of his nature, upholding the universe by his word of power. When he had made purification for sins, he sat down at the right hand of the Majesty on high." (Verse 3)

Christ was an exact representation of God's nature. The idea here is the impression a seal made on wax. Jesus is the exact image and expression of God. If you look at Jesus, you see exactly what God is like. Christ sat down at the right hand of Majesty after He fulfilled His purpose of redemption. We can reflect the glory of God in kindly acts, sincere prayer, sacrifice and triumph over sin.

The Prologue

"That which was from the beginning, which we have heard, which we have seen with our eyes, which we have looked upon and touched with our hands, concerning the word of life . . ." (Verse 1)

Christ coming into the world expresses, in terms understandable by man, the thoughts of God. God becoming man opens the way for man to understand God. John was sharing the message about Jesus. Christ was not only "from the beginning" of eternity, but was also manifested in flesh.

John says, "We have heard, seen, and touched." "Looked upon" carries the idea of close scrutiny or detailed examination. There was no question, to the apostles, that Jesus was human as well as divine. The Apostles and men associated with them bore witness to the revelation of God in Jesus Christ. The record of this witness became our New Testament. The New Testament is the record and interpretation of the life and work of Jesus by men who had seen it all happen.

Personal experience—"We have seen, we have heard"—marks authentic religion. The Christian message must be believed and experienced. Those who have seen and heard, and those who have believed and experienced, have had possession—in Christ's life, death and resurrection—of God's eternal life and truth.

"The life was made manifest, and we saw it, and testify to it, and proclaim to you the eternal life which was with the Father and was made manifest to us." (Verse 2)

"Manifest" means something made visible or known which had been hidden or unknown. "Manifest" also means "to make plain to the sight or understanding."

The invitation of the Gospel is to live in the eternal life now. "Eternal life" means more than life after death. It is more than life that lasts forever. It has quality of eternity in it. "Eternal" is unending and of the character of the life Christ lived. It is life with God now. It can be a present possession and a present experience. It is a resurrection with Christ now.

The Purpose in the Gospel

John 20:30–31

"Now Jesus did many other signs in the presence of the disciples, which are not written in this book." (Verse 30)

The important thing about each miracle was what it signified. These miracles pointed to a deep spiritual truth. Therefore, John prefers the word "sign."

These miracles of Jesus were performed in the presence of His disciples so that the testimony is of eyewitnesses.

"But these are written that you may believe that Jesus is the Christ, the Son of God, and that believing, you may have life in his name." (Verse 31)

Here, we have two words found frequently in the Gospels— "believe" and "life." "Believe" is found ninety-eight times in John's Gospel and the word "life," thirty-six times.

These passages sum up the aim of the writers of the Gospel. When we read the Gospels, we must read them primarily as men and women seeking God.

Here, John states the purpose in writing the Gospel—to induce faith in Jesus as the Messiah, "the Christ," the Son of God. Here, the word "belief" indicates a deepening faith and trust which will result in a truer knowledge of Him. Belief in Jesus as the Christ, the Son of God, brings life with God. Those that believe will enjoy that spiritual and eternal life which He possesses. It is a life now which is like life in heaven. It is a foretaste of glory divine.

If one reads the Bible as history or literature, he may miss its divine purpose. The greatest fact in history is that God exists. Another fact is that God has spoken and revealed Himself to man.

God has revealed Himself progressively and in many different ways. He has revealed Himself supremely in Christ. The Bible is the record of God's revelation. The purpose of God's revelation is redemptive.

God has spoken to men so that they may believe in His love from which comes our redemption. Man is responsible for what he does about this revelation. It is tragic and dangerous to refuse to believe the revelation that God has given. Unbelief is a great sin. We need to believe with our head and heart. If we do not know Christ, we know but little of God's revelation.

The Christian is responsible to see that this revelation is given to the world. This can be done by the lives we lead: witnessing, teaching and giving.

The Divine, Human Book

The Bible is a divine book written by men as they were inspired by the Holy Spirit. The Bible also needs to be interpreted under leadership of the Holy Spirit.

Inspiration describes the way in which the Bible came to be written. It is the doctrine of how men came to understand the revelation of God, and how it was put down and preserved for future generations. In this devotional, we will study the meaning of inspiration.

The Bible was inspired by the Spirit of God. Therefore, it is divine. It was also written by men and so is human.

Human Investigation

Luke 1:1-4

"Inasmuch as many have undertaken to compile a narrative of the things which have been accomplished among us . . ." (Verse 1)

God selected men for the writing of the Scriptures—men who were spiritually suited for their task.

Luke was a physician and a traveling companion of Paul. In the introduction to his Gospel, Luke tells how his book came to be written. The Gospel of Luke was divinely inspired. Yet, it was the product of careful research. He was writing God's message to men. Many others had engaged in a similar task.

"Just as they were delivered to us by those who from the beginning were eyewitnesses and ministers of the word . . ." (Verse 2)

Luke had prepared himself for this important work. He investigated everything "from the beginning." He goes far back into the story of Jesus, back to the very "beginning." He presented everything orderly, read previous accounts, and questioned witnesses carefully.

7

Luke had trustworthy eyewitnesses and received accurate information from them. These eyewitnesses were close companions of Jesus. "Ministers of the word" served under Jesus and thus had information based on their own personal knowledge.

We are responsible to tell this Gospel to others. We should follow the example of Luke by doing thorough and accurate research so we can instruct others on such an important subject. Christians also should help newer Christians better know and grow in Christ.

Spiritual Illumination

I Corinthians 2:12–13

"Now we have received not the spirit of the world, but the Spirit which is from God, that we might understand the gifts bestowed on us by God." (Verse 12)

Paul is saying that one must have the Spirit of God if he is going to understand God's spiritual truth.

This is a tremendous passage. When men receive the Spirit, they have received God's self-consciousness and are able to understand His secret wisdom.

God chose men well-suited for their task in writing the Scriptures. Paul wanted the Corinthians to know that God gave his messengers their message. It was not just his personal interpretation; rather, it was a message from God. The words were of Paul. The truth was from God.

The message of God can only be understood by the presence and guidance of the Holy Spirit.

Treasure in Earthen Vessels

II Corinthians 4:7

"But we have this treasure in earthen vessels, to show that the transcendent power belongs to God and not to us." (Verse 7)

This verse has given rise to many sermons. The treasure here referred to is the great truths of God, the Gospel of Christ, and "the light of the knowledge of the glory of God" (II Corinthians 4:6) revealed to us in Jesus Christ.

Paul carried within his heart this treasure. He had suffered many things. The message is divine; the messenger is human.

We have this heavenly treasure in "earthen vessels"—the frail weak body of man. We humans have imperfections—physical, mental, emotional, and spiritual.

The closer we live to Christ, the more we are conscious of our spiritual inadequacy. Someone said that the true saint is the last to claim sainthood. If he made such a claim, it would be evidence of spiritual blindness.

We Christians should tell these great truths to others. God can use those unworthy vessels when they are totally surrendered to him. It is amazing what He can do with these imperfect earthen vessels.

At this time, a clay lamp was used. As clay lamps hold the oil for light, so our "earthen vessels" hold His light. Our vessels are His and we are to reflect His light.

Divine Inspiration

II Timothy 3:14–16

"But as for you, continue in what you have learned and have firmly believed, knowing from whom you learned it." (Verse 14)

Timothy was the product of a home divided racially and religiously. His father was a Greek and his mother was a Jewess. However, he was taught the Scriptures by a devout mother and grandmother. Later, he had learned from the inspired apostle Paul.

Timothy is told to hold fast to his convictions, and to remember who his teachers have been. This revelation is to be learned, held intact and transmitted to others. These passages should be a great incentive to Christian parents.

"And how from childhood you have been acquainted with the sacred writings which are able to instruct you for salvation through faith in Christ Jesus." (Verse 15)

The Christian faith is established on authoritative sacred writings. In these, Timothy has been acquainted from infancy. What he has received is sufficient for salvation. There is no need to run after new ideas or the fads of the hour. The Christian's Scriptures are adequate to convey the knowledge which leads to salvation. Salvation comes from faith. To understand how we can be saved comes from the Scriptures.

"All Scripture is inspired by God and profitable for teaching, for reproof, for correction, and for training in righteousness . . ." (Verse 16)

The work of inspiration was the work of the Holy Spirit. "Inspiration" means "breathing in." "Inspiration of God" literally means "God breathed." God has breathed into or inspired it. This is one of the most important statements in the Bible regarding the inspiration of the Scriptures.

Doctrine is teaching. The Bible is profitable and useful for teaching.

"Reproof" is from a verb meaning "convict," "to convict of sin," and "to show what is wrong." The word "correction" is used in Greek literature and refers to a ship correcting his course from the stars when storms have drawn him out of his right course. "Correction" has to do with setting the misguided right.

"Training in righteousness" means that the word of God teaches us what is right and gives power to do right. The Bible is the Christian's book of instruction. The purpose of the Scriptures is to bring one under the judgment and correction of God leading to righteousness.

Understanding the Bible

II Peters 1:20–21

"First of all you must understand this, that no prophecy of scripture is a matter of one's own interpretation . . ." (Verse 20)

Because the prophets were moved by the Holy Spirit, their words were a message from God. The authors were God's spokesmen. In Peter's day, some people were interpreting the Scriptures to suit themselves and bolster a false doctrine. Peter denounced this.

"Because no prophecy ever came by the impulse of man, but men moved by the Holy Spirit spoke from God." (Verse 21)

Prophecy never came by the impulse of man; so then, it is not a matter of one's own private opinion. These Scriptures have a meaning. Discovery of this meaning is the duty of the believers. The proper understanding will require divine guidance.

LESSON IN LIFE

Our Bible has a divine origin. Therefore, we should earnestly and consistently read and meditate upon it. We have more things to interfere with our reading the Scriptures than ever. It is God's book. There is a difference between the books that men make, and the Book that makes men.

The New Testament opens its treasures to the man who comes in faith and prays for the inward witness of the Holy Spirit. Inspiration is important to interpretation. It is as necessary that one have the Holy Spirit aid him in the interpretation, as it was for the Holy Spirit to aid the men who wrote the Bible.

God inspired men to commit His word to writing. To the Christian, he has given the task of conveying His written word to His world. It is a privilege to share this task, but with this privilege comes a responsibility.

It is possible for us to enter into the great work of carrying the message. Over the years, members of a worthy group have risked their all to reach the world with the word. It is a great honor if one can be numbered among such a group.

The Authority of the Bible

The authority of the Bible stems from the fact that it is the word of God. This is the message of one who is the source of all authority. The Bible is the living word because it is the product of the living God. It is the authority for the people of God. Someone has said that what we think of the Bible reflects what we think of God.

In this devotional, let us try to understand what is meant by "the authority of the Bible." Let us apply this authority to our daily living, and accept the responsibility of communicating Biblical truth to others.

Men can accept the Bible as having come from God, but still not follow its teaching.

The Great Commandment

Deuteronomy 6:4–7

"Hear, O Israel: The Lord our God is one Lord . . ." (Verse 4)

This passage in Deuteronomy contains words that have been uttered frequently and earnestly by the Hebrew people.

To Jews, Verses 4–9 were, and are, the primary confession of faith to be recited twice daily. These verses are known as the "Shema," the Hebrew word meaning "hear." In the religious life of the Jews, it is the first scripture taught to their children. It opens the synagogue service. There is one God.

At this time, many of Israel's neighbors had many gods—polytheism. This creed, given by Moses to the people of Israel, was binding on every true follower in Israel.

To my mind, the greatest contribution of Israel to the world was its religious insight. The Greeks gave culture, the Romans gave law and government, but from Israel, the true and living God.

"And you shall love the Lord your God with all your heart and with all your soul, and with all your might." (Verse 5)

Supreme love to God is the first requirement of true religion. Love for self must be replaced by love for the Lord.

The "heart" in Hebrew psychology is the seat of mind, will,

12

and emotion. The "soul" is the source of vitality—the center of the personality. These two words, "heart" and "soul," mean that one is to love God with his whole being. This is reinforced "with all your might," with all your force and strength. There is one true God, and therefore, no reason for any divided love and devotion to Him. Love of God without obedience is not love.

The importance of this great Commandment is made plain in Verses 6–9. The words are to "be upon your heart." (Verse 6)

One's love for God is to be central.

"And you shall teach them diligently to your children, and shall talk of them when you sit in your house, and when you walk by the way, and when you lie down, and when you rise." (Verse 7)

The Commandments were to be taught diligently to the children so that they became the children's way, habit and practice of life. The word "diligently" was used when referring to the sharpening of weapons. The Scriptures "shall be sharpely impressed" upon their minds so that they will not forget them. The parents accepted the responsibility of teaching their children to love God, not only in the home, but in the streets, in the fields, early in the morning and at the close of the day. This instruction was to be a part of daily life. The love of God was to be the control and absorbing interest in life.

The Christian parent has the same obligation to share with his children, Jesus Christ, the truth of the Bible, and his faith. A Christian home should have discussion of religious matters, prayers, Bible reading and family worship.

Christ and Biblical Authority

Romans 16:25–27

"Now to him who is able to strengthen you according to my gospel and the preaching of Jesus Christ, according to the revelations of the mystery which was kept secret for long ages . . ." (Verse 25)

Paul was persuaded that God had entrusted to him the message of a salvation for all mankind conditioned upon belief in Jesus. The "preaching of Jesus Christ" means the preaching about Jesus, His person and His work.

Mystery is something hidden and unknown, but later revealed and understood. The Gospel, as Paul understood it, was a mystery because it could not have been known except through divine revelation. The mystery is God's plan to save all men. This was kept secret until Jesus came—and then it was revealed.

"But is now disclosed and through the prophetic writings is made known to all nations, according to the command of the eternal God to bring about the obedience of faith." (Verse 26)

These are words of benediction to Paul's letter. This is an involved passage. The mystery of the ages is at last made known— all believers are one in Christ. The apostle says that this truth goes back to the "prophetic writing." Always, God's salvation has been conditioned upon "the obedience of faith." Faith and obedience are inseparable. One cannot really believe without obeying. The glory of salvation is that it is offered "to all nations." All men may be saved through faith in Jesus Christ.

Reliability of Biblical Authority

II Peter 1: 16–19

"For we did not follow cleverly devised myths when we made known to you the power and coming of our Lord Jesus Christ, but we were eyewitnesses of His majesty." (Verse 16)

Heathen religions had many myths about their gods. Some scoffers said that the Bible was a book of myths. The apostle Peter knew of this criticism. To combat this false teaching, he wrote the words in our lesson passage.

Peter said that there had been eyewitnesses. Men of unbelief had been transformed from what they had seen to men of faith. Jesus Christ had lived, died, and been raised from the dead. Peter was saying that Christianity is a real genuine religion. The message of Christ was concerned with things that really happened. Reliable witnesses gave testimony to his majesty.

"For when he received honor and glory from God the Father and the voice was borne to him by the Majestic Glory, 'This is my beloved Son, with whom I am well pleased.'" (Verse 17)

In this passage, when Peter spoke of being an eyewitness of his majesty, he had in mind one glorious event—our Lord's Transfiguration. Before the eyes of Peter, James, and John, our

Lord was bathed in glorious light. His face shone like the sun and His garments white like the snow.

The voice came out of heaven. The eternal God had spoken. His word gave absolute authority to His Son.

Out of their personal experience with Jesus Christ, the apostles were even more sure of the message of the Scriptures.

"And we have the prophetic word made more sure. You will do well to pay attention to this as to a lamp shining in a dark place, until the day dawns and the morning star rises in your hearts." (Verse 19)

The revelation which Christ made to His apostles confirmed the prophecies of the Old Testament. The prophet had foretold His coming. The final fulfillment would come to pass in the second coming of the Lord. The prophets filled their books of Jesus' coming, and He fulfilled their prediction by this coming. The voice heard on the "Holy mountain" had the same origin as that heard by the prophets. The life of Jesus proved Old Testament prophetic Scriptures.

God's Word dispels the gloom. The indwelling spirit is like the morning star in that he illuminates the meaning of prophecy for the believer. Jesus brings the brightness of day. He is the "morning star." Jesus in your heart gives light for your needs. It will grow into a full day at His return.

We are to hold our mind upon these Scriptured truths, as one holds a lamp to illuminate a dark room, until the light of Christ's glory appears.

Early Christians pictured the Missions Age in terms of light. "The day" refers to the Second Coming and the inauguration of that age. "Dawn" describes the sunlight breaking through the vanishing night. The "morning star" usually precedes the sunrise. Here, it is referring to the illumination of the inner life of the believer by the Spirit. The morning star pictures religious experience.

LESSON IN LIFE

We grow old. Our home, our clothes, and our car grow old. The Bible's message never grows old. It is as appropriate to us as it was to our ancestors. It is the eternal light.

The Bible is good news of what God has done in Jesus Christ for man's salvation. It is a trustworthy authority.

The Bible speaks with authority about Christ, the church and salvation. God spoke His work that men might be saved. It gives us encouragement and hope. The way revealed to us in God's word is the way of life. We need to read and follow it.

Your children need to be taught the Bible. It is important as a parent, however, that you practice what you teach. Otherwise, the teaching may be ignored. Life service is more important than lip service.

The Bible speaks with authority about God. When we read the Bible about God, we come to know God. In knowing Him, we can have fellowship with Him. Unless we read the Bible, it will not become the authority of our lives.

Actual acknowledgment of the authority of the Bible becomes a reality when we submit to its demands and accept its gifts.

The Formation and Preservation of the Bible

The Bible is a collection of sixty-six books written by many different writers over many centuries. They were written on parchment or papyrus scrolls.

In 1947, a number of scrolls containing portions of many of the books of the Old Testament were found in a cave in the region of the Dead Sea.

The word "Bible" is derived from Byblos, a town in Phoenicia. "Byblos" is the Greek word for "papyrus." The word "Bible" actually means "little papyrus books." For us, it means the collection of Jewish and Christian writings accepted by Christians as their sacred Scriptures.

The word "canon" comes from a Greek word which originally meant "a staff" or "reed." In time, it came to mean "measuring rod" or "rule." It is the "rule" by which the books recognized as Holy Scriptures were selected and recognized as inspired and authoritative. It was a very long and complicated process. "Canon" means the official group of books that are included in our Bible. "Canonicity" of a book means the qualities which made it accepted as a part of the divine library.

God guided the formation of the canon as surely as He inspired the writers of its books.

The Scripture passages in this devotional give us three examples of how God's message to man was placed on written record and preserved.

Preservation of the Message of the Prophets
Jeremiah 36:27–32

"Now, after the king had burned the scroll with the words which Baruch wrote at Jeremiah's dictation, the word of the Lord came to Jeremiah." (Verse 27)

17

These passages in Jeremiah illustrate the formation and preservation of Scripture.

The Lord had told Jeremiah to write down His message. The prophet dictated the prophetic message that God had given him to Baruch, a scribe. Jeremiah had stressed that repentance and return to faith in God was necessary.

Baruch read this scroll in the temple. The king sent for the scroll to be read in his presence. The king slashed the scroll with a knife and then burned it. At this point, the printed lesson begins.

"Take another scroll and write on it all the former words that were in the first scroll, which Jehoiakim the king of Judah has burned." (Verse 28)

The Lord commanded the prophet to again dictate his prophecies. The written record was gone, but the inspired message was still fresh in the mind of the prophet, and the Spirit would guide him again.

"Then Jeremiah took another scroll and gave it to Baruch the scribe, the son of Neriah, who wrote on it at the dictation of Jeremiah all the words of the scroll which Jehoiakim king of Judah had burned in the fire; and many similar words were added to them." (Verse 32)

God spoke to Jeremiah, who in turn spoke to Baruch, who wrote them in the book. There was also included in this scroll prophecies that had not been included in the scroll that the king had burned.

This verse shows how carefully God guarded His word. God does not allow His official message to be destroyed. In spite of human opposition, the Scriptures have endured through many centuries. If it had not been God's Book, the Bible would probably have disappeared long ago.

Preservation of Teachings of Jesus

John 21:24–25

"This is the disciple who is bearing witness to these things, and who has written these things; and we know that his testimony is true." (Verse 24)

The reputation of the Beloved Disciple for truth is well-known in the church at large. His testimony lies behind this written Gospel. He was a guarantee that it was worthy of acceptance. John had been very close to Jesus and there was no question that "His testimony is true." The author was not only an eye-witness, but the writer of the Gospel.

"But there are also many other things which Jesus did; were every one of them to be written, I suppose that the world itself could not contain the books that would be written." (Verse 25)

The Gospel records do not try to include all that Jesus said and did. They were written to make-believers. The material that was recorded was under the inspiration of the Holy Spirit.

Preservation of God's Message to the Early Church
II Peter 3:15–18

". . . So also our beloved brother Paul wrote to you according to the wisdom given him . . ." (Verse 15)

Peter, the writer of this epistle, refers to Paul as "our beloved brother." This shows a fine Christian spirit of fellowship between these two great leaders. It is thought that both later were put to death in Rome by the emperor.

"Speaking of this as he does in all his letters. There are some things in them hard to understand, which the ignorant and un-stable twist to their own destruction, as they do the other scriptures." (Verse 16)

Paul's letters are classified with the other Scriptures. These verses indicate that Paul's writings already were recognized by the Christian community as Scripture. Some of Paul's ideas were hard to understand. Twisting of these writings because of ig-norance of Paul's teachings, or because they were unsteadfast in their own lives, would sew seeds of their own destruction. They should beware of false interpretations of the Scriptures that might lead men into a denial of saving truth.

"You, therefore, beloved, knowing this beforehand, beware lest you be carried away with the error of lawless men and lose your own stability." (Verse 17)

There is an old saying that "to be forewarned is to be fore-armed." Foreknowledge is no automatic protection against error. We need to be careful of our commitment.

"But grow in the grace and knowledge of our Lord and Savior Jesus Christ. To him be the glory both now and to the day of eternity." (Verse 18)

Grace is the undeserved kindness of God by which men are redeemed. The word can also mean those fine traits of Christian character and life by which men referred to God's saving grace. To grow in grace may be to become more like Christ.

Knowledge is more than accumulation of facts. It is to know Him as the divine Son of God and the Savior of men. It is to know His will and do it.

The antidote for sin is to continue to grow spiritually. When we stop growing, we are in danger of sin.

LESSON IN LIFE

The Bible contains the words of God revealed through the Holy Spirit for the salvation of man and the glory of God.

Men can try to destroy the Word, or ignore it—but they accomplish nothing. The Word stands true. The Word of God is eternal.

Memory Selection: "Heaven and earth will pass away, but my words will not pass away." (Mark 13:31)

We need to study the Scriptures—which sometimes are difficult to understand. However, not trying to understand them can be disasterous.

We can grow in a knowledge of Christ as we read, study and meditate upon the revelation of Christ in the Holy Scriptures.

This growth is not automatic. God has spoken and guides us through His Word as we read and pray. Bible readings and prayers are two sources for growth in grace.

As we come to know Christ better, we will love Him better. By growing in knowledge and in loving obedience to Him, we shall increase in our knowledge of Him and become more like Him. As we grow, we will glorify Him and point others to Him.

The Bible in the Language of the People

I read of a man who went into a book store to buy a Bible. He looked at the different versions and translations, and asked the clerk which one was the Bible. The clerk replied that all were Bibles. He then said that he wanted the Bible as originally written. The clerk then brought out a copy of the Old Testament in Hebrew, and a copy of the New Testament in Greek. The man, of course, could not read or understand this.

Few of us can read Hebrew or Greek, so we owe a great deal to translators who have labored to convey the meaning of the oldest manuscript by using words that we can understand.

I will try to suggest answers as to why there are so many translations and versions.

Reading the Scriptures

Nehemiah 8:8

"And they read from the book, from the law of God, clearly; and they gave the sense, so that the people understood the reading." (Verse 8)

Nehemiah read the Scriptures to the people in the square before the Water Gate. Since these books were written in Hebrew, the Hebrew people had some understanding of what was being read. Even so, some of the teachings were difficult to understand, and it was necessary to have certain qualified persons help them understand "the readings."

As time went on, many Jews left Palestine, settled in various parts of the world, and became more familiar with the Greek language.

A group of approximately seventy men set about translating the Hebrew Old Testament into Greek in the third century B.C. Their translation was called the Septuagint, meaning "seventy." The Septuagint became widely known.

The Coming of the Spirit

Acts 2:1-6

"When the day of Pentecost had come, they were all together in one place." (Verse 1)

Pentecost is derived from a word meaning "fifty." In the Old Testament, it is known as the Feast of Weeks. This feast came on the fiftieth day after the second day of Passover. "They" probably refers to the apostles. These people loved Jesus. They were there because they adored Him. Christians have been drawn together for the same reason ever since. Jesus draws men together.

"And suddenly a sound came from heaven like the rush of a mighty wind, and it filled all the house where they were sitting." (Verse 2)

Suddenly, there was a sound such as a mighty wind would make.

"And there appeared to them tongues as on fire, distributed and resting on each one of them." (Verse 3)

The promise of baptism "with the Holy Spirit and with fire" (Luke 3:16) is fulfilled.

There was visible and audible evidence of the Spirit's presence. There was sound like that of wind. An appearance like that of fire rested on each apostle.

"And they were all filled with the Holy Spirit and began to speak in other tongues, as the Spirit gave them utterance." (Acts 2:4)

The essential thing that happened on the day of Pentecost was that the waiting disciples were filled with the Holy Spirit.

Each year on this day, people from many different parts of the world were gathered here in Jerusalem to offer their thanksgiving to God for the harvest which had been gathered.

"Other tongues" refers to languages other than Hebrew. The apostles were praising God in many different languages and dialects. Each person in the large crowd heard in his own language the wonderful message of God.

The speaking of tongues symbolized the great truth that the Gospel was for all languages and should be proclaimed to all nations.

"And at this sound the multitude came together, and they were bewildered because each one heard them speaking in his own language." (Acts 2:6)

The Holy Spirit spoke through the tongues of men of God. Every person heard the Gospel in his own tongue. Everyone heard the disciples speaking in his language.

One of our great concerns should be that every person should hear the Gospel in his own language.

If men are to be together as one people, they must do so under the inspiration of the Holy Spirit.

This was one of the most important meetings in Christian history. It was the beginning of putting the Gospel in the language of the people. The Word was to be translated again and again into the languages of the earth.

There were many people in Jerusalem on that day. Some of the earliest translations of the Scriptures after Pentecost were made in these languages.

Some of the ancient non-English translations were:

1. Septuagint—This was a translation of the Old Testament from Hebrew to Greek.

2. Aramaic—Many of the New Testament books were translated into Aramaic, the common language spoken by the Jewish people.

3. Vulgate—As more and more Latin-speaking people embraced the Christian faith, there arose a need to have the Scriptures translated into their own tongue. In the fourth century A.D., the devout scholar Jerome translated the entire Bible into Latin from Hebrew and Greek. Vulgate was the chief Bible of the Christian world for more than a thousand years.

Shortly after the end of the Middle Ages, another non-English version evolved:

Luther's Translation—Martin Luther felt the need of giving the German people the Bible in their own language. The work took him from 1521 to 1534 A.D. to complete.

Some of the English versions which evolved include:

1. *Wycliffe*—The first English Bible was published in the late fourteenth century. In doing this work, Wycliffe did more than just give the people the Scriptures. He sent "poor priests"

throughout the land to expound the Word. They dressed in rough garb, lived simply and took nothing for this ministry of the Word of God.

2. *William Tyndale*—This translation was completed about 1535. Tyndall died a martyr's death—on his knees while praying for the opening of the eyes of the king of England who had opposed his project to translate the Bible for the people.

3. *Geneva Bible*—This version was published in 1560 at Geneva, Switzerland by English-speaking Christians. It was very popular until issuance of the King James version.

4. *King James Version*—In 1607, forty-seven scholars were commissioned by James I of England to prepare a translation. It has remained the most beloved of all the English versions.

5. *American Standard Version* (1901)—This was a revision of the King James Version.

6. *Revised Standard Version* (1952)—This is a revision of the King James Version. The work is classified as an authorized version because it is the product of a group of scholars, rather than an individual scholar.

In addition, other English translations have been made—a few of them being *Phillips, Moffatt Goodspeed, Weymouth, The New English Bible, The Living New Testament Paraphrased, Amplified Bible* (1965), and *Good News for Modern Man,* a translation of the New Testament published by the American Bible Society.

LESSON IN LIFE

Very few of us in any age are able to examine and understand the earliest manuscripts in the original languages—so we must depend upon that small group of scholars who have done these things for us. Each Christian must find the version or versions that speaks to him, in his language, and makes his understanding most effective.

Billy Graham said that a working toward clearer translations does not necessarily alter the content of the Bible. He likes the King James translation and uses it in the pulpit because more people are familiar with it, but he finds that some of the newer translations, like that of *Phillips* and the *Living New Testament*, make some passages clearer. When he speaks in a foreign country, he speaks through an interpreter or translator. The interpreter does not change his words. He simply puts them into the language of the people.

We need to become more serious students of the Bible. We have the many translations that make more vivid the divine truth. It has been said that the Bible is more up-to-date than the morning newspaper.

The apostles spent their lives transmitting the Word to the world. Some people have died in bringing the Bible to the people. Others have died for just having a Bible in their possession.

A higher price has been paid to give us the Bible. Because of what the Bible does for us and the price paid to give the Bible to us, we should consider the Bible so precious that we measure it and use it in our daily lives.

People to whom God has given the Bible are responsible to give it to others. We can translate God's Word in two ways: the way you explain it, and the way you live by it.

Every Christian should be translating the commands and teachings of the Bible into everyday actions.

Keys to Understanding the Bible

There is a difference between simple reading and actually studying the Bible. The Christian should carefully study it eagerly and expectantly. He should be ready to receive its message and willing to obey the Word. We should read prayerfully and under the guidance of the Holy Spirit. We should try to get a deeper understanding of the Bible. It is very important that one has a proper true understanding of what God has said to men.

Illumination of the Holy Spirit
John 16:12–15

"I have yet many things to say to you, but you cannot bear them now." (Verse 12)

Jesus is on His way to the garden of Gethsemane on the night before His crucifixion. He was near the end of His earthly mission.

During His earthly ministry, Jesus spent much time in teaching His disciples. He knew that they could not grasp all the truth of His Kingdom. What was true of His disciples during his earthly ministry is true of us today. No one has attained all knowledge. A Christian must be taught as he grows spiritually and gains understanding.

Revelation is the bringing of God's truth to man. This is the work of the Spirit. Revelation is a progressive process. Therefore, Jesus could not tell His disciples everything at one moment because they were not ready. It is only possible to tell a man as much as he can understand. However, there is no end to God's revelation. God is always revealing Himself.

"When the Spirit of truth comes, he will guide you into all the truth; for he will not speak on his own authority, but whatever he hears he will speak, and he will declare to you the things which are to come." (Verse 13)

"The spirit of truth" is the Holy Spirit. The Holy Spirit would guide the earnest inquirer "into all the truth." This phrase refers to the truth about Jesus. When Jesus' disciples were filled with the Holy Spirit, they were able to understand spiritual truths. Truth is not man's discovery. It is God's gift. Truth is waiting to be discovered. The Holy Spirit brings us the truth of God. At the back of truth is God. This same Spirit which was in Christ was coming, in time, to be with them.

The nearer we live to Jesus, the better we will know Him. The more we become like Him, the more He will be able to tell us. To a man of God, His truth can be revealed.

Jesus Christ was to die and be resurrected. The Spirit would help them to understand this. They would understand something of God's plan for the ages, including such things as the Lord's return and the Judgment.

"He will glorify me, for he will take what is mine and declare it to you." (Verse 14)

As Christ glorified the Father, so the Spirit would glorify Christ by making clear the meaning of Jesus Christ and His work.

The purpose of the Holy Spirit is to glorify Christ. If we are filled with the Spirit, we shall glorify our Lord, not ourselves. When we reveal Christ to others, we glorify Him. What the Spirit shows to us, we should show to others.

Christ is the key to the Bible. To unlock Bible truths, we need to begin with the message of Christ. To make Christ known through His word is the task of the Holy Spirit.

Willingness and Diligence

Acts 17:10–12

"The brethen immediately sent Paul and Silas away by night to Beroea; and when they arrived they went into the Jewish synagogue." (Verse 10)

Silas was Paul's companion on Paul's second missionary journey. They had crossed Asia Minor (modern Turkey) and sailed to Europe. They had preached in Philippi, where they were beaten and jailed. They had then gone to Thessalonica and then to Beroea. Beroea was about forty-five miles west of Thessalonica and was described as a town off the road. As was Paul's custom

on the Sabbath, he went to the synagogue and taught. If there
were ten male Jews in a community, they were supposed to or-
ganize a synagogue. In these passages are found a beautiful picture of an early church.

"Now these Jews were more noble than those in Thessalonica,
for they received the word with all eagerness, examining the
scriptures daily to see if these things were so." (Verse 11)

"Noble" means "liberal" in the sense that these people were
more free from prejudice than were the Thessalonican Jews.

These people from Beroea received Paul's word "with all
eagerness." They wanted to know the truth. I think one of the
tragedies of today is there are so many who seem to have no
desire to understand divine truth. We need to have an eagerness for spiritual matters. The Lord promised a blessing on
"those who hunger and thirst for righteousness."

They wanted to be sure of Paul's teachings, so they "examined
the Scriptures daily to see if these things were so."

The word "examine" is a strong word meaning that they in-
tensely studied the Scriptures. Sometimes a church gives the
Bible secondary importance. However, nothing is more important
than searching out the truths of the Bible.

One does not have to commit intellectual suicide to be a good
Christian. The great commandment interpreted by Jesus was,
"You shall love the Lord your God with all your heart, with all
your soul, and with all your mind." Note that it says, "with all
your mind." The right kind of intellectualism takes this command
seriously.

"Many of them therefore believed, with not a few Greek
women of high standing as well as men." (Verse 12)

As a result of careful searching of the Old Testament writings,
they became convinced of the truth of Paul's Gospel and "many
of them believed."

We should use every possible aid in studying the Bible. There
are many books available, such as a Concordance, Bible Dictionary, and Commentary.

The people of Beroea had none of these aids, but they were
apparently familiar with the Scripture. Today, so many of us
are not familiar with the Scriptures, yet so much spiritual help

is available through His word. There is nothing which will stimulate faith more than honest study of the Bible. Those who search the Scriptures will find Christ there, and finding Him can believe in Him.

These Beroeans are worthy of imitation. They eagerly listened and carefully examined the Scriptures. The Spirit will bless such people.

Hearing and Doing

James 1:22–25

"But be doers of the word, and not hearers only, deceiving yourselves." (Verse 22)

Hearing the word is not enough. That which is heard must be put into practice.

"For if any one is a hearer of the word and not a doer, he is like a man who observes his natural face in a mirror." (Verse 23)

The mirrors of the day were small and made of polished metal. Usually, they had to be held in the hand. The "natural face" is the face as seen with all its defects.

"For he observes himself and goes away and at once forgets what he was like." (Verse 24)

The man looks in the mirror, may see some dirt on his face, and instead of washing it off, he just walks away and forgets it. Anyone who hears the word, and does not act on what it tells him, is compared to a careless and unconcerned person who looks into a mirror and does not act on what the mirror reveals to him.

The Word of God is here likened to a mirror which reveals to us the kind of people we actually are, and the ideal of what we ought to be.

A mirror does not remove the speck of dirt; it just reveals it. Merely reading the Bible, then turning aside and forgetting, will not be of much help. Seeing must lead to believing. This must lead to doing. We need to do what the Word teaches.

"But he who looks into the perfect law, the law of liberty, and perseveres, being no hearer that forgets but a doer that acts, he shall be blessed in his doing." (Verse 25)

The attitude of the person here is in contrast to the one previously mentioned. Here, the man looks intently into "the perfect law of liberty" and instead of forgetting, he becomes "a doer that acts." It is perfect because it is the new covenant, final and complete. James was convinced that the truth of the Bible stood as the final standard by which all actions of life are to be judged. The true believer is eager to obey. The full blessing of God comes to such a man.

LESSON IN LIFE

We cannot study the Bible as we would any other book, for we cannot, by ourselves, grasp divine reality. Since the Bible is a revelation of spiritual truth, its message must be spiritually discerned through the leadership of the Holy Spirit. If we try to read the Bible without the guidance and illumination of the Holy Spirit, then we will fail to grasp its eternal truth.

In Acts is found an account of Jews in the synagogue at Beroea. They not only "received the Word," but also were "examining the Scriptures daily."

The people at Beroea are a good example for us—a daily commitment to the Bible. Reading the Bible calls for obedience to whatever God calls upon us to do. If a person is morally serious about following the truth, he will find it. Real believing involves real obedience.

We cannot know the Bible unless we have the illumination of the Holy Spirit, a serious intent to study, and a heart willing to obey truth when it has been discovered.

People and Places of the Bible

The Bible is a book of life. It is concerned with the hopes and fears of people. It is also concerned with the relationship of people with God and His relationship to them. The Bible was written to, and about, people in many places.

For adequate interpretation, it is helpful to know the background of Biblical events. People referred to in the Bible lived at a certain time and in certain geographical areas. It would be helpful if all Christians could visit these areas as my wife and I did a few years ago. Geography, history, customs, culture, local conditions and prejudices can help one understand certain Biblical passages.

Interpreting the following verses will demonstrate how a knowledge of historical, geographical, and cultural background can give us a better understanding of Scripture.

Interpretation Aided by Knowledge of Geography
John 4:3–6

"He left Judea and departed again to Galilee. He had to pass through Samaria." (Verses 3–4)

A glance at this passage demonstrates that the study of the life of Jesus can be helped by the use of a map. Palestine was about 130 miles long. The area west of Jordan was divided into three parts. The northern part was called Galilee and bordered the sea of that name. The southern part was called Judea, where Jerusalem and the temple were located. Between these two lay Samaria.

There was a century-old feud between the Jews and Samaritans, the cause of which will be discussed later.

The trip from Judea to Galilee could be made in about three days, going by way of Samaria. The bitter rivalry between the Jews and Samaritans led to violent attacks upon pilgrims journeying from Galilee to the temple feasts at Jerusalem. Therefore, when the Jew traveled north, he usually took an alternative route by crossing the Jordan River, going up the eastern side of the river to avoid Samaria, and then recrossing the Jordan River north of Samaria to enter Galilee. Jesus took the shorter route to Galilee, which was by way of Samaria.

"So he came to a city of Samaria, called Sychar, near the field that Jacob gave to his son Joseph." (Verse 5)

There was a piece of ground there which had been bought by Jacob. Jacob had bequeathed this ground to Joseph. On Joseph's death in Egypt, his body had been taken back to Palestine and buried here. This was a place of memories.

"Jacob's well was there, and so Jesus, wearied as he was with his journey, sat down beside the well. It was about the sixth hour." (Verse 6)

Just short of Sychar, the road to Samaria forks. At this fork, there is a well known as Jacob's well. The well still stands today, and is one of the sites we visited and drank from while on our trip.

When Jesus came to the fork in the road, He sat down to rest for He was travel-weary. The sixth hour is twelve o'clock noon. At this time, the heat was at its greatest.

Interpretation Aided by Knowledge of Social Customs
John 4:7–8

"There came a woman of Samaria to draw water. Jesus said to her, 'Give me a drink.'" (Verse 7)

The request for a drink was natural, since Jesus had neither the skin bucket nor the rope for drawing water from so deep a well. In Biblical times, women were the drawers of water. Usually, they came early in the morning or late in the afternoon to avoid the heat of the day. It was possible that this woman had such a reputation that other women avoided her, so she came at a time when she would not be embarassed to meet anyone else at the well.

In that day, women were not looked on as equal to man. Rabbis were not to talk to them in public. This was a woman of notorious character. Jesus did more to enable womanhood than any person who ever lived. Here is God loving the world, not only in theory, but in practice.

Interpretation Aided by Knowledge of History
John 4:9–20

"The Samaritan woman said to him, 'How is it that you, a Jew, ask a drink of me, a woman of Samaria?'" (Verse 9)

The Samaritans were a mixed breed. The Assyrians conquered the northern kingdom of Samaria in 722 B.C., and after some of the population were moved out of the area, foreigners came in and intermarried with the remaining Samaritans—resulting in a mixed race.

Babylonia later defeated the southern kingdom—and when the Jews later returned from Babylon, where they had been captives, the Samaritans opposed them. They even built a rival temple on Mount Gerizim.

Just as the Jews had no dealings with the Samaritans, the Samaritans avoided the Jews. Hatred had built up over the years.

"Jesus answered her, 'If you knew the gift of God, and who it is that is saying to you, 'Give me a drink,' you would have asked him, and he would have given you living water.'" (Verse 10)

The woman did not understand what Christ was saying. Jesus was referring to the grace and love of God offered in salvation to everyone. Had the woman realized to whom she was talking, she would have asked for the living water of life.

There is the thirst which only Jesus Christ can satisfy.

"Our fathers worshiped on this mountain; and you say that in Jerusalem is the place where men ought to worship." (Verse 20)

The Samaritan woman meant Mount Gerizim when she said, "this mountain."

When we were at Jacob's well on our trip, we could see Mount Gerizim and Mount Ebal. Here geography and history blend together. These two mountains had a significant role in the history of Israel. When Israel entered the Promised Land, Moses commanded all the people to stand between these two mountains. One group of Levites stood on Mount Gerizim and enunciated the principles by which the Lord would bless the nation. The other group of Levites stood on Mount Ebal, declaring what things would bring the curse of God upon the nation. Since Mount Gerizim was the mountain of blessing, it became the place of worship.

Christ and the woman sat at the foot of the mountain around which so much of the history of Israel had gathered.

Religious Barriers Removed

John 4:21–26

"Jesus said to her, 'Woman, believe me, the hour is coming when neither on this mountain nor in Jerusalem will you worship the Father.'" (Verse 21)

Worship had come to be identified with a place. The woman had been brought up to regard Mount Gerizim as the most sacred spot in the world. Jesus was telling her that she did not have to go anywhere special to find God. True worship can find God in any place.

"But the hour is coming, and now is, when the true worshipers will worship the Father in spirit and truth, for such the Father seeks to worship him." (Verse 23)

The woman had talked about the place of worship. Jesus moved from the place of worship to the way a person worshiped. Value in worship is not determined by where we worship, but rather, how we worship. We can worship God at our job, at our home, and in every aspect of our life.

True worship comes from the heart. It is spiritual worship.

True and genuine worship is not coming to a certain place and going through a certain ritual. True worship is when the immortal and invisible part of man—the spirit—meets with God who is Spirit.

"The woman said to him, 'I know that Messiah is coming (he who is called Christ); when he comes, he will show us all things.'" (Verse 25)

From the Samaritan literature, we find that they expected a Messiah. ("Messiah" means "annointed one.") Throughout all Israel, men were looking for a divine deliverer to come. This remark by the woman opened the way for the announcement of Jesus.

"Jesus said to her, 'I who speak to you am He.'" (Verse 26)

Jesus made this startling declaration. The amazing thing was that Jesus revealed Himself as the Messiah to such a person. Does this not indicate the willingness of Christ to reveal Himself to a sinner's soul!

Jesus seeks sinners in unexpected places. He cannot enter unless there is a desire and sense of need. He will receive the outcast, the rejected and lonely.

We, too, should overcome prejudices toward others. Jesus will cross all barriers of prejudice and race.

LESSON IN LIFE

In understanding the Bible better, it would be helpful to know more of the history, geography, customs and political conditions. A Christian would profit to have books on these subjects.

The Twenty-third Psalm has won for itself a supreme place in the religious literature of the world. "The Lord is my shepherd, I shall not want . . ." (Psalms 23:1)

This could not have been written very well in the heart of a city. Did not the place where the author of this psalm lived have anything to do with the kind of psalm he wrote?

The loyalty and devotion of the good shepherd was a matter of common knowledge in the ancient Near East. His first interest was to supply the sheep with all it needed for its well-being. In order, then, to describe God's care for him, the psalmist used the shepherd.

A knowledge of Bible traditions, customs, geography and history will enrich the study of the Scriptures.

These people of the Bible were of high intelligence. Their cultures were great. The Bible people were real people—persons with problems similar to ours.

Literary Forms in the Bible

The Bible is a collection of books written over many hundreds of years and is a progressive account of God's revelations to man.

When we read the Bible, we find many different types of literature. There are books of history, law and poetry. The Bible contains short stories, letters, gospels, drama, devotional literature, prophecy and apocalypse.

God inspired the Bible and led His writers to use these different forms because of the complex need of people. Some find help in the letters of Paul, others from the Gospels, and others from Psalms. We can be thankful for all, or a part of this great book, *The Bible*.

A correct understanding of the message of the Bible often depends on knowing the literary form used by the writer.

The Scripture for this devotional puts before us several different types of literature in both the Old and New Testaments.

A Song of Victory

Exodus 15:1-2

"Then Moses and the people of Israel sang this song to the Lord, saying, 'I will sing to the Lord, for he has triumphed gloriously; the horse and his rider he has thrown into the sea.'" (Verse 1)

This song is a splendid example of biblical poetry. Chapter 15, often called the "Song of Moses," describes how Moses must have felt after the victory at the Red Sea when the people of Israel were delivered from the bondage of Egypt. The Red Sea opened before them and they marched safely to dry ground. The Egyptians rushed into the sea after them, but the water came together and destroyed them.

"The Lord is my strength and my song, and he has become my salvation; this is my God, and I will praise him, my father's God, and I will exalt him." (Verse 2)

The Lord has saved the poet and Israel. This joyful song describes God as the source of strength and salvation. The God of their fathers was personal to them. Each one could say, "My God."

From this brief example of poetry in the Bible, we can see how beautifully poetry expresses man's thought toward God.

Parable of the Lost Sheep

Luke 15:3–7

"So he told them this parable . . ." (Verse 3)

The Greek word for "parable" means "to place alongside of." A parable takes an earthly story and places along beside it a spiritual meaning. It is an earthly story with a heavenly meaning. A parable usually has one truth which it is attempting to teach. Jesus used the parable frequently.

"What man of you, having a hundred sheep, if he has lost one of them, does not leave the ninety-nine in the wilderness, and go after the one which is lost, until he finds it?" (Verse 4)

Luke 15 has three parables on lostness—the lost sheep, the lost coin, and the lost son.

In this parable, the regard of a shepherd for a lost and help-less creature portrays the love of God for lost and helpless humanity. This tells of the worth of one soul as God evaluates life. There is no limit to God's search for one who is separated from Him.

"And when he has found it, he lays it on his shoulders, re-joicing." (Verse 5)

God rejoices when a lost sinner is found, even as the shepherd who finds a sheep that has strayed. It is the teaching of the Old Testament that God, as a shepherd, cares for His own. The picture of Jesus as the Good Shepherd was dear to the early church.

"And when he comes home, he calls together his friends and his neighbors, saying to them, 'Rejoice with me, for I have found my sheep which was lost.'" (Verse 6)

In ancient times, sheep were often brought at night to the village for safekeeping. If the shepherd had to search for a lost sheep, he sometimes was late in returning to the village. The village would watch for him and rejoice with him on his return.

"Just so, I tell you, there will be more joy in heaven over one sinner who repents than over ninety-nine righteous persons who need no repentance." (Verse 7)

Jesus said that there is rejoicing in heaven over the salvation of one sinner. A point that stands out is the love that God has for each individual soul.

Parable of the Lost Coin
Luke 15:8–10

"Or what woman, having ten silver coins, if she loses one coin, does not light a lamp and sweep the house and seek diligently until she finds it?" (Verse 8)

These two parables, the lost sheep and the lost coin, have been called twin stories. One makes a man the chief actor; the other, a woman.

The coin was precious to the woman. She seeks "diligently until she finds it." As the woman sought the lost coin, so God seeks the salvation of one lost sinner. Each soul has that preciousness in the sight of God. There is accent on the search, as well as on the value of the individual. God seeks the lost.

"And when she has found it, she calls together her friends and neighbors, saying, 'Rejoice with me, for I have found the coin which I had lost.'" (Verse 9)

Everybody knows the joy of finding things that have been lost. When the woman found the coin, she had the same reaction as the shepherd. She calls together her friends and neighbors for a time of rejoicing.

"Even so, I tell you, there is joy before the angels of God over one sinner who repents." (Verse 10)

That God loves sinners was proven by His sending His Son.

One soul coming to God brings joy to earth and heaven. Those who seek the lost know such joy when a sinner repents. The word "repentance," as translated in the New Testament, means "turning from sin" and "a turning to God."

Law, Prophecy and Psalms in the Bible

Luke 24:44

"Then he said to them, 'These are my words which I spoke to you, while I was still with you, that everything written about me in the law of Moses and the prophets and the psalms must be fulfilled.'" (Verse 44)

This is one of the last appearances of Jesus to His disciples after His Resurrection. Jesus reminded them that before His Crucifixion, He had told them that all which had been written about Him in the Law of Moses, by the prophets and in the psalms would eventually be fulfilled.

The Jews divided the Scriptures into three parts: (1) the Law, consisting of the five books of the Pentateuch, became the first five books of the Bible; (2) the Prophets, which included Joshua, Judges, Samuel, Kings and the major and minor prophets (except Daniel, which was placed in the third group); (3) poetry or writings, including Psalms, Proverbs, Job, the Song of Songs, Ruth, Lamentations, Ecclesiastes, Esther, Daniel, Ezra, Nehemiah, and Chronicles.

This passage, then, sets before us the three groups of literature in the Old Testament—law, prophecy, and writings or poetry. In the Septuagint, the Old Testament was divided into the Law (five books), history (twelve books), poetry (five books) and prophecy (seventeen books).

All Scripture must be read and interpreted in the light of the Revelation of the Father through Jesus Christ, our Lord.

Letters

Philemon 1–3

"Paul, a prisoner for Christ Jesus, and Timothy our brother, to Philemon, our beloved fellow worker . . ." (Verse 1)

Thousands of papyrus letters have been found in the dry sands of southern Egypt. These letters begin with the name of the writer, which seems a little more sensible than the way it is done now.

These passages are offered to illustrate the letter or epistle form in the New Testament. This is a private or personal letter.

The letter was addressed to Philemon, a Christian at Colossae, in behalf of a runaway slave named Onesimus. Onesimus had robbed his master and fled to Rome. There, he became a Christian under the influence of the imprisoned Paul. Paul asks Philemon to forgive the runaway and accept him as a brother. This letter has been an inspiration to readers of the Bible through the centuries. It has meaning for all Christians.

"And Apphia, our sister, and Archippus, our fellow soldier, and the church in your house." (Verse 2)

Note the words of affection and honor—"beloved," "fellow worker," "fellow soldier." Paul's heart was full of love for another whose heart was also full of love.

Many times, in the first century, the congregation met in some large room of the house of a member.

"Grace to you and peace from God our Father and the Lord Jesus Christ." (Verse 3)

This is the regular Paul-type salutation. The usual salutation in an ancient Greek letter was simply the word, "Greetings." Paul substitutes for this word "grace," which here means "the free, unmerited favor of God toward us." He adds the word "peace," which primarily means "reconciliation with God," but also, "inner serenity and harmony with others which come from this reconciliation."

LESSON IN LIFE

An understanding of the Bible is helped by knowing the various literary forms in which its message is presented.

The Bible is a divine library consisting of sixty-six books of the best literary forms known to men.

However, we must not consider the Bible simply as a collection of various types of literature. Each literary form is a way to give God's word to man. The Bible says that God loves us and has a plan for our lives. The Scriptures are spiritual and written to make us wise unto salvation.

The Unity of the Bible

Many writers, over a span of at least 1,500 years, wrote the books of the Bible. Among these writers were kings, shepherds, secretaries, scholars, peasants and fishermen. One was a physician, one a scribe and another a king's cupbearer. The Bible was written in different lands and languages under varied circumstances. Many of the people who wrote the Bible never met, and were separated from each other by hundreds of years. In spite of all this, there is a remarkable unity in the Bible. The central figure is Christ, and the theme is the salvation of mankind.

The word "testament" in Biblical use means "covenant," and with this comes the word "redemption."

The Scripture passages of this devotional trace the doctrine of redemption from very early times until the first century B.C.

Redemption from Egyptian Bondage
Deuteronomy 26:5–9

"And you shall make response before the Lord your God, 'A wandering Aramean was my father; and he went down into Egypt and sojourned there, few in number; and there he became a nation, great, mighty, and populous.'" (Verse 5)

Jacob lived a seminomadic life. The word "wandering" suggests "being lost" or "about to perish." God saw to it that they survived. He redeemed or saved them.

These verses tell how Moses instructed the people to celebrate their deliverance from Egypt. This was, and is, an illustration of "redemption." As God delivered Israel from bondage in Egypt, so God continues to deliver men from the bondage of sin.

Jacob went into Egypt with a small number of people— estimated at seventy. They miraculously increased during their sojourn in Egypt to around 600,000.

"And the Egyptians treated us harshly and afflicted us, and laid upon us hard bondage." (Verse 6)

The story is told in detail in Exodus. When a pharaoh arose who had not known Joseph, he oppressed the people and reduced them to slavery. Terrible years of bondage and slavery were endured by the Hebrew people.

"Then we cried to the Lord, the God of our fathers, and the Lord heard our voice and saw our affliction, our toil and our oppression." (Verse 7)

The oppression was severe and the Hebrews cried to God. He acted to relieve the oppression. Sometimes the hard things of life cause us to cry to God.

"And the Lord brought us out of Egypt with a mighty hand and an outstretched arm with great terror, with signs and wonders." (Verse 8)

Moses received his call at the Burning Bush. He said to Pharaoh, "Thus saith the Lord, let my people go." Pharaoh refused and added more burdens to the Israelites.

Ten plagues fell on the helpless Egyptians. The Red Sea opened, allowing the Jews to escape from the Egyptians. God had showed His "mighty hand" and "outstretched arm."

"And he brought us into this place and gave us this land, a land flowing with milk and honey." (Verse 9)

His people came from slavery in Egypt to the Promised Land. "Milk and honey" described the richness and abundance of Canaan.

Verses from Deuteronomy 26 contain a confession recited by the Jewish people. It is an old ritual—reminding them that God had, and would save them from destruction, but that they must remain faithful to the laws and covenant of Sinai.

Redemption Through Jesus Christ

Acts 13:17, 32

"The God of this people Israel chose our fathers and made the people great during their stay in the land of Egypt, and with uplifted arm, he led them out of it." (Verse 17)

Paul is preaching in the synagogue of Antioch in Pisidia in Asia Minor. This is his first recorded sermon. He refers his hearers back to the covenant recorded in Deuteronomy 26 and proceeds to build a new covenant on the old one. The sermon is a review of the history of Israel. Paul showed that this was a preparation for the Messiah's coming. Through the ages, God was preparing the people for the coming of the Saviour. He was trying to convince the Jews that Christ was the promised Messiah.

"Of this man's posterity, God has brought to Israel a Savior, Jesus, as he promised." (Verse 23)

After telling some of the highlights of God's leadership of Israel, Paul then announced that God was faithful to his promise in sending Jesus into the world. "Jesus" means "Savior."

We read in Matthew 1:21, "You shall call his name Jesus, for he will save his people from their sins."

Paul traces Hebrew history from the covenant with Abraham directly up to Jesus Christ. Paul had no doubt about unity.

Redemption Foretold by Moses and the Prophets
Luke 24:25–27

"And he said to them, 'O foolish men, and slow of heart to believe all that the prophets have spoken.' " (Verse 25)

These verses are the record of one of Christ's appearances after his death and resurrection. Two men were walking along the road toward Emmaus. Jesus joined these men and asked them what they had been discussing. They told him of their hopes and expectations in Jesus as the Messiah. These hopes had been shattered by the crucifixion. They had also heard of the empty tomb.

Christ reproves them for being so slow to believe the prophetic Scriptures of the Old Testament. These prophecies had been fulfilled in Him. We also can study the Bible and see how perfectly Christ fulfilled these prophecies.

"Was it not necessary that the Christ should suffer these things and enter into his glory?" (Verse 26)

The Passion and Resurrection were in accordance with Old Testament prophecy.

Many learned men have interpreted the prophets. But this Interpreter was the Christ. Human ears and hearts had never heard an exposition of the Holy Scriptures as this Interpreter gave to these men on the way to Emmaus.

It was hard for most of the people to accept the idea of a suffering Messiah. However, both the glory and the sufferings of the Messiah had been foretold by the prophets.

If the disciples had understood the prophecies, they would not have been so depressed by His death or puzzled by the empty tomb.

"Christ should suffer." Over the years, Christians had to suffer. Many years ago a king tried, by torture, to make God's faithful people forswear their faith. An old man wrote a poem which is now Psalm 37. It is about the meek and their inheritance. Jesus quoted it one day. The writer of this psalm tells the faithful that God reigns, and that prosperous wickedness does not last. He tells them to "Wait for the Lord, and keep his way."

"And beginning with Moses and all the prophets, he interpreted to them in all the Scriptures the things concerning himself." (Verse 27)

This was a great and rare experience for these men on the road to Emmaus. Jesus taught the unity of the Bible, the promises of the New Testament, and "the things concerning himself."

The Scripture tells of the prediction, birth, work, death and resurrection of the Redeemer. This is the truth on which the Bible is built.

LESSON IN LIFE

When you consider that the Bible was written by about forty men of various backgrounds over a period of about 1,500 years, then you can realize the miracle of the unity of this book.

It does not seem possible to explain the unity of the Bible, other than that the Holy Spirit has directed the hand of every author. The Bible was divinely inspired and as we read it, we find the message of redeeming love in Christ.

The word "redeem" can mean the recovery of something for the original owner by a payment. The term is used in the Old Testament when we refer to the Lord's deliverance of His people from Egypt. It was also used to describe the deliverance of Israel from Babylonian exile. It was used when referring to deliverance of individuals from trouble.

In the New Testament, "redemption" implies deliverance from sin and its effects, rather than merely from death or trouble.

God's saving work among men, as a process of redemption, is one of the fundamental concepts of the Bible.

Forgiveness is given to those who believe on the Lord Jesus Christ, repent of their sin, confess Christ before men, and are buried with Him in Christian baptism. The redeemed are those who have put their trust in God and seek to do His will.

This subject of redemption runs through the Bible, reminding us that God is love and that He makes it possible for us to come to Him.

Redemption, then, is the main theme of the Gospel. This is why the Bible was written.

The Bible in the Life of the Church

In our church, we are dependent on the Bible for preaching, teaching, doctrines, sacraments, conducting business and understanding the mission of the church.

We should find our inspiration and authority in the Word of God in all of our service to God. The Bible is the Christian's rule of faith and practice, and it should also be the authoritative rule of faith and practice for the Christian Church. If the Church stands under this authority of God's word, it can become a redemptive society—which it is supposed to be. The Church then can be live and vital, and not as one critic said, "The clock struck twelve and the Church gave up her dead."

The church that tries to function by giving the Bible a secondary place will weaken and die as a spiritual influence. When a church tries to live in harmony with the revelation of the Bible, it will grow and thrive.

There are millions of Bibles sold, but men remain sinful. Millions of bars of soap are sold, but the presence of a bar of soap in the house does not guarantee that the people will be automatically cleansed. One has to use the soap to be clean, and one must use—and know how to use—the Bible to be convicted and cleansed of sin. Let us learn to use the Bible more effectively.

In this devotional, we want to stress that the Bible should serve as the rule of faith and as a guide for our lives.

The Minister as Example

I Timothy 4:10–16

"We have our hope set on the living God, who is the Savior of all men, especially of those who believe." (Verse 10)

"Command and teach these things." (Verse 11)

Timothy was to "command and teach" the sentiments in Verse 10.

Paul was in prison in Rome while writing these words to Timothy. Timothy was at Ephesus where Paul left him to straighten out some trouble in the congregation. These are personal words to Timothy, who was an evangelist and minister of the Word of God. What Paul says then has special significance for the Church. These passages tell us the place the Bible held in the public services of the Church.

In the early church, certain things were stressed: reading of the Scripture, teaching, practice and prayer. The reading of the Scriptures was the basic element of worship.

"Let no one despise your youth, but set the believers an example in speech and conduct, in love, in faith, in purity." (Verse 12)

The word "youth" could mean anyone up to the age of forty. The term could be used in referring to the age of Timothy in respect to his position in the Church. Timothy was rather young to have the responsibility of such a large congregation. Elders were usually mature men of advanced years.

The word "example" in Greek is the word from which we get our word "type." Timothy was to be an example in speech, conduct, love, faith and purity.

"Till I come, attend to the public reading of Scripture, to preaching, to teaching." (Verse 13)

Timothy was to give attention to public, as well as private reading of the Scriptures.

In the first-century church, an important part of the service was the reading of the Scriptures. In the synagogue, services in which Jesus himself participated during the entire service was built around the reading of God's Word.

Timothy is also told to preach. We must remember that great preaching in the Biblical sense is not necessarily popular preaching.

God's Word should be studied, explained and applied to life. This can be done in Sunday School. Christians should know the Bible and have a firm basis for their Christian faith.

The synagogue was both church and school, so it was natural that preaching and teaching continued side by side in the church. Today, teaching and preaching go together in Sunday School and Church.

"Do not neglect the gift you have, which was given you by prophetic utterance when the elders laid their hands upon you."

Paul is telling Timothy not to neglect the ministerial duties, particularly the teaching and preaching for which he had been ordained.

"Practice these duties, devote yourself to them, so that all may see your progress." (Verse 15)

"Practice" is a strong word meaning "to be diligent in" or "to practice as an athlete does." These duties refer to public reading, preaching and teaching. "Devote yourself" means to let these duties absorb you, or to live in them.

Timothy must dedicate himself wholly to his task. If Timothy devoted himself to the ministry, others would be able to see the progress he was making in Christian experience.

"Take heed to yourself and to your teaching; hold to that, for by so doing you will save both yourself and your hearers." (Verse 16)

The teacher must be concerned with his own spiritual welfare, as well as with his teaching.

Here, Paul brings creed and conduct together. It is as important for a man to be right in the way he lives, as to be right in what he believes. What a man believes should make a difference in his life. The Bible must be translated into life.

The Bible As Source Book of the Church's Preaching Ministry
Ephesians 3:7–9

"Of this gospel I was made a minister according to the gift of God's grace which was given me by the working of his power." (Verse 7)

Paul is explaining his call to the ministry. He received his calling by the grace of God and carried out his task by the power of God.

A minister is one who helps others. The Greek word for "minister," *diakonos,* means "servant." "Diakonos" also is the word from which our word "deacon" is derived.

No Christian should feel egotistical if his service places him in the center of public attention. He should remember that his calling was through the grace of God, and he is effective because of God's power, not his own.

"To me, though I am the very least of all saints, this grace was given, to preach to the Gentiles the unsearchable riches of Christ." (Verse 8)

"Saints" is the New Testament word meaning Christians. Paul is saying that he was less worthy than the least of all the followers in Christ. He was saying that despite his unworthiness, he was chosen as a minister.

The Greek word for "preach," from which we derive our word "evangelist," literally means "to announce good news."

"And to make all men see what is the plan of the mystery hidden for ages in God who created all things." (Verse 9)

Paul is expressing his profound gratitude to God for having called him to be the apostle to the Gentiles. The mystery was the mystery of redemption that had been concealed, but now made known through the Gospel. All men can be saved through Jesus Christ. God's plan, which had been hidden, is now revealed to us in Jesus Christ.

The Ministry of Music
Colossians 3:16

"Let the word of Christ dwell in you richly, as you teach and admonish one another in all wisdom, and as you sing psalms and spiritual songs with thankfulness in your hearts to God." (Verse 16)

The presence of Christ contributes to the higher life of everyone. The Christian ideal is that all members of the church should accept some responsibility for the spiritual welfare of everyone else.

"Dwell" indicates a continual dwelling. The gospel is to be constantly at home in the minds of the believers. "Richly" suggests a great or abundant indwelling of the Word of Christ.

"Psalms and spiritual songs" indicates the richness of Christian worship at this early time. These songs are to be sincere "in your hearts." Where Christ reigns, there should be radiance of spirit. The early Christians impressed the pagan world with the joy of their new life.

Not only were the Scriptures read, but they were sung.

Many Biblical scholars believe that the psalms were words of Scripture set to music. Therefore, the Bible played a big role in the music of the early church.

Faith is a happy thing and calls for joyous gratitude to God. One way to express this gratitude is through song.

Paul indicates that the Christian should find instruction and spiritual guidance in every part of the service.

LESSON IN LIFE

Every Christian should study the Bible and let its teaching guide him. We need to watch the way we walk, the way we talk, and the way we work. We need to pay attention to our conduct and character.

By studying the Bible, we are better able to understand God's plan for the world. We are also challenged to live a righteous life.

The purpose of the Bible is to bring us salvation. However, it also enables us to bring salvation to others.

God's Word is important to the life of His church. The Church lives only as the Bible is obeyed. Revivals are started when fresh attention is given to the Word of God. Spiritual revival and devotional reading of the Bible go hand in hand.

The Bible, A Personal Book

True Hope

Romans 15:4

Memory Selection: "For whatever was written in former days was written for our instruction, that by steadfastness and by the encouragement of the scriptures we might have hope." (Verse 4)

This passage by Paul is, to my mind, one of the great verses regarding the Bible. Paul says that the usefulness of the Scriptures was not just limited to the times in which they were written. They were to bring light to people over the ages.

The demands of daily life are changeable and trying. It is sometimes difficult to stand firm, and easy to be discouraged. The scriptures speak to us and fortify in us the qualities for perseverance. "Steadfastness" and encouragement are a present experience of the Christian.

Hope is a distinctive quality of the new life. True hope is grounded in God. Since God's Word reveals his nature and teaches us to trust in his purpose, it is the surest means of training us to place our confidence in Him.

Many read the Scriptures regularly and gain inspiration and strength for each day. Start daily reading of a portion of the Scripture now. Let us study and learn the Scriptures. Only God's Word can teach us patience and give us comfort.

We all need to use the Bible for guidance and inspiration.

Religion is Personal

II Timothy 3:16

"All scripture is inspired by God and profitable for teaching, for reproof, for correction, and for training in righteousness." (Verse 16)

Read the Bible ardently and listen for what God is saying to

51

you. All genuine religion must be personal. No one can live our lives for us. No one can answer for us at the Judgment. Each must do this for himself. The Bible is a personal book which can help you in your personal experiences.

D. L. Moody wrote in his Bible: "This book will keep you from sin, and sin will keep you from this book."

The Bible Speaks to Every Generation
Deuteronomy 5:1–6

"And Moses summoned all Israel and said to them, 'Hear, O Israel, the statutes and the ordinances which I speak in your hearing this day, and you shall learn them and be careful to do them.'" (Verse 1)

The word "Deuteronomy" means "second law" and is primarily a record of three farewell addresses made to Israel by Moses as Israel planned to enter the Promised Land. Knowing that death was near, Moses has summoned all Israel that he might rehearse the Law in their hearing.

There is a reason for the second giving of the Law. Most all the adults who have been at Sinai when the covenant was made had died in the wilderness. Moses was now facing a new generation. In a few days they would be entering Canaan. They needed to be instructed in the law of the Lord before they began the conquest of this heathen land. Moses emphasized the responsibility and obligation of the people under the covenant.

The ancient Israelites understood that hearing the Word of God involved obeying it also. When God speaks, He expects to be obeyed. God's Word is still applicable to all generations. It still speaks to our needs. Man's spiritual needs are basically unchanged.

As Moses told the people, so do we also need to study the Bible. We need to study the Bible to know God's Word. We cannot "do them" until we have first "learned them."

"The Lord our God made a covenant with us in Horeb." (Verse 2)

A covenant is an agreement between two or more parties. Horeb is another name for Sinai. There, God made a covenant with the people of Israel. They were to be His people and He their God, conditioned on their faithfulness and obedience to His Law.

"Not with our fathers did the Lord make this covenant, but with us, who are all of us here alive this day." (Verse 3)

The covenant was made at Sinai about forty years earlier, but it was made with all the nation of Israel. It was binding on everyone who stood in the presence of Moses on the day of his address.

God is concerned about His people. The fact that God is willing to make a covenant with a sinful people reveals His deep love and concern for them.

"The Lord spoke with you face to face at the mountain, out of the midst of the fire." (Verse 4)

The account of this in the Book of Exodus is very vivid.

"While I stood between the Lord and you at that time to declare to you the word of the Lord; for you were afraid because of the fire, and you did not go up into the mountain." (Verse 5)

Moses had reported the words of God to the people. God spoke to Moses. He speaks to us today. He speaks to us individually although He may not come to every man in the same way.

"I am the Lord your God, who brought you out of the land of Egypt, out of the house of bondage." (Verse 6)

Before giving the Law to the people of Israel, God recalled what He had done for them.

Moses then repeated the Ten Commandments to a new generation of Israelites. It is from this "second statement" of the Law that the title of the book, Deuteronomy, meaning "second law," is derived.

The Choice Is Between Life and Death
Deuteronomy 30:15-20

"See, I have set before you this day life and good, death and evil." (Verse 15)

Once again, Israel is urged to a serious and deliberate choice. This was an important moment in the life of Israel. The path of life and the path of death lay before them.

They were offered life as a nation if they kept the law. Death here refers to the death of a nation. Good here means prosperity.

There was to be no compromise. The choice was theirs to make—life or death. If they remained true to God, life would be good. If they were untrue, death awaited them.

Moses recognized that men, by acceptance or rejection of the divine Word, would bring upon themselves either a curse or a blessing.

Life is a matter of one choice after another. The way of obedience to God's will is the way of "life and good."

"If you obey the commandments of the Lord your God, which I command you this day, by loving the Lord your God, by walking in his ways, and by keeping his commandments and his statutes and his ordinances, then you shall live and multiply, and the Lord your God will bless you in the land which you are entering to take possession of it." (Verse 16)

To enjoy the blessing of God, then, Israel was to love the Lord their God, to walk in his ways to keep his statutes, his commandments and his judgments.

The first requirement for us is to love the Lord. When we truly love God, it is not hard to walk in His ways and keep His commandments. Love and obedience always bring life and blessing. The love that God requires is a deep devotion that is shown in the way one lives. It is useless to talk of love of God and ignore what He said. A love that does not show itself in obedience and service is not real love. Love and duty belong together.

"But if your heart turns away, and you will not hear, but are drawn away to worship other gods and serve them . . ." (Verse 17)

In Canaan, the Israelites would be surrounded by nations who worshiped false gods. A temptation to worship these false gods would face Israel as she entered the new land.

"I declare to you this day, that you shall perish; you shall not live long in the land which you are going over the Jordan to enter and possess." (Verse 18)

Obedience brings life and to disobey brings death. If the Israelites did not obey God and turned to false gods, then they would perish and not live long in the land that God was about to give to them.

"I call heaven and earth to witness against you this day, that I have set before you life and death, blessing and curse; therefore, choose life, that you and your descendants may live." (Verse 19)

The God of the covenant demands a definite concrete decision. One is required to make a decision and a commitment. The choice is either for God or for idols. The Bible understands this as the real decision which must be made.

LESSON IN LIFE

Man has before him the choice of life and death. He makes his own decision which way he will go. If he chooses life, he must love God, walk in His way and keep His commandments.

The heart of religion is to love God. We must give ourselves in service to Him.

"Walk" is a way of describing man's way of life. It is leading a life that is in fellowship with God. It is knowing and living the teachings of our Lord.

When we keep His commandments, we do so because of a deep and abiding love.

The Bible is God's personal message to each of us and our response is personal. We should personally meditate upon the things we read in the Bible. A person should read the Bible as if it were directly addressed to him. You can never tell when the Bible will come alive for you and suddenly illuminate your problems. The Bible speaks to us today even as it has spoken to men and women in every era of history.

The Bible Speaks to Our World

The Bible speaks to the world in which we live. It has been relevant for the church throughout the ages and for individuals in every generation. The Bible is also relevant for the present troubled times. God has a remedy for our moral and spiritual ills. The Bible speaks to each of us in a personal way.

We should love God and we should love our neighbor. We should witness to our neighbor and we should be willing to help our neighbor.

The Bible needs to speak to many more who are in need of its message. Invite people to church, Sunday School or to a Bible study group.

The Bible Speaks to Spiritual Needs of Our Times
Luke 4:16–18

"And he came to Nazareth, where he had been brought up; and he went to the synagogue, as his custom was, on the sabbath day. And he stood up to read . . ." (Verse 16)

Jesus had grown up in Nazareth. He returned to his home town for a visit. Here at Nazareth, Jesus began his public ministry in Galilee by going to the synagogue.

Worship in a synagogue consisted of the recitation of the Shema, a prayer, Scripture lessons from the Law and Prophets, an explanation and application of one or both of the Scripture passages, and a blessing by a priest or a prayer by a layman. The Scripture was read in Hebrew and a translator turned it into Aramaic. An invitation to read and to preach could be given by the ruling elders to a competent member of the congregation or visitor. It was the practice to stand up to read, and to sit down to preach.

Jesus came to the place where he had been brought up in order

56

to announce the purpose of his Messianic mission. In these passages, we see our Lord's concern for the needs of the people.

"As his custom was," Jesus honored the Sabbath by worshiping. It was a practice of Jesus to attend the synagogue services. It is still good to go into the house of the Lord and worship Him.

"And there was given to him the book of the prophet Isaiah. He opened the book, and found the place where it was written." (Verse 17)

The ancient books were not like those that we use today. They consisted of large skins or papyrus sheets rolled on a roller and kept in a case. The roll of the prophet Isaiah was handed to Jesus and He unrolled it.

"The Spirit of the Lord is upon me, because he has anointed me to preach good news to the poor. He has sent me to proclaim release to the captives, and recovering of sight to the blind, to set at liberty those who are oppressed." (Verse 18)

The greater part of this is from Isaiah 61:1–2.

Jesus proclaimed Himself as the fulfillment of the prophecy in Isaiah 61. He came as the Servant of God, bringing the blessing of spiritual light and liberty to the poor and the afflicted.

Priests, kings and prophets were designated to their office by being anointed with oil. Jesus had been anointed with the Holy Spirit as the Christ. The Spirit of the Lord had come to Him at His baptism.

The word "anointed" is derived from the same Greek word from which we have the word "Christ" which means "anointed." "Messiah" is from the Hebrew word with the same meaning.

The passage read by Jesus was an announcement of the year of Jubilee. In the Old Testament, there was a decree that on the fiftieth year all slaves should be released and all property should revert to its original owner. It was against the background of this joyful year of liberation that Jesus set his ministry. He was to bring the day of deliverance.

Many of us are enslaved by harmful habits. Jesus can deliver us from these habits if we act in faith. Sinners are captives of Satan. Christ came to deliver sinners from this captivity.

His was a mission of love. Christ came to those poor in spirit.

He preached a message of hope and redemption to the poor in spirit.

Blind men came to Jesus for help and He healed them. Jesus not only physically opened the eyes of those who were blind, but He opened men's eyes to the wonder, majesty, and nearness of God. He gave spiritual insight to those who were spiritually blind. He opens their eyes to a new life in the Kingdom.

So much of the time we see people physically—not as they really are. We do not see their souls or the way they are within. Many are blinded by prejudices, selfishness, hatred, animosity and fear. Jesus can heal this blindness. The healing touch of Jesus may allow us to see these souls as they really are.

Jesus came into the world and set men free in the fullest sense of the Word.

"And he began to say to them, 'Today this scripture has been fulfilled in your hearing.'" (Luke 4:21)

Jesus is saying that this Scripture, which they had just heard, has been fulfilled. This was, according to Luke, Jesus' first public announcement claiming that He is the fulfillment of the Old Testament prediction. The Messiah has come, and with Him, the new era of "the acceptable year of the Lord"—the Kingdom of God.

Jesus was the one whom God had sent to minister to the spiritually distressed and those enslaved by sin.

Those who have believed in Him have been released from captivity of sinning, have had their eyes opened to the truth and received the blessing of spiritual light.

The Holy God

Isaiah 5:16

"But the Lord of hosts is exalted in justice, and the Holy God shows himself holy in righteousness." (Verse 16)

Isaiah was sure of God. He saw Him as the God of Holiness who hated sin. Isaiah wanted the people to understand the high ideals of God in their lives and their relations with other people. He denounced sin. He wanted to hold before the people the greatness and majesty of God who required them to practice their religion. God is a Holy God, a God of righteousness, a God of justice. He demands of man both justice and righteousness.

Sinful Man

Isaiah 5:18

"Woe to those who draw iniquity with cords of falsehood, who draw sin as with cart ropes." (Verse 18)

This is a picture drawn from rural life showing how men are attached to their sins. The people were tied to an evil way of life. They are bound to their sins as the oxen were bound to the farm wagons which they pulled. The cart ropes can be referred to as ropes of wickedness.

Sins that a Holy God Must Condemn

Isaiah 5:20–23

"Woe to those who call evil good and good evil, who put darkness for light and light for darkness, who put bitter for sweet and sweet for bitter!" (Verse 20)

It is indeed tragic when people are so evil that they are unable to know right from wrong.

"Woe to those who are wise in their own eyes, and shrewd in their own sight!" (Verse 21)

Pride is a sin. The self-righteous may end up worshiping himself. God warns proud sinners of the judgment which is to fall upon them. Jesus said, "For every one who humbles himself will be exalted." (Luke 18:14)

"Woe to those who are heroes at drinking wine, and valiant men in mixing strong drink . . ." (Isaiah 5:22)

It has been estimated that there are 6,900,500 people in the U.S. addicted to alcohol, and that such a person consumes $25,000 worth or more if he lives as long as 50 years of age. Everyone who drinks alcohol does not become a progressive drinker. Many who have a susceptibility to alcohol addiction are unaware that alcohol is for them an addictive drug.

"Who acquit the guilty for a bribe, and deprive the innocent of his right." (Verse 23)

Bribery is one of the oldest sins of mankind. It is practiced in every country and nearly every area of life. The taking of a bribe indicates a love of money. Money is a good servant, but a poor master.

LESSON IN LIFE

Christian faith is relevant to our times. A true Christian does not close his eyes to the suffering, oppressions and injustices in the world.

Jesus gave us an example of the kind of witness we should have in the world and the attitude we should have toward others. He was sensitive to the needs of others. His concern led Him to the Cross.

When one gets right with God, he will get concerned with man.

The Story of God and His People

This study of "The Story of God and His People" is designed to give an overall view of the message of the Bible, and to help the reader discover the record of God having revealed his seeking love and redemptive purpose for all mankind. We also will see the unity of the Old Testament, and will discover the workings of the redemptive purpose of God in the unfolding history of the Hebrew people.

God's Plan and Man's Rebellion

Genesis 1:1, 2:7–9, 3:1–8

The word "Genesis" is the Greek word for "beginning." Genesis is a book of beginnings. It records the beginning of time, of the heavens, of the earth, of man, of sin, of death, and of redemption. It is an important book of the Bible.

Chapters 1–11 contain the account of primeval history from the beginning of time to the time of Abraham. Chapters 12–50 contain the story of the patriarchs Abraham, Isaac, Jacob and Joseph.

God Created the Heaven and the Earth

Genesis 1:1

"In the beginning God created the heavens and the earth." (Verse 1)

These are great words with which the Bible opens: "In the Beginning God." This expresses the Hebrew faith in the foundation of all life. The Bible begins with a short, but profound statement.

The Bible never tries to prove that God exists. This is accepted as a basic presumption of faith. The opening words of the Bible simply state that God was in the beginning, and that He brought all things into existence.

61

Does the universe have a meaning? The Bible is sure it does—and the meaning is a heavenly one.

God is responsible for all things. He created the universe. Only God could create. Man can make, form or fashion.

When scientists have learned everything there is to know about the universe, the first statement of the Bible will stand unshaken. Men of faith will still be able to say, "In the beginning God created the heavens and the earth."

God Created Man

Genesis 2:7–9

"Then the Lord God formed man of dust from the ground, and breathed into his nostrils the breath of life; and man became a living being." (Verse 7)

The body of man had a very humble beginning with the dust of the ground. This human body, however, was given the very breath of the living God and man became a "living being." Man, then, is a unity of matter and spirit.

Jesus said, "God is spirit." (John 4:24)

Man was created a spiritual being. He is a creature with a soul and has the capacity to have fellowship with God who is his creator. This image included likeness in power of thought, communication and self transcendence. Man has the ability to reason, understand and think. Man alone has the ability to make moral decisions. This places enormous responsibility on him to make the right decisions.

God made man in His own image. "So God created man in His own image, in the image of God He created him; male and female He created them." (Genesis 1:27)

This is a stupendous passage. If we though more of this, perhaps one would take much better care of his body and what he does with it. Man is set apart from all creation. Of no other created being was it said that he was created in the image of God.

"And the Lord God planted a garden in Eden, in the east; and there He put the man whom He had formed." (Genesis 2:8)

In Hebrew, the word "garden" does not have the meaning

that we think of today. It probably means a place that is hedged about, covered or protected. Eden means "pleasure," "delight" or "enchantment." God created man to live in this beautiful, delightful and protected place in fellowship with Him.

"And out of the ground the Lord God made to grow every tree that is pleasant to the sight and good for food, the tree of life also in the midst of the garden, and the tree of the knowledge of good and evil." (Verse 9)

This was a favored and well-watered area. There were many trees in the Garden of Eden—the tree of life and the tree of knowledge of good and evil. These two trees are related to the moral tests man face.

Man's Rebellion

Genesis 3:1–8

"Now the serpent was more subtle than any other wild animal that the Lord God had made. He said to the woman, 'Did God say, "You shall not eat of any tree of the garden?"'" (Verse 1)

In the world's writings, it would be difficult to find so brief a passage that has had so much influence upon human thought.

"Serpent" in Hebrew means "to hiss," and in another form it means "to whisper," "to use sorcery." In another, it means "to shine," especially in referring to the serpent's bright glistening eye.

Many think Satan took the form of a serpent or spoke through a serpent. This serpent became the instrument of temptation.

Later, Biblical revelation identified the serpent with Satan. "That old serpent, called the Devil, and Satan, which deceiveth the whole world." (Revelation 12:9)

He stands as the adversary of God and of man.

It was in this beautiful garden that evil entered into the world.

Satan began with a question to raise doubt as to what God said, and to the love, wisdom and justice of God. This same doubt comes to man when he is tempted. Satan wanted her to think it was unfair, and Satan still approaches man in much this same way today. Satan showed surprise that there was any restriction on enjoyment. Man wants to believe that he has the right to enjoy all the pleasures in the world.

"And the woman said to the serpent, 'We may eat of the fruit of the trees of the garden?'" (Genesis 3:2)

Eve made her first mistake in choosing to carry on a conversation with the devil. What the woman should have done was to immediately denounce Satan.

When one is tempted, one of the first steps in giving in to sin is to begin an argument or discussion. No discussion is necessary in resisting temptation. One word is better than many—and much more effective. This word is "no."

"But God said, 'You shall not eat of the fruit of the tree which is in the midst of the garden, neither shall you touch it, lest you die.'" (Verse 3)

God had warned the man and woman that if they should eat of the fruit of the forbidden tree, they would die. It is clear that Eve understood God's command.

"But the serpent said to the woman, 'You will not die.'" (Verse 4)

When Eve corrected the serpent, he assured her that her disobedience would go unpunished.

The same temptation today says that there is no punishment for sin, especially if one is not caught. One who believes this has fallen to the same temptation that overcame Eve. We are in a universe which God controls—not we. We need to grow up spiritually.

The serpent appeals to the human desire to be like God. This is a right desire. We should all want to try to be like God in character. "Ye shall be holy, for I the Lord your God am holy." (Leviticus 19:2)

To try to be like Him, we must submit to God's will.

The serpent told the woman that to be like Him, she was to defy His command.

"So when the woman saw that the tree was good for food, and that it was a delight to the eyes, and that the tree was to be desired to make one wise, she took of its fruit and ate; and she also gave some to her husband, and he ate." (Genesis 3:6)

So Eve yielded to temptation and took of the fruit, and ate it, and gave some to Adam, "and he ate."

The nature of temptation is pictured vividly in these passages.

There is the look, the longing, then the rationalization, and finally, yielding to temptation.

Eve gazed with fascination at the forbidden fruit. She should have fled from it.

When one begins to discuss a temptation or to consider its merits, he is already weakening.

Someone once said, "I can resist everything but temptation." Many act as if no one could resist temptation.

The great sin was disobeying God. This still is a great sin. This is what sin is now and then.

"Then the eyes of both were opened, and they were naked, and they sewed fig leaves together and make themselves aprons." (Verse 7)

The things that stand out in this passage are man's shame. The eyes of Adam and Eve were opened and they knew that they were naked.

Satan promised one thing, but they received another. Temptation is like this. There is a promise of one thing, but it gives another.

"And they heard the sound of the Lord God walking in the garden in the cool of the day, and the man and his wife hid themselves from the presence of the Lord God among the trees of the garden." (Verse 8)

"The man and his wife hid themselves" records their sense of guilt. There was now shame and fear.

Here we see the separation of God and man. Sin had broken the fellowship with God. The rest of the Bible tells of God's provision for bringing man back into fellowship with Him.

LESSON IN LIFE

Why do we disobey God? This is what sin is. Like Eve, we find reasons to go our own way. We will say that this evil is a delight to the eyes—will make us wise or good. We are also like Adam when we give excuses for our behavior. We like to blame it on society, friends and circumstance.

What has happened to Adam has happened in one way or another to each of us. All of us are sinners and have come short of the glory of God. But through faith in Jesus Christ, we can have fellowship with God.

By disobeying God, we are drawing further away from Him. By doing His will, we can walk with Him. It is good to walk with Him every day.

When we submit ourselves to God's will, we are living as men created in God's image.

It would be good if all of us read the Bible through this coming year. It would be impossible for every verse to be covered in these devotionals, but it would not be impossible to read through the Bible. If you have not read through the Bible before, try it now. If you have read through the Bible before, do it again.

God Chooses A People

From the earliest times, God has depended on faithful followers to make His name known and witness to His redemptive purpose in the world.

To be chosen of God to accomplish a special work in life is the greatest privilege an individual can know. Abraham had that privilege. "Abraham believed God." From this belief, all the world was influenced. By this kind of faith, we too can become useful in the hands of God.

God called Abraham to cut his ties with the past and to begin a new life of service in covenant with God. Today, God calls Christians to a new life and covenant with Him. Obedience is an expression of faith. God expects action to go along with faith.

The Call of Abraham

Genesis 12:1–3, 7

"Now the Lord said to Abram, 'Go from your country and your kindred and your father's house to the land that I will show you.'" (Verse 1)

The name Abram is made up of two parts. "Ab" means "father." "Ram" means "exalted" or "high." Abram was later changed to Abraham meaning "father of a multitude."

Abram had a call to leave his country, relatives and his father's house. He was from Haran or Ur of the Chaldees near the Euphrates River in Mesopotamia—now Iraq. Abram was to go into a land that God would show him.

The glory of human history is in its pioneers. The pioneer goes out ahead. He prepares the way for others to follow. He may be a pioneer in the physical, mental or spiritual realm.

Spiritual pioneers may not have proof of their hopes fulfilled while they are still alive. Such a pioneer does not need quick results if he knows that he is doing God's will.

Always, the pioneer will have discouragements. The man who goes ahead has a difficult way. Many times, a pioneer is not realized for who he is and what he is doing.

Abraham was a man of righteousness and faith. God was able to make him such a man. God can do this with us if we will let Him. We must always remember, however, that God chooses men so that through them, they can bring blessings to others.

"And I will make of you a great nation, and I will bless you, and make your name great, so that you will be a blessing." (Verse 2)

God promised Abraham four things. Abraham would be the founder of a great nation, he would receive divine blessing, his name would be widely known, and many people would be blessed because of his faithfulness.

"I will bless those who bless you, and him who curses you I will curse; and by you all the families of the earth will bless themselves. (Verse 3)

God would bless Abram abundantly. Through Abram and his people, all the families of the earth will be blessed. This could have referred to the prophets, the Scriptures, the heritage of a belief in one true God, and also could have referred to Jesus Christ who was of the lineage of Abraham.

"Then the Lord appeared to Abram, and said, 'To your descendants I will give this land.' So he built there an altar to the Lord, who had appeared to him." (Verse 7)

At Shechem, the Lord appeared to Abraham and told him that to his descendants would be given this land. Abraham responded by building an altar and worshiping there.

The Covenant

Genesis 17:1-8

"When Abram was ninety-nine years old the Lord appeared to Abram and said to him, 'I am God Almighty; walk before me and be blameless.'" (Verse 1)

Many years have passed since God called His servant out of Ur of Chaldees. Abraham was now ninety-nine years of age. He discovers the faithfulness of God as never before. "God almighty" describes the mighty power of God who is able to do all things.

To "walk before" God was to have fellowship with Him, to live as if God was watching, to be upright and sincere, and to surrender completely to His will.

Abraham was to reflect the character of God and become His instrument of blessing to others. Christians are to do this also.

"And I will make my covenant between me and you, and will multiply you exceedingly." (Verse 2)

The covenant with God is initiated by God. God moved toward man. In return for Abraham's complete obedience, God promised to multiply his seed "exceedingly."

When God called Abraham, He made a covenant with him. That is, He made promises to Abraham that He would fulfill if Abraham followed His guidance and submitted to His will.

"Then Abram fell on his face; and God said to him," (Verse 3)

Abraham prostrated himself in reverence.

"Behold, my covenant is with you, and you shall be the father of a multitude of nations." (Verse 4)

Abraham did become the father of many nations. The Ishmaelites, as well as the Israelites, acknowledge him as a father.

"No longer shall your name be Abram, but your name shall be Abraham; for I have made you the father of a multitude of nations." (Verse 5)

When God renewed the covenant with him, then his name was changed from Abram, "a high father," to Abraham, "father of a great multitude."

God's covenant was made with Abraham, but was to be effective throughout the ages.

Those who do the will of God by faith are the descendants of Abraham and heirs of the promise.

Birth of Isaac

Genesis 21:1–3

"The Lord visited Sarah as he had said, and the Lord did to Sarah as he had promised." (Verse 1)

As He had promised, He gave Abraham a son. Twenty-five years before, God had promised to make of Abraham a great nation. God did "as he had said." He always does. He is completely faithful and reliable. We need to have absolute confidence in the Word of God. Isaac was a child of promise. God's choosing a people involved making good a promise.

"And Sarah conceived, and bore Abraham a son in his old age at the time of which God had spoken to him." (Verse 2)

God changed Sarai's name to Sarah. Sarah means "princess." Abraham and Sarah were both old. Abraham was about one hundred years old, and Sarah, ninety years old. This birth, then, was a miracle. God made it possible for them to have a son. The covenant, which God had made with Abraham to make of his seed a great nation, began to be fulfilled when his son was born.

"Abraham called the name of his son who was born to him, whom Sarah bore him, Isaac." (Verse 3)

The name Isaac means "laughter." Isaac may have been so-named in that when Sarah was informed by the messenger of God that she was to bear a child in her old age, she "laughed within herself." It was hard for her to believe that such a thing was possible. The name Isaac may have meant that the coming of a son brought great joy to his parents in their old age and to their friends.

LESSON IN LIFE

Abraham was indeed a special man. He was called for a special purpose. He responded to this call.

I think it would be good to review some of his qualities that helped him answer God's call, and try to make these qualities our qualities.

Abraham was great in faith, commitment, obedience, and courage. To be great in God's sight, one must be willing to do bold and daring things.

Abraham had a vision. It has been said that a man is what his dreams make of him, and he is no greater than his vision of the future.

Abraham must walk and live as if before God and in His presence. He would be stronger if he walked before God. We need to walk and live daily as before God because we are in His presence.

Abraham was patient and waited a long time on the promise

of God. He not only endured trustingly, but he also obeyed the call of God. He trusted and obeyed. Faith and works go together.

God wants each of us to do something. Let us seek His will in our lives, and strive for those qualities which will enable us to respond to His call.

Heirs of the Covenant

Abraham had a son called Isaac. Isaac had two sons, Esau and Jacob.

Jacob, under the direction of his mother, deceived his father and received the blessing that would have gone to his twin brother, Esau. When Esau learned of this, he vowed to kill his brother after their father died.

Jacob's mother, Rebekah, and Isaac, his father, felt it best for him to leave home and go to Haran. Haran had been the home of Abram, and also was the home of the kinfolk of Jacob's mother. Rebekah thought that Esau would seek revenge against his brother, and Isaac did not want Jacob to "take a wife of the daughters of Canaan." (Genesis 28:1)

Jacob then set out for Haran, a journey of some four hundred miles, to visit his uncle, Laban.

Jacob's Encounter with God

Genesis 28:10–14

"Jacob left Beer-sheba, and went toward Haran." (Verse 10)

Beer-sheba is in the desert, southwest of the Dead Sea. It marked the southern boundary of the traditional territory of Israel.

"And he came to a certain place, and stayed there that night, because the sun had set. Taking one of the stones of the place, he put it under his head and lay down in that place to sleep." (Verse 11)

The meaning of "a certain place" can mean a well-known sanctuary. Later, Jacob called the place Bethel. Bethel means "the house of God."

Scattered about were large stones. Jacob took one of the stones for a pillow and went to sleep.

"And he dreamed that there was a ladder set up on the earth, and the top of it reached to heaven; and behold, the angels of God were ascending and descending on it!" (Verse 12)

As Jacob slept, he dreamed that he saw a ladder or stairway to heaven with angels going up and down on it.

"And behold, the Lord stood above it and said, 'I am the Lord, the God of Abraham your father and the God of Isaac; the land on which you lie I will give to you and your descendants.'" (Verse 13)

Here, the Lord reveals that He is the same God who covenanted with Abraham and Isaac. He now makes the same covenant promise to Jacob.

Jacob was by himself, frightened and lonely. He was fleeing the wrath of Esau. He lay down in "a certain place" and dreamed one of the famous dreams of history. Frightened and lonely when he went to sleep, he awoke with a new strength of faith in a God who would not let him go.

Like Jacob, we need to trust God completely. We need a strong faith for troubled times. When our lives are shaken, we need an unshakeable faith. Jesus told a parable of two houses—one built on sand and the other on rock. When the weather is good, it is difficult to tell the difference between the two; but when there is a storm, then one can see the difference.

We need to be able to see, in faith, what is unshakeable. We need to hold tight to Him in the time of trouble. We need a faith in Him who is "from everlasting to everlasting . . . the same, yesterday, today and forever."

Paul met Jesus on the road to Damascus in a sudden blinding flash of light. Jacob had his dream where he met God and came away a much stronger man in his faith. These were divine human encounters. All through the Old and New Testaments, God was trying to bring man into right relationship with himself and his fellowmen. This is the story of the Bible.

God spoke to these men. He speaks to different men in different ways. God will come to each man in his own way. He will speak to us if we will let Him.

Jacob Becomes Israel

Genesis 35:9–12

"God appeared to Jacob again, when he came from Paddan-aram, and blessed him." (Verse 9)

Jacob left Bethel and went to Haran. Here he met, loved and finally married Rachel, one of the daughters of Laban. He had agreed to work for Laban for seven years for the hand of Rachel in marriage. Laban deceived Jacob and gave him Leah, another daughter, instead. Jacob served Laban seven more years for Rachel. After twenty years, Jacob left Haran with his family and possessions.

Many years have gone by since Jacob first met God at Bethel. He had become the father of eleven sons and at least one daughter. In Chapter 35, four burials took place. Jacob buried the foreign gods of some of his family. He buried Rebekah's nurse. He buried his wife Rachel, who died in childbirth. Finally, he buried his father, Isaac. One by one, those closest to Jacob were called home in death. At such a time, he needed a new experience with God.

Once again, at Bethel, God spoke to Jacob and blessed him.

"And God said to him, 'Your name is Jacob; no longer shall your name be called Jacob, but Israel shall be your name.' So his name was called Israel." (Verse 10)

No longer would he be called Jacob, which probably originally meant "may God protect." He would be called Israel, meaning "prince of God," "warrior of God," "God strives" or "may God rule."

This name, "Israel," became the collective name of Jacob's descendants and of the nation.

Jacob Enters Egypt

Genesis 46:1–4

"So Israel took his journey with all that he had, and came to Beer-sheba, and offered sacrifices to the God of his father Isaac." (Verse 1)

Of Jacob's twelve sons, one was Joseph. Joseph was sold by his brothers to a group of merchants who took him to Egypt where he was sold into slavery. Through a series of events, Joseph was made governor of Egypt. Joseph interpreted dreams. One of these dreams told of a famine. When that famine came, "all countries came into Egypt to Joseph for to buy corn." (Genesis 41:57)

Jacob sent his sons into Egypt. They did not at first recognize Joseph, whom they had sold into slavery. Joseph revealed his identity and invited the whole family to Egypt.

Jacob was traveling once again. Now, as an old man, he was going to Egypt. To Joseph he would go. "Joseph my son is still alive; I will go and see him before I die." (Genesis 45:28)

On the way, at Beer-sheba, Jacob faithfully offered sacrifices "to the God of his father Isaac."

It seemed that Jacob was frequently saying good-bye, as we all are. Some of these good-byes are temporary—and some permanent. The word "good-bye" is a contraction of "God be with you." Would it not be better if we used the full expression? Would not all partings be a little easier if we reminded ourselves that God is with us and with those from whomever we part?

"And God spoke to Israel in visions of the night, and said, 'Jacob, Jacob,' and he said, 'Here am I.' " (Genesis 46:2)

"Here am I" is the response of faith and obedience. In the Scripture are instances of individuals who, hearing the voice of God, gave this meaningful response. God does not ask about our ability or inability, but about our availability.

"Then he said, 'I am God, the God of your fathers; do not be afraid to go down to Egypt; for I will there make of you a great nation.' " (Verse 3)

We can sense something of the tenderness of God toward His servant in the calling of his name, "Jacob, Jacob," and the way He identifies Himself as the "God of your fathers." We see here the tenderness of a great God as He deals with one who has followed Him a long time.

A boy is sold into slavery. He became a great man in Egypt. His family followed him there. The family and clan grew to be a numerous people. From their sojourn in Egypt comes Moses, the Passover, the Exodus, and the road to the Promised Land. God assured Jacob of what would happen. Jacob was told not to be afraid to go down to Egypt. God saw what Jacob could not see.

"I will go down with you to Egypt, and I will also bring you up again; and Joseph's hand shall close your eyes." (Verse 4)

These words must have been reassuring to Jacob. He was not to go alone. God comforted Jacob with the assurance that Joseph would be near him at the time of his death.

LESSON IN LIFE

Once there was a little boy playing on the deck of a ship in a severe storm. One of the passengers asked him why he was not scared. He replied that his father was the captain of the ship.

God can be the captain of your life and guide you as He guided Jacob.

God's guidance may be as real an experience today as then. The guidance is promised to us through the Holy Spirit.

Is the God of Jacob your God? If not, take Him by an act of faith and commitment.

God Delivers His People

We now come to an important event that contributed to Old Testament faith—the Exodus from Egypt. Not many stories in the Bible have more drama than the deliverance of Israel from Egypt. The Exodus is a picture of God's redemption and concern for men. A person's bondage to sin is as real as the slavery was in Egypt.

Historical Setting

The call of Abraham has been roughly dated at about 2000 B.C. Jacob entered Egypt with all of Israel around 1700 B.C. The book of Genesis closes with the death of Joseph.

The early days of Israel in Egypt were marked with hospitality. Changes occurred later.

"Now there arose a new king over Egypt, who did not know Joseph." (Exodus 1:8)

The new pharaoh "set taskmasters over them to afflict them with heavy burdens." (Exodus 1:10).

The Israelites were treated like slaves and their lives became intolerable.

Meanwhile, in Midian, God was preparing a man named Moses.

The God Who Delivers His People

Exodus 2:23

"In the course of those many days the king of Egypt died. And the people of Israel groaned under their bondage, and cried out for help, and their cry under bondage came up to God." (Verse 23)

Israel was severely oppressed by the king of Egypt. The Israelites in their great misery cried out for help. God heard Israel's crying and groaning. He heard them and listened.

God will listen to each one of us. He will be attentive toward

77

the prayers of His saints. He will also listen to those who repent and ask for His forgiveness and believe in His name. Do not hesitate. Lay your whole case before Him.

God Remembers

Exodus 2:24–25

"And God heard their groaning and God remembered his covenant with Abraham, with Isaac, and with Jacob." (Verse 24)

The covenant was that agreement which God had made with his people—that He would bless them and use them to bless all nations. God would stand by them.

"God remembered His covenant." God does not forget any of the promises He makes to any of us. Someone has estimated that there are more than 7,400 promises in the Bible. Think what a source of grace and strength this should give to us. These promises come from a God who never forgets.

"And God saw the people of Israel, and God knew their condition." (Verse 25)

Nothing lies beyond the knowledge of God. This passage was written to tell what happened to the oppressed Hebrews. It was also written to be read by all the oppressed. They can know that God hears, remembers, sees, and knows their sufferings and cries. Yes, our God knows and cares.

God Sees and Hears

Exodus 3:7

"Then the Lord said, 'I have seen the affliction of my people who are in Egypt, and have heard their cry because of their taskmasters; I know their sufferings.'" (Verse 7)

God calls Israel "my people." He was aware of their troubles. He had seen and understood. "I know their suffering." He knows of your suffering. He cares. He is a God of love. God always hears the laments of His suffering people.

God Delivers

Exodus 3:8

"And I have come down to deliver them out of the hand of the Egyptians, and to bring them up out of that land to a good and broad land, a land flowing with milk and honey." (Verse 8)

"A land flowing with milk and honey" became an expression for the Promised Land.

God was saying that He would deliver them. What God says He will do, He *will* do.

The Passover

Exodus 12:21, 23–27

"Then Moses called all the elders of Israel, and said to them, 'Select lambs for yourselves according to your families, and kill the passover lamb.'" (Verse 21)

In the previous chapters in Exodus, God had commissioned Moses to represent His people before the pharaoh. Moses begged a stubborn pharaoh to let his people go. A series of plagues failed to change the pharaoh's mind. Now a plague of the killing of the first-born of Egypt is announced. God remembers the descendants of Abraham, Isaac and Jacob, and spares their first-born.

Moses was advised by God on how to proceed in preparing His people for their escape from Egypt. Moses and Aaron so instruct the Israelites.

Only homes with the blood of the lamb on their doorways would be passed over on the night of death.

The Israelites were to select a lamb which was without blemish, and was a male of the first year. The lamb was to be killed on the evening of the Passover, and the blood was to be sprinkled on the doorposts and lintel of each house as a sign of their obedient faith. Faith must be exercised, and this was an outward sign of an inner faith. When the angel saw this sign, he would spare the first-born in that house. The lamb was to be roasted whole and eaten with unleavened bread and bitter herbs The people were to be fully dressed with staff in hand, ready to leave in haste. It became memorialized as a continued observance.

This was a beautiful picture of the work of Christ on the Cross, shedding His blood in order that we, by faith in Him, might be cleansed from sin. It was at the Passover supper that our Lord chose to institute His own memorial supper. When we confess Christ before men, this is an outward sign of an inner faith.

The Israelite on that night believed God's word. He may have not understood how the blood of the lamb could protect him, but because of his faith, he obediently followed the instruction.

We may not completely understand the mystery of the cross. Even though we cannot understand, we believe that in the sacrifice of Jesus, our sins were taken away. The Lamb of God shed His blood for the release of all men from the bondage of sin.

The Salvation of God

Exodus 14:30–31

"Thus the Lord saved Israel that day from the hand of the Egyptians; and Israel saw the Egyptians dead upon the seashore." (Verse 30)

Chapter 14 of Exodus gives a description of Israel's departure from Egypt: They came to the Red Sea, followed by the pharaoh's army. They successfully crossed the sea just before the waters came together to destroy pharaoh's army. The Lord saved Israel that day out of the hand of Egypt.

"And Israel saw the great work which the Lord did against the Egyptians, and the people feared the Lord; and they believed in the Lord and in his servant Moses." (Verse 31)

These mighty acts of God led to more belief and faith. The three key words in this verse are "saw," "feared" and "believed." The people had an increased fear of, and reverence for, the Lord. As an example, note the words of Proverbs 1:7, "The fear of the Lord is the beginning of knowledge."

LESSON IN LIFE

God delivered the Israelites from bondage. His deliverance did not cease with the Reed Sea.

Many men today are in the bondage of sin. We are still being delivered daily from sin, guilt and death, by the shedding of His sacrificial blood, the blood of the Lamb of God. There is no salvation without faith in Christ. It is the blood of Christ that is the price of redemption for sinners today. We are saved by the sacrifice of Jesus on the Cross.

He can make you a free man—but you must repent and believe. The one who believes is eager to obey. Trusting God and obeying God go together.

Deliverance from sin will come when one obeys the commandment of God to believe on Christ, and to receive Him as personal Saviour. When we do this, God's deliverance will bring the end of bondage and the beginning of freedom.

God's Covenant and Law

The Exodus, or God's deliverance of His people from bondage in Egypt, was an important event in Hebrew history and faith.

In the following devotional, God renews His covenant with all the people of Israel. This was the end of the time of bondage and a beginning of time of freedom and responsibility. They were to no longer be servants of the pharaoh, but were on their way to becoming servants of God.

When the Israelites left Egypt, they headed for Mount Sinai and arrived there about three months later after many tribulations.

Basis of the Covenant

Exodus 19:3–4

"And Moses went up to God, and the Lord called him out of the mountain, saying, 'Thus, you shall say to the house of Jacob, and tell the people of Israel.'" (Verse 3)

The people of Israel camped at the base of Mount Sinai. Moses went up into the mountain. God calls out to him to make a covenant with the people of Israel. God took the initiative in proposing the covenant.

"You have seen what I did to the Egyptians, and how I bore you on eagles' wings and brought you to myself." (Verse 4)

The pledge for God's faithfulness and power in the covenant is His redemptive action already seen in the deliverance.

The memories of Egypt were still in the minds of the Israelites. God had brought them out of Egypt. He had gone with them. He had given them water when they thirsted and food when they starved. God had carried them "on eagles' wings" safely beyond the reach of their enemies. The phrase "eagles' wings"

82

denotes the strong and loving care of God. He had done His part. They needed to do theirs.

Conditions of the Covenant

"Now therefore, if you will obey my voice and keep my covenant, you shall be my own possession among all peoples; for all the earth is mine." (Verse 5)

The covenant was between Yahweh and His servants. Obedience was the central role of Israel. This obedience is expressed in faith and loyalty. To "keep my covenant" probably meant obeying the Law.

God loved the people of Israel with a special love and had helped them in special ways. If they would respond as He desired, they would be His "own possessions."

Despite the fact that God created them and redeemed them from Egypt, the people were free. Their decision to obey God's voice and to enslave themselves to Him was a free decision. By keeping the covenant, the people became God's possession.

"And you shall be to me a kingdom of priests and a holy nation. These are the words which you shall speak to the children of Israel." (Verse 6)

The covenant is with the people and Israel will fulfill the role of priest in the world.

It will be a "holy nation" set apart for a peculiar task. Israel was to be the church. They were to be God's ministers on earth.

Response

"So Moses came and called the elders of the people, and set before them all these words which the Lord had commanded him." (Verse 7)

Moses communicated the message of God to the elders and they gave it to the people.

"And all the people answered together and said, 'All that the Lord has spoken we will do.'" (Verse 8)

Having witnessed the gracious movement of God on their

behalf, they felt compelled to say, "All that the Lord has spoken, we will do." They committed themselves to their side of the agreement. They promised to obey the Lord and to keep His covenant.

God's Revelation of Himself to His People
Exodus 19:16–17

"On the morning of the third day there were thunders and lightnings, and a thick cloud upon the mountain, and a very loud trumpet blast, so that all the people who were in the camp trembled." (Verse 16)

After the people accepted the covenant, Moses commanded them to undergo a ceremonial purification for three days. Moses then brought them to the foot of Mount Sinai to meet God.

Mount Sinai was bathed in lightning and sounds of thunder filled the air. Thick clouds covered the mountain. God was revealing Himself in a mighty power. They did not see God, but felt His presence—and the people "trembled."

The People's Fear of God
Exodus 20:18–20

"Now when all the people perceived the thunderings and the lightnings and the sound of the trumpet and the mountain smoking, the people were afraid and trembled; and they stood afar off." (Verse 18)

For this narrator, awe and respect are taken as the normal mood of religion. God is holy.

The Ten Commandments had been given to Moses on Mount Sinai. Moses returned from the mountain and found the people still gathered together. The people were some distance from the mountain because of their fear. Awe and fear caused the Israelites to move from the mountain.

"And they said to Moses, 'You speak to us, and we will hear; but let not God speak to us, lest we die.'" (Verse 19).

The people of Israel were overwhelmed with the sense of the presence of God. They asked Moses to become the mediator of the Law to the people. They promised to "hear," that is, to obey His words.

We, too, are furnished a mediator between ourselves and the Father: Jesus Christ. "For there is one God, and there is one mediator between God and men, the man Christ Jesus." (I Timothy 2:5)

"And Moses said to the people, 'Do not fear, for God has come to prove you, and that the fear of Him may be before your eyes, that you may not sin.'" (Exodus 20:20)

Moses explains the terrible scene as a manifestation of God's goodness to Israel. It is another sign of His power so "that you may not sin." Sin is understood as a lack of faith in God. To have "the fear of Him" is to live by faith in His power and reality.

God came to test or prove Israel, and not to frighten them. He wanted them to respect Him and have reverence for Him. The fear of the Lord can be defined as a respect for God's holiness, God's righteousness and God's judgment. To fear God is to have a genuine reverence for God, and to desire to do His will. Moses said that God's appearance on Sinai was to test whether they truly believed in the majesty, power and holiness of God. Israel must now have the fear that would result in obedience to God and His commandments.

The presence of God, the deliverance of His people, and the giving of the Law had the purpose of leading man away from sin to the higher life of covenant fellowships with Him.

LESSON IN LIFE

Sometimes I feel there is too much familiarity when we speak of God. One such example is the use of the expression "the man upstairs."

At Mount Sinai, the people were filled with great awe before God. Reverence and honor are due God.

"The fear of the Lord is the beginning of wisdom." (Proverbs 1:10)

He is always approachable, but He is to be approached with awe. The Christian has immediate access to the throne of grace, but this does not mean he should walk arrogantly into God's presence.

We need to stand with Israel at the foot of the mountain and see the smoke and lightning and listen to the thunder roll and feel the mountain quake. Reverence for God is a sign of Christian maturity.

God is so great that the heavens cannot contain Him. Yet, He can reign inside your heart.

God's Presence With His People

G od revealed Himself to the people in the thunder, lightning and fire of Mount Sinai. He then gave to them the Ten Commandments. While Moses was on Mount Sinai, God also gave him certain laws, regulations and directions for constructing the Tabernacle.

The covenant was made between God and Israel.

From Exodus 25 through Numbers 10, the people remained at Sinai.

The great strength of the people of Israel was a sense of the presence of their God among them.

The strength of a Christian is the sense of God's presence— when he trusts in God through faith in Jesus Christ. Awareness of the presence of God is the greatest experience of all times.

Preparing for God's Presence
Exodus 25:1-2, 8-9

"The Lord said to Moses." (Verse 1)

Moses had entered the cloud to receive "the tables of stone." (Exodus 24:12)

Now God spoke once again to His servant Moses.

"Speak to the people of Israel, that they take for me an offering; from every man whose heart makes him willing, you shall receive the offering for me." (Exodus 25:2)

Moses is to ask the people for "an offering" that will make construction of the Tabernacle possible. The offering was a voluntary, free-will offering. The people responded so generously that Moses finally found it necessary to call a halt to their giving.

"And let them make me a sanctuary, that I may dwell in their midst." (Exodus 25:8).

The word for "sanctuary" means "holy place." In this verse we have the great purpose for which the Tabernacle was erected. Here, God would manifest Himself in a special way.

87

"According to all that I show you concerning the pattern of the Tabernacle, and all of its furniture so you shall make it." (Exodus 25:9)

The pattern of the Tabernacle was from God. He gave Moses the divine pattern for everything. The Tabernacle, the portable sanctuary of the people who went forth from Egypt, was constructed after the solemn making of the covenant between God and Israel at Mount Sinai. It accompanied the Israelites throughout the period of their wanderings. After the conquest of Canaan, it was set up at Shiloh.

The Tabernacle was followed later by the Temple in Jerusalem and, at last, to the perfect Tabernacle of Hebrews 9:11; Revelation 21:3.

The Promise of the Presence of God
Exodus 29:43–46

"There I will meet with the people of Israel, and it shall be sanctified by my glory." (Verse 43)

God had given to Moses the specifications for the building of the Tabernacle and its furnishings. God also gave the purpose for the Tabernacle. It was to be the place for the sons of Israel to meet God.

"Sanctified" means to be "made holy," "separated," or "set apart." Sanctified things are those which are set apart for God's exclusive use.

A Christian is sanctified when he accepts Jesus as Saviour and Lord. God sets apart the believer to Himself.

"I will consecrate the tent of meeting and the altar; Aaron also and his sons, I will consecrate, to serve me as priests." (Verse 44)

This was to be a most holy place, with definite rules for its use. God also promised to sanctify the men who ministered in the priestly office.

"And I will dwell among the people of Israel, and will be their God." (Verse 45)

Again, God promised to be near and accessible to His people.

There is a special need in these hectic days to feel His presence and to be assured that He dwells among us and is our God.

The words of Jesus comes to mind: "Lo, I am with you always, even unto the end of the age." (Matthew 28:20).

"And they shall know that I am the Lord their God, who brought them forth out of the land of Egypt that I might dwell among them; I am the Lord their God." (Exodus 29:46)

Through worship, Israel would know that God was its God. They would see that He cared for them, just as when He led them from Egypt.

God's Continuing Presence with His People
Exodus 40:34–35

"Then the cloud covered the tent of meeting, and the glory of the Lord filled the Tabernacle." (Verse 34)

The children of Israel followed God. The cloud rested on the tent. God had promised to come and dwell with His people. Here His coming is described.

The cloud had been the mark of God's presence. The children of Israel were led during their wilderness wandering by a pillar of cloud by day, and a pillar of fire by night.

When people come together and worship God, they should have the feeling that they will meet God. For those people of Israel, God's presence was real and awesome.

For those who have faith in Christ, God lets us know through the Holy Spirit that He is still with us, and still in the midst of His people to give them strength and encouragement.

Practicing the Presence of God
Leviticus 16:29–30

"And it shall be a statute to you for ever that in the seventh month, on the tenth day of the month, you shall afflict yourselves, and shall do no work, either the native or the stranger who sojourns among you." (Verse 29)

The day of atonement was instituted in Israel, at which time the high priest made atonement for himself, for the Tabernacle, and for the people.

In preparation for the day, the children of Israel were to "afflict yourselves." They were to carefully examine their moral state, to humble themselves and to fast.

Like the Sabbath, the Day of Atonement was to be observed by not working. The Day of Atonement was to be kept as a sabbath and fast day.

The word "atone" may mean "to cover," "to make amends for," "to reconcile." The word came to be used in a general sense of removing the effects of sin.

"For on this day shall atonement be made for you, to cleanse you from all your sins you shall be clean before the Lord." (Verse 30)

The Bible assumes the need for some atoning action if man is to be right with God. The barrier raised by man's past sins must be removed.

The sins of the people were "washed away" in the sacrifices of the bullocks and goats, and there the priest "made atonement" for his people. In this sacrifice, man was made clean and reconciled with God.

The Christian sees atonement in the sacrifice of Christ on His Cross, reconciling men to God.

One of the prayers still used by the Jews when they keep the Day of Atonement reads:

"O my God, before I was formed I was nothing worth, and now that I have been formed I am but as though I had not been formed. Dust am I in my life; how much more so in my death. Behold I am before thee like a vessel filled with shame and confusion. O may it be they will, O Lord my God and God of my fathers, that I may sin no more, and as to the sins I have committed, I purge them away in thine abounding compassion, though not by means of affliction and sore diseases."

LESSON IN LIFE

At the center of the Jewish camps in the wilderness was the Tabernacle. This was appropriate, for at the center of Jewish life was an awareness of the presence of God.

What is at the center of your life? Is it an idol of money, social prestige, greed, or any of the many materialistic idols that we have today?

Make God the center of your life and you, too, will have an awareness of the presence of God.

I will close with one verse from the Old Testament and another from the New Testament.

Memory Selection: "I will walk among you, and will be your God, and you shall be my people." (Leviticus 26:12)

"Behold the Tabernacle of God is with men and He will dwell with them and they shall be His people and God Himself shall be with them and be their God." (Revelation 21:3)

The Hebrews' Lack of Faith

In this devotional, we see the tragic consequences of unbelief.

The Hebrews were at the place where they could move forward into Canaan, however, they could not enter the Promised Land because of their unbelief.

"So we see that they were unable to enter in because of unbelief." (Hebrews 3:19)

The children of Israel came to their hour of destiny and drew back. The results were tragic.

The Israelites failed God because of their lack of faith. "Without faith it is impossible to please God." (Hebrews 11:6)

Christians often fail God because of a lack of faith. We need to remember that we belong to Christ, and that He is ever with us and ready to help us. Apart from faith, there is failure. Faith is taking God at His word. God's promises to his people are fulfilled only when His people have had the faith to lay hold upon that which He has offered them.

The pertinent Scripture comes from the Book of Numbers. This book is called "Numbers" because of the two numberings of the people found in Chapters 1 and 26. The work covers a period of about forty years.

After leaving Mount Sinai, the Israelites came to Kadesh-barnea. This location was suitable for invasion of the Promised Land.

Briefing of the Spies

Numbers 13:17–20

"Moses sent them to spy out the land of Canaan, and said to them, 'Go up into the Negeb yonder, and go up into the hill country.'" (Verse 17)

Israel is to send out twelve princes to "spy out the land of Canaan." The "land of Canaan" is a term for the Land of

Promise. "The Negeb" is a term for the country south of Judah. "Negeb" meant "parched" or "dry." Today, this land is a large barren area.

"And see what the land is, and whether the people who dwell in it are strong or weak, whether they are few or many." (Verse 18)

The spies are to find out if the land is fertile or barren. They were to take note of the people, how many there were, whether they were warlike or peaceable, and whether they lived in open or strongly fortified cities.

The Spies Report

Numbers 13:25, 30–33

"At the end of forty days they returned from spying out the land." (Verse 25)

After forty days (a sacred number and associated with a solemn revelation from God), the spies returned to Paran.

The spies reported that the land was flowing with milk and honey. They returned with some of its fruit.

"Yet the people who dwell in the land are strong, and the cities are fortified and very large; and besides, we saw the descendants of Anak there." (Verse 28)

This majority report had three mistakes. It overestimated the enemy, underestimated themselves, and underestimated God.

"But Caleb quieted the people before Moses; and said, 'Let us go up at once, and occupy it; for we are well able to overcome it.'" (Verse 30)

Caleb intervenes to present a minority report. Caleb saw no need for delay. They had started out for the Promised Land. It was now before them. Caleb was confident that the time was right for them to go in and take over, according to God's promise. Caleb trusted in God's promise of the land, and so advised conquest. This is a covenant trust.

Caleb was a man of great faith. His faith made him a man of action.

"Then the men who had gone up with him said, 'We are not able to go up against the people; for they are stronger than we.'" (Verse 31)

Here we have an opposite interpretation of the situation. This was the majority report.

Breaking Faith With God

Numbers 14:1–3

"Then all the congregation raised a loud cry; and the people wept that night." (Verse 1)

These people were easily discouraged. Doubt, fear and despair prevented them from seeing the power of their God.

"And all the people of Israel murmured against Moses and Aaron; the whole congregation said to them, 'Would that we had died in the land of Egypt! Or would that we had died in this wilderness!'" (Verse 2)

The people would rather have death in Egypt or the desert in Canaan. Such an attitude has its roots in a lack of trust in God.

"Why does the Lord bring us into this land, to fall by the sword? Our wives and our little ones will become a prey; would it not be better for us to go back to Egypt?" (Verse 3)

Here stands a terror-stricken people. Unbelief brought them fears.

The people longed to go back to Egypt. Once, they had cried out to God and He had heard their prayers. They seemed to have forgotten the bitterness of their bondage and their oppressors. They also forgot the mighty power of God in delivering them. This was a sin of forgetfulness.

The price of progress in the Kingdom of God is not easy. When suffering and sacrifice is demanded, how many times do we want to "go back to Egypt?" What a tragedy it would have been if the children of Israel had gone back to Egypt.

Results of Disobedience

Numbers 14:26–32

"And the Lord said to Moses and to Aaron," (Verse 26)

The Lord responds to the murmurings and grumblings. The people had considered appointing another leader to replace Moses. The people were ready to stone Joshua and Caleb. This was prevented by the appearance of "the glory of the Lord." (Numbers 14:10)

The Lord threatened to smite the people with a "pestilence and disinherit them" (Numbers 14:12), and to create a new people from Moses. In a great intercessory prayer, Moses pleads for his people. God responds with an undertaking not to obliterate the Israelites, but He says that none of the rebels and doubters shall see the Land of Promise. (Numbers 14:13-23)

"Not one shall come into the land where I swore that I would make you dwell, except Caleb the son of Jephunneh and Joshua the son of Nun." (Numbers 14:30)

Israel is sentenced to wander for forty years in the wilderness until the present generation is dead. All males of twenty years of age and upward are to be excluded from Canaan, except for Caleb and Joshua.

"But your little ones, who you said would become a prey, I will bring in, and they shall know the land which you have despised." (Verse 31)

During the next forty years, a new generation would be prepared to enter the Promised Land.

The Promised Land is not for those who have no faith.

LESSON IN LIFE

Many Christians are bogged down in the wilderness of fear and doubt. God can lead every Christian across the wilderness and into the Land of Promise. Faith is needed to accomplish this. Unbelief can prevent the realization of the purpose of God in our lives.

The faith that we need is the kind that takes God at His Word and acts upon it. The more we act on the promises God has made to us in Christ, the surer we become of this truth. Not acting on faith is like one believing that an airplane will fly safely, yet he is not willing to get inside the plane.

The world moves forward on the faith of persons who see beyond the present. Because Caleb was a man of God, he placed the future in God's hands.

We first accept Christ by faith and then through His help, walk with Him. We know the meaning and joy of truth only when we practice the truth. It is one thing to talk about love and another thing to love.

A knowledge of God must be achieved personally. We must commit ourselves to Him and do His will. Meditation, contemplation, prayer and doing His will can help us sense unity with Him.

Companionship with Him will change weak and frightened souls into joyous, radiant creatures who are willing to move forward with Him to the Promised Land.

Possessing the Promised Land

The Israelites refused to enter the Promised Land because of their lack of faith, and God condemned them to wander in the wilderness some forty years. At the end of wandering, Moses led the children of Israel to the plains of Moab.

Here Moses died. With his death, the nation lost a great leader and a man who loved both his God and people.

Sometime before Moses' death, the Lord selected Joshua to succeed him.

The Book of Joshua opens upon a new Israel having a new opportunity to possess Canaan. The book has historic significance. The events it records are believed to have occurred between 1250 and 1225 B.C.

Does God reveal himself in history? Is history the story of God's dealing with men? To these questions, the Old Testament gives an affirmative answer.

Joshua Assumes Command

Joshua 1:1–6

"After the death of Moses the servant of the Lord, the Lord said to Joshua the son of Nun, Moses' minister, 'Moses my servant is dead . . .'" (Verse 1)

The title "the servant of the Lord" (as well as "my servant") as applied to Moses stresses that quality in Moses most pleasing to God—his obedience to the commands of God.

There are some men to whom it is almost impossible to find successors. Such a man was Moses.

Now the command of the Lord comes to Joshua to take up the work which Moses has laid down. Joshua is here called "Moses' minister." Here the term "minister" means "lieutenant." Association with God-inspired men is a good preparation for leadership.

The name Joshua means "Salvation." Joshua had proved himself to be the kind of a man God could use. He and Caleb had shown their faith and courage when they had advised against retreat at Kadesh-barnea.

"Moses my servant is dead; now therefore arise, go over this Jordan, you and all this people, into the land which I am giving to them, to the people of Israel." (Verse 2)

Again, faith with courage was needed—that which had been lacking years previously at Kadesh-barnea. The time for action and fulfillment had come. The walled cities, with obstacles that had faced the people a generation before, were still there.

Joshua was to lead the people "into the land which I am giving to them." God promised to give Joshua and his people the land which lay before them if they had the courage and and faith to possess it. This is to be a leap of faith. This is the kind of faith a follower of God must have.

"Every place that the sole of your foot will tread upon I have given to you, as I promised to Moses." (Verse 3)

All the land was theirs, if they were willing to set foot upon it. God promised Joshua victory wherever he went. God calls leaders to a specific responsibility. He began by giving him a great vision.

"From the wilderness and this Lebanon as far as the great river, the river Euphrates, all the land of the Hittites to the Great Sea toward the going down of the sun shall be your territory." (Verse 4)

This was the promise which God made to Joshua. These were to be the boundaries of the new nation.

"No man shall be able to stand before you all the days of your life; as I was with Moses, so I will be with you; I will not fail you or forsake you." (Verse 5)

No enemy was to be able to resist Joshua and Israel.

The Lord was with Moses and He would also be with Joshua. God had called him and he would equip him. God's great promise, "I will not fail you or forsake you," must have encouraged Joshua and given him courage and peace of mind. God does not walk out on his promises or let us down.

"Be strong and of good courage; for you shall cause this people to inherit the land which I swore to their fathers to give them." (Verse 6)

With God's help, Joshua would also be strong and courageous. The promises of God imply a call to courage.

Covenant Renewal

Joshua 24:1–2

"Then Joshua gathered all the tribes of Israel to Shechem, and summoned the elders, the heads, the judges and the officers of Israel; and they presented themselves before God." (Verse 1)

Joshua had neared the end of his days. Canaan had been conquered. Joshua called the people together at Shechem, located between Mount Ebal and Mount Gerizim.

This place has sacred memories. Abraham and Jacob had built an altar here. Joseph was also buried here. Here is located Jacob's well where Jesus talked to the Samaritan woman.

"And Joshua said to all the people, 'Thus says the Lord, the God of Israel, 'Your fathers lived of old beyond the Euphrates, Terah, the father of Abraham and of Nahor; and they served other gods.'" (Verse 2)

This verse begins a recital of the mighty acts of God in connection with the history of these people. He reminded them that they had been called out of heathenism and were now the covenant people of God.

Many years had passed since God's call of service to Joshua. The enemies had been defeated. Physical battles had been won, but now they would have spiritual battles to face.

Appeal for Decision

Joshua 24:14–18

"Now therefore fear the Lord, and serve him in sincerity and in faithfulness; put away the gods which your fathers served beyond the River, and in Egypt, and serve the Lord." (Verse 14)

"Fear the Lord"—To fear the Lord was to reverence Him.

"Serve Him in sincerity and truth"—The Latin word from which our "sincerity" comes denotes honey without wax or unmixed purity. The Greek word referred to something without flaw. Sometimes cracks in a house were covered with wax to hide flaws. When the sun shone on these areas, the wax would melt revealing the flaws. The Greek word refers to something held up in the rays of the sun and proved to be without speck or flaw.

"Serve the Lord"—There was the true and living God who

had revealed Himself to them as their great deliverer. Joshua calls for undivided loyalty to God. The people are invited to commit themselves anew to the Lord.

"And if you be unwilling to serve the Lord, choose this day whom you will serve, whether the gods your fathers served in the region beyond the River, or the gods of the Amorites in whose land you dwell; but as for me and my house, we will serve the Lord." (Verse 15)

A choice must be made: "The Lord" or "the gods which your fathers served" or "the gods of the Amorites." The choice was to be personal and immediate.

Life is always confronting us with choices—God or mammon. All too often we try to live by half-choices.

"But as for me and my house, we will serve the Lord." Joshua had already decided the course of his life. His choice was also the choice of his household.

Even if the whole nation turned away from God, Joshua would still follow God completely. Joshua had been loyal to God all of his life and now in his old age, he is prepared to stand alone rather than dishonor God.

Choice was imposed on the people of Israel and this choice is imposed on each of us. We need to say with sincerity, "We will serve the Lord."

"Then the people answered, 'Far be it from us that we should forsake the Lord, to serve other gods.'" (Verse 16)

Joshua made a convincing argument. He also set an example. The response of the people was immediate. The people recognized that it is indeed the Lord who has done all these mighty acts. They promised to serve Him not only because of what he had done for them, but also because He was the only true God. They would "serve the Lord, for he is our God." (Verse 18)

LESSON IN LIFE

One of the greatest invitations in the Old Testament is from Joshua: "Choose this day whom you will serve."

There are many forks in the road of life. Many times the Scriptures emphasize the need to take a stand for God.

Decisions of our life determine our destiny. Events of life are usually the result of the direction we choose. Will it be God or the world!

"As for me and my house, we will serve the Lord" is the sign of a God-centered life.

Criswell ends his book, *Why I Preach That the Bible is Literally True,* with these words: "In the spirit of the captain of the conquering armies of Israel, Joshua of old, I am prepared to say that as for me and my people, we shall serve the Lord, stand by the Book, preach its treasures, love its words, serve its Savior and humbly seek to obey his mandates. Will you?"

God's People in Confusion

The Book of Judges deals with the years after Israel had conquered Canaan. This book covers Israel's history from the death of Joshua to the birth of Samuel. This was the period of tribal league. Each tribe operated almost independently of the others. Each tribe had its own boundaries and leaders.

The Book of Judges receives its name from the men who freed Israel from her enemies. The bulk of the book tells the story of the chief Israelite leaders who are called "judges," and of the experiences of the various tribes under their leadership. These leaders judged men, but their first task was to deliver their people from their enemies.

Sin and violation of the commandments of the Lord brought dire consequences. Yet, the Lord is not resentful. He hears the cries of the people and raises up for them a deliverer. There is mercy and forgiveness, and always the opportunity to return to the Lord and make a new beginning.

God's Patience with Israel
Judges 2:16–19

"Then the Lord raised up judges, who saved them out of the power of those who plundered them." (Verse 16)

Israel had conquered, but had not completely subdued the land. Thus, she was surrounded by enemies. This was no time of security.

The Jews repeatedly called on God. When they cried, He answered. "The Lord raised up judges." The judges were people aroused by God to deliver the people of God in response to God's call. "Judges" were leaders who came from almost every walk of life. They were leaders or persons of power and not necessarily lawyers.

These judges were military leaders endowed by the grace of

God to deliver and govern his people in times of oppression. The people recognized the ability of these judges and obeyed their commands.

"And yet they did not listen to their judges; for they played the harlot after other gods and bowed down to them; they soon turned aside from the way in which their fathers had walked, who had obeyed the commandments of the Lord, and they did not do so." (Verse 17)

The Israelites were living among people whose religion was different from theirs. There was a temptation for the Israelites to serve the foreign gods. Even though God raised up deliverers, the people would not at first listen and continued to practice idolatry. The Hebrew word "to hear" means "to hear and obey." Hebrew and Greek biblical language meant that one hears only when he obeys what he hears.

"Whenever the Lord raised up judges for them, the Lord was with the judge, and he saved them from the hand of their enemies all the days of the judge; for the Lord was moved to pity by their groaning because of those who afflicted and oppressed them." (Verse 18)

In Verses 16–18, we find what happened again and again in this period. The cycle of unfaithfulness, punishment and restoration repeated again and again is the story of a saving, redeeming God. It is the lesson of all scriptures that God will never let his men go. He is with them as a shepherd is with his sheep. "He saved them" is the whole lesson of Judges.

"But whenever the judge died, they turned back and behaved worse than their fathers, going after other gods, serving them and bowing down to them; they did not drop any of their practices on their stubborn ways." (Verse 19)

As soon as each judge died, the generation he delivered would turn away from God and return to a worse moral condition than previously.

Call of Gideon

Judges 6:11–15

"Now the angel of the Lord came and sat under the oak at Ophrah, which belonged to Joash the Abiezrite, as his son

Gideon was beating out wheat in the wine press, to hide it from the Midianites." (Verse 11)

Here is an example of a judge and his call from the Lord. Again there is deliverance by a man chosen for the task.

The circumstances calling forth Gideon were the raids of camel riders who seized the hard-earned products of the Israelites. The desperate situation was shown by Gideon threshing his wheat in the secrecy of a wine press. Usually the wheat was threshed on the top of a hill where the wind could blow away the chaff. Gideon hid in a valley and threshed in secret because he was afraid.

God sent a messenger to speak to Gideon. Gideon may hide from the Midianites, but he could not hide from God. God had work for Gideon. Gideon saw the messenger sitting under an oak tree. This oak tree was considered a sacred tree and a place where oracles or pronouncements were given.

Gideon was the fifth of the judges who delivered Israel from her enemies. Gideon's name means "cutter down" or "hewer" or "One who cuts off." The name may have been given to him prophetically, because he was a great warrior or because he cut down the image of Baal.

"And the angel of the Lord appeared to him and said to him, 'The Lord is with you, you mighty man of valor.'" (Verse 12)

The Lord knew the Gideon of yesterday and tomorrow. God knew that Gideon would deliver his people with divine help so that Gideon was rightly called "man of valor."

"And Gideon said to him, 'Pray sir, if the Lord is with us, why then has all this befallen us? And where are all His wonderful deeds which our fathers recounted to us, saying 'Did not the Lord bring us up from Egypt?' But now the Lord has cast us off and given us into the hand of Midian.'" (Verse 13)

Gideon was like many people when they are reminded of God and his support. If he is like that, why has he not helped us before this? Gideon seemed to believe that good times were a sign that God was with them and bad times meant that God had forsaken them. Gideon knew of God's "wonderful deeds," but he was not interested in the good old days. He was interested in the present. He seemed to have given up hope. He was in a state of spiritual depression.

"And he said to him, 'Pray, Lord, how can I deliver Israel? Behold, my clan is the weakest in Manasseh, and I am the least in my family.'" (Verse 15)

Gideon knew of his weakness before God and was therefore in a place where God could help and use him. Gideon was afraid and he was humble.

Gideon struggled against unbelief. He was a man of faith. It was faith that helped him win mighty victories. In us, as in Gideon, there is also a mixture of unbelief and faith.

Gideon admitted his faults and fears, but he was great because in spite of his doubts, he obeyed God and put his trust in Him.

"And the Lord turned to him and said, 'Go in this might of yours and deliver Israel from the hand of Midian; do not I send you?'" (Verse 14)

The Lord sees the deep faith behind Gideon's words. God gives Gideon strength. God was with him. When later Gideon was to win the victory over Midian, it would be the shout of victory, "the sword of the Lord, and of Gideon." (Judges 7:20)

The idea that he should "deliver Israel" struck him as fantastic. It has always been this way when humble men face a great task.

It was the assurance of divine support which convinced Gideon that he must do his task. The important matter was that the Lord had asked, "Do not I send you?"

God calls us to do tasks both small and great. We need to be ready for the task and to say, "Here am I! Send me." (Isaiah 6:8)

We can do anything when God is with us.

Israel's Forgetfulness

Judges 8:33-35

"As soon as Gideon died, the people of Israel turned again and played the harlot after the Baals, and made Baal-berith their God." (Verse 33)

Gideon had won a great victory against the Midianites and had turned the people away from Baal. As soon as he died, the people forgot what he stood for and turned their back upon the Lord.

They returned to the worship of Baal whose shrine was located at Shechem.

"And the people of Israel did not remember the Lord their God, who had rescued them from the hand of all their enemies on every side;" (Verse 34)

They had no sense of loyalty or gratitude for God "who had rescued them from the hand of all their enemies."

God was forgotten. God had not wanted to forsake Israel. He was waiting for a cry from his people in time of need.

"And they did not show kindness to the family of Jerubbaal (that is, Gideon) in return for all the good that he had done to Israel." (Verse 35)

Although Gideon was forgotten by the people of his own day, he has been remembered through the years as a man of faith who trusted in the power of God to deliver his people.

LESSON IN LIFE

In the Old Testament is His command, "Thou shalt have no other gods before me." (Exodus 20:3)

In the New Testament, Christ tells us, "No man can serve two masters: for either he will hate the one and love the other, or else he will be devoted to the one and despise the other. You cannot serve God and mammon." (Matthew 6:24)

Are we like the Israelites? We accept Christ as Lord. Do we then adopt the ways of the world?

The book of Judges has many examples of people forsaking God. The period of Judges has been called the "dark ages of Hebrew history."

Even in such a period, God did not forsake the people.

Many Christians find themselves in situations similar to Gideon. When sickness or misfortune strikes, there may be the feeling that God is nowhere to be found.

Someone has said that an interpretation of life is that it came to pass—not to stay.

We need to go forward in faith. If we do, we will be able to look back and see that God was with us all the time.

The man who has a spiritual reserve is able to have help through each crisis. We can build up this spiritual reserve through studying the Bible and prayer.

To the Christian, Jesus says, "Lo, I am with you always, even unto the end of the world."

God Grants Israel A King

Samuel was a prophet and the last of the judges. He lived in the eleventh century B.C. He annointed first Saul and later David as king over Israel.

The name Samuel means "name of God" or "his name is God." Samuel was dedicated to the Lord before his birth by his mother Hannah. In his early years, he was placed in the house of God at Shiloh where the arc of the covenant rested. Here he received his prophetic call.

The tribes of Israel had little unity during the time of the judges. They demanded a king "like all the nations." Samuel did well as a prophet, but Israel wanted a king.

It was the people who asked for a king. In doing so, they rejected God's plan for ruling them. The nation suffered because of their decision to set up a king.

The first book of Samuel reports the life and deeds of Samuel. The reign of Israel's first king is also considered in this devotional.

The Demand for a King

I Samuel 8:4–7

"Then all the elders of Israel gathered together and came to Samuel at Ramah." (Verse 4)

The elders were the heads of families or clans. An important matter was to be brought to Samuel since "all the elders" came to Samuel. Ramah was the birthplace of Samuel.

"And said to him, 'Behold, you are old and your sons do not walk in your ways; now appoint for us a king to govern us like all the nations.'" (Verse 5)

Samuel himself was held in high esteem by the people. However, his sons did not follow in the steps of their father.

The elders wanted Israel to be "like all the nations." Israel lived under the threat of war from surrounding nations. The people thought that if they had a king like the other nations, they would have someone to lead them in war. Israel wanted to conform to her neighbors. The elders were calling for a new political era. The nation had had a theocratic form of government based on God's laws and under his guidance. Now they wanted a king.

The big difference between Israel and the heathen nations was that the Lord was their king. They were a people chosen of God, a God who had led them from slavery to freedom, and who had bound himself to them by a covenant.

Israel made a contribution of spiritual strength to religion, not because it had a king like other nations, but because it had God and prophets to tell of Him.

"But the thing displeased Samuel when they said, 'Give us a king to govern us.' And Samuel prayed to the Lord." (Verse 6)

This request of the people for a king displeased Samuel who may have thought that he was now being rejected by the people that he had served over the years. Also, the leaders were not consulting God in the matter. Samuel wanted to know God's will in this matter. Therefore, he laid it before God in prayer. At one moment, he stood before the elders—the next, he stood before God.

"And the Lord said to Samuel, 'Hearken to the voice of the people in all that they say to you; for they have not rejected you, but they have rejected me from being king over them.'" (Verse 7)

God assured Samuel that the people had not rejected him. God comforted Samuel. Israel's action was not against Samuel, but against Israel's God. Israel was rejecting the leadership of God.

Anointing of Israel's First King

I Samuel 9:27, 10:1

"As they were going down to the outskirts of the city, Samuel said to Saul, 'Tell the servant to pass on before us, and when he has passed on, stop here yourself for a while, that I may make known to you the word of God.'" (I Samuel 9:27)

By the providence of God, Saul was led to Samuel. Saul was a mighty man physically. He was a head taller than the crowd. The prophet had given a feast and entertained Saul. Early the next morning, Samuel escorted Saul and his servant out of the city. Samuel ordered Saul's servant to go on ahead so that he may talk to Saul about God's Word.

"Then Samuel took a vial of oil and poured it on his head, and kissed him and said, 'Has not the Lord annointed you to be prince over His people Israel? And you shall reign over the people of the Lord and you will serve them from the hand of their enemies round about. And this shall be the sign to you that the Lord has annointed you to be prince over his heritage.'" (I Samuel 10:1)

Saul is anointed. The act of anointing was done in Egypt as well as in Israel. Oil was smeared or poured on the head or body of a person. To the Jews, the act of anointing showed that the power of God had come upon the anointed one.

God's Continued Concern for His People
I Samuel 12:19–22

"And all the people said to Samuel, 'Pray for your servants to the Lord your God, that we may not die; for we have added to all our sins this evil, to ask for ourselves a king.'" (Verse 19)

In Chapter 12, Samuel is making his farewell speech to the people at Gilgal. He reminds the people that they have sinned in asking for a king. Samuel calls out to God to send a thunderstorm.

The storm came, which showed to the people that God disapproved. The people were frightened and begged Samuel to pray "to the Lord your God, that we may not die." This was a moment of awful truth for Israel. In their desire to be like other nations and have a king, they had rejected God.

"And Samuel said to the people, 'Fear not; you have done all this evil, yet do not turn aside from following the Lord, but serve the Lord with all your heart.'" (Verse 20)

In demanding a king, the people stood against the will of God. The people realized their mistake and come before Samuel and poured out their confession that they have sinned against God.

Samuel assured them that God would forgive their failures if they would serve the Lord with all their hearts. Once more, they experienced the forgiveness of God.

"And do not turn aside after vain things which cannot profit or save, for they are vain." (Verse 21)

Samuel told the people to turn aside from "vain things." The Hebrew root of "vain" is to make hollow or to be empty. "Things" are empty. They cannot prolong life or give peace. A vain man is hollow or empty. When a man disregards God, he is empty and without heart. Such a person does not understand life.

"For the Lord will not cast away his people, for his great name's sake, because it has pleased the Lord to make you a people for himself." (Verse 22)

Samuel reminds the people that they are the chosen people of God. God is faithful to the covenant. We can see the beautiful living relationship that exists between God and His people.

In Christianity, there is a personal relationship between the believer and his Lord. Christianity is personal and centered in Jesus Christ.

Saul's Jealousy

I Samuel 18:8–9

"And Saul was very angry, and this saying displeased him; he said, 'They have ascribed to David ten thousands, and to me they have ascribed thousands; and what more can he have but the kingdom?'" (Verse 8)

The bitter feelings of Saul toward David started early in their relationship. David served Saul as musician and armorbearer, and then as military leader. David is appointed a leader in the army. He is so successful that he is a national hero. It must have been irritating for Saul to hear the women singing, "Saul has slain his thousands, and David his ten thousands." (Verse 7)

His envy grew.

Saul seems to have changed as he grew older. He became more unstable emotionally. He became a brooding man.

"And Saul eyed David from that day on." (Verse 9)

This signals the beginning of a tragic conflict between Saul and David.

LESSON IN LIFE

The Israelites wanted to be "like all the nations" who lived near them. Israel wanted to keep up with the Joneses. Conformity is a sin that still plagues God's people. Many times Christians try to conform to the world and let the world decide their standards of behavior.

There is one conformity, however, that is right. He to whom we shall be conformed is Jesus Christ.

David's Reign, Israel United

Saul became increasingly jealous of David. Finally, David fled to the Philistine city of Gath. He was not favorably received here, so he took refuge in a cave. With him were his family and some four hundred men.

Saul continued to pursue David. More than once David could have killed Saul, but he did not.

Saul and three of his sons were killed at Gilboa in a battle with the Philistines. When David heard of Saul's death, he went to Judah where he was proclaimed king of Judah. He set up his government at Hebron, nineteen miles south of Jerusalem.

David King of Israel

II Samuel 5:1–5

"Then all the tribes of Israel came to David at Hebron, and said, 'Behold, we are your bone and flesh.'" (Verse 1)

David made Hebron his capital for seven and one-half years while he reigned over Judah.

One thing that broke down the resistance of the tribes to David's being their ruler was the fact that David belonged to them by birth.

"In times past, when Saul was king over us, it was you that led out and brought in Israel; and the Lord said to you, 'You shall be shepherd of my people Israel, and you shall be prince over Israel.'" (Verse 2)

The leaders of the tribe also remembered David's military victories. David had proved his ability as a leader. The people knew that the brilliant part of Saul's reign was when David stood by his side. During Saul's reign, David had been the military leader.

Also, God had ordained that David become king. The people knew that David was to reign by divine right.

Here David, the political leader, is called a shepherd. This was an appropriate term for David who had been a shepherd in earlier years.

The people had three reasons for wanting to draft David as leader: (1) common ancestry, (2) his military victories, and (3) the call of God.

"So all the elders of Israel came to the king at Hebron; and King David made a covenant with them at Hebron before the Lord, and they anointed David king over Israel." (Verse 3)

David was called king because he was already king of Judah. He was now being anointed as king over all the tribes of Israel.

David made a covenant with the elders. The people agreed to obey David as long as he ruled in accordance with the divine law. David and the people recognized God as the real ruler of the nation.

"David was thirty years old when he began to reign, and he reigned forty years." (Verse 4)

The age of thirty seemed to be the age when Hebrew men began their life work. The Levites entered the ministry at age thirty (Numbers 4:3). This also was the age at which Jesus began his public ministry.

"At Hebron he reigned over Judah seven years and six months; and at Jerusalem he reigned over all Israel and Judah thirty-three years." (II Samuel 5:5)

David reigned seven and one-half years over the tribes of Judah. Later, he was crowned king over all the tribes and reigned thirty-three years over the unified kingdom.

David, Blessed of God

II Samuel 5:9–12

"And David dwelt in the stronghold, and called it the city of David. And David built the city round about from the Millo inward . . ." (Verse 9)

When David was elected King, he decided to make his capital a stronghold of the Jebusites located on Mount Zion. David led his army to Mount Zion and defeated the Jebusites. David lived here in the fort.

The word "Millo" means "the fillings." It was thought that the Jebusites stronghold had a gully or ravine that separated it from a ridge, and because of this it was difficult to get into the fortress.

It is thought that Solomon filled up this gully, giving it the name of "the filling." Solomon "closed the gap of the city of David his father." (I Kings 11:27)

David did not continue to reign in Hebron because it had been recognized as the special capital of Judah, the southern kingdom. The city of David was located in the southeastern corner of present-day Jerusalem, and was located more centrally than Hebron. Jerusalem was not within the territory of any one of the tribes since it was a Jebusite fortress until its capture. The "City of David" was to be the capital of *all* Israel. David was trying to break down any jealousy.

"And David became greater and greater for the Lord, the God of hosts, was with him." (II Samuel 5:10)

David increased in greatness because God was with him.

"And Hiram king of Tyre sent messengers to David, and cedar trees, also carpenters and masons who built David a house." (Verse 11)

Hiram, king of Tyre, was a close friend of David. The king sent messengers and "cedar trees." The trees were known for their strong and durable wood. Hiram also sent skilled workmen, carpenters and masons to help in the building of David's house. In the time of David, Tyre was a flourishing Phoenician port midway between Carmel and Beirut.

"And David perceived that the Lord had established him king over Israel, and that he had exalted his kingdom for the sake of his people Israel." (Verse 12)

David was an instrument in the hand of God. God had exalted David's kingdom "for the sake of his people Israel." David's accomplishments were a part of God's purpose for His people.

David Restores the Ark to Israel

II Samuel 6:12–15

"And it was told King David, 'The Lord has blessed the household of Obed-edom and all that belongs to him, because of the ark of God.'" (Verse 12)

The ark of the covenant was the symbol of God's presence

among His people. The ark was captured by the Philistines. The Philistines later sent the ark back to Israel because they felt it brought evil to them. While bringing the ark back to Jerusalem, a man died when he touched the ark, as it was being hauled by oxen in a cart. The ark was then left temporarily at the home of Obed-edom.

After three months, David again decided to bring the ark to Jerusalem. He had heard that Obed-edom and his household had been greatly blessed because of "the ark of God." David determined to make Jerusalem not only the political capital, but the religious capital as well. There was great gladness as the procession brought the ark to Jerusalem.

"And when those who bore the ark of the Lord had gone six paces, he sacrificed an ox and a fatling." (Verse 13)

Those who carried the ark were instructed to lift the ark and walk six paces in the direction of Jerusalem.

By the time six paces were taken, David felt that the journey to Jerusalem had the blessing of God upon it. David thanked Him with sacrifices.

"And David danced before the Lord with all his might; and David was girded with a linen ephod." (Verse 14)

David was rejoicing. "David danced." The Hebrews had their sacred dances. David performed a sacred dance clothed in an "ephod." The "ephod" was a type of garment worn by priests during religious functions.

"So David and all the house of Israel brought up the ark of the Lord with shouting, and with the sound of the horn." (Verse 15)

Thus with sacrifices, with a royal dance in a priestly garment, with shouting and with trumpet, so "David and all the house of Israel" brought the ark to the City of David.

LESSON IN LIFE

Israel achieved glory because she had a leader who was faithful to God's purposes. David ruled well because God ruled in his heart. Before David had the kingdom of Israel, he had the kingdom in his heart. David considered the will of God for himself and for His people Israel.

David, the king, was important—but the kingdom was more important. God did not prepare the Kingdom for David, but he prepared David for the Kingdom's sake. There was a motto that I once read that reminded me of David: "God first, others second and myself last."

His Kingdom and His people should come first with Christians.

Each of us as individual citizens should put our trust in God and seek His will in our lives.

We need to choose leaders today who will guide the people to the Lord. God should be in the heart of our national life today as it was in David's Kingdom.

A Nation Under God

David wanted to build a house of worship for the Lord. David told Nathan the prophet about this. When Nathan took this to God, the prophet was told by God that David would not be permitted to build a temple. Solomon, David's son, would build the temple.

As Moses was denied the privilege of entering Canaan, David was denied the privilege of building a temple.

David's Prayer

II Samuel 7:18–19, 27–29

"Then King David went in and sat before the Lord, and said, 'Who am I, O Lord God, and what is my house, that thou hast brought me thus far?'" (Verse 18)

God promised to build David a house or dynasty which would be established forever. "And your house and your kingdom shall be made sure forever before me; your throne shall be established forever." (Verse 16)

Upon hearing these words from the Lord, David went into the temple where the ark was housed and worshiped God.

David "sat before the Lord." What is probably meant is a kneeling position in which the worshiper sat back on his heels.

David was a great king, but he was greatest when he kneeled before his God. He did not take a step without consulting God.

David confessed his unworthiness as he knelt before God. He recognized that he was what he was because of the blessing of God.

"Who am I?" David was greatly humbled by the message from God. He is filled with wonder of the past and the future. David expressed wonder that God took notice of him. It reminds one of his words in Psalm 8:4, "What is man that thou art mindful of him? And the son of man, that thou visitest him?"

118

Paul was of similar spirit when he said that he was the least of all the saints. (Ephesians 3:8)

Jesus said, "For every one who exalts himself will be humbled, and he who humbles himself will be exalted." (Luke 14:11)

"And yet this was a small thing in thy eyes, O Lord God; thou hast spoken also of thy servant's house for a great while to come, and has shown me future generations, O Lord God!" (II Samuel 7:19)

God had brought David from a little shepherd boy to king of Israel. This was a "small thing" for the power of God. David knew that God had led him in the past, and had the assurance of God's presence in the future. David had been promised a long dynasty, and that members of his family would rule Israel "for a great while to come."

"For thou, O Lord of hosts, the God of Israel, has made this revelation to thy servant, saying, 'I will build you a house; therefore, thy servant has found courage to pray this prayer to thee.'" (II Samuel 7:27)

David was filled with joy because of God's promise to him. After David recognized his unworthiness, he thanked God again that his house would continue to rule. The note of praise is seen all through David's prayer. So many times, thanksgiving is found lacking in our prayers. We are frequent in asking and infrequent in gratitude.

"And now, O Lord God, thou are God, and thy words are true and thou hast promised this good thing to thy servant." (Verse 28)

David believed God. He had faith in Him. His words and promises are true. David had always found God to be faithful to His word. David did not doubt. David acted upon the promises of God. David believed that what God promised, He would do.

"Now therefore may it please thee to bless the house of thy servant, that it may continue for ever before thee; for thou, O Lord God, hast spoken, and with thy blessing shall the house of thy servant be blessed forever." (Verse 29)

David know that God had blessed him. Now he was asking God to bless his descendants.

Solomon's Temple Dedicated

I Kings 8:62-63, 65-66

"Then the king, and all Israel with him, offered sacrifice before the Lord." (Verse 62)

David died—and his son, Solomon, was made king. Solomon built the Temple and had a dedication ceremony. Many people came to Jerusalem for the dedication.

When the Temple was completed and the furnishings installed, the ark of the covenant was put in place. Then, there was a prayer of dedication.

After the dedication service, the people, led by King Solomon, offered sacrifices to God.

"Solomon offered as peace offerings to the Lord twenty-two thousand oxen and a hundred and twenty thousand sheep. So the king and all the people of Israel dedicated the house of the Lord." (Verse 63)

A large number of animals were offered at the dedication of the Temple. Animal sacrifices were customary in observance of festive occasions.

The first sacrificial offering of the dedication service was the peace offering.

The peace offering was symbolic of the peace between the one who offered, and God. It also symbolized the peace between man and man. Participation in the peace offering drew the members of the community together.

The king and the people took part in the dedication. The fat was consumed on the altar. The peace offerings were later used for a great feast in which all the worshipers shared.

"So Solomon held the feast at that time, and all Israel with him, a great assembly, from the entrance of Hamath to the Brook of Egypt, before the Lord our God, seven days." (Verse 65)

It was thought that this feast celebrated the dedication of the Temple, as well as being the Feast of the Tabernacle. The Feast of Tabernacles celebrated the end of the agricultural year and the gathering in of the crops.

"From the entrance of Hamath" is the northern boundary of the Holy Land and is between Mount Hermon and the Lebanon mountains, north of the Sea of Galilee.

The "Brook of Egypt" was a desert stream which was usually dry and formed the boundary between Israel and Egypt.

"From the entrance of Hamath to the Brook of Egypt" meant that people came to the dedication of the Temple from all over Israel.

"On the eighth day he sent the people away; and they blessed the king, and went to their homes joyful and glad of heart for all the goodness that the Lord had shown to David his servant and to Israel his people." (Verse 66)

On the eighth day, the people went to their homes. They were "joyful and glad."

LESSON IN LIFE

Why attend church? Since the first church was established, there have always been difficulties involved in going to church. Early Christians were tortured and killed, but Christians continued attending church and rejoiced through their suffering.

Going to church in the winter in colonial days took courage and determined devotion. The distance was often great and the sanctuary was unbearably cold.

In our own days, we are less likely kept from church by cold sanctuaries than by other interests.

The great danger of our church today is not that it will be criticized or persecuted, but rather, that from indifferent and preoccupied friends who believe worship is valuable but inconvenient.

Millions attend worship services because they wish to be led into the presence of the Most High, and to be shown the meaning of life and how to live better.

When we observe a congregation leaving church, we cannot help but wonder sometimes if they have been in mourning. True worship brings true happiness. Great joy and gladness come from an experience with God and the realization of "all the goodness that the Lord has shown."

"Make a joyful noise to the Lord, all the lands."

"Serve the Lord with gladness! Come into his presence with singing!" (Psalm 100:1–2)

See you in church!

A King's Glory and Corruption

Why does a good person, who seems so stable and strong, sometimes go to pieces? Why does he lose his ideals and character?

When I was in high school, a friend of mine was the captain of the football team. He was voted as the boy most likely to succeed, and also, the boy with the best personality. Yet, he now is spending more time in jail than out—and has no permanent job.

A good beginning is important—but to start, and then quit, is tragedy.

Jesus told the parable of a great house built upon the sand (Matthew 7:24–27), and another house built on rock. When the wind, rain and floods came, the house that was built on rock did not fall, but the house that was built on sand fell.

Growth is a fact of life, but so is degeneration. No matter who the man is, he must take care lest he fall. We can all fail and fall.

In this devotional, we will discuss the rise and fall of Solomon.

Israel's Prosperity

I Kings 4:20–21

"Judah and Israel were as many as the sand by the sea; they ate and drank and were happy." (Verse 20)

The southern tribes were called Judah, and the northern tribes, Israel.

Times were good and the people were happy. The reign of Solomon was characterized by peace and prosperity.

"Solomon ruled over all the kingdoms from the Euphrates to the land of the Philistines and to the border of Egypt; they brought tribute and served Solomon all the days of his life." (Verse 21)

Solomon was the third and last king of the united kingdom. David had established the kingdom. When Solomon inherited it, he organized the kingdom, built up commerce and industry, and formed commercial and political relationships with other nations.

The kingdom stretched from the Euphrates River to the Egyptian border, with the exception of the strip of land along the Mediterranean coast that was held by the Philistines.

The Wisdom of Solomon
I Kings 4:29–30, 32–34

"And God gave Solomon wisdom and understanding beyond measure, and largeness of mind like the sand on the seashore." (Verse 29)

In a dream at Gideon, God had appeared to the king and asked him what he needed most. Solomon requested wisdom. "Give thy servant therefore an understanding mind to govern thy people." (I Kings 3:9)

The monarch's wisdom was a marvel of the ancient world.

"So that Solomon's wisdom surpassed the wisdom of all the people of the east, and all the wisdom of Egypt." (I Kings 4:30)

Many kings had their wisemen, but they were no match for Solomon because of the source of his wisdom. Wisdom in its fullest sense has to do with character, as well as intellect.

"He also uttered three thousand proverbs; and his songs were a thousand and five." (I Kings 4:32)

A proverb is a short pithy saying, comparison or question. The book of Proverbs contains many of Solomon's proverbs. Solomon was the author of three thousand proverbs and one thousand songs.

"He spoke of trees, from the cedar that is in Lebanon to the hyssop that grows out of the wall; he spoke also of beasts, and of birds, and of reptiles, and of fish." (Verse 33)

His knowledge of botany ranged all the way from the beautiful cedar trees in Lebanon to the lowly hyssop often seen in the midst of old ruins. He was a great expert in botany and zoology.

Solomon's wisdom was not limited to these fields. In I Kings 3:16–28, there is another type of wisdom. Two women approached Solomon with an infant child, each claiming that the child was hers. Solomon asked for a sword to cut the child in half. Only the real mother objected, and was willing to let the other have the whole child.

The last verse concludes with, "they perceived that the wisdom of God was in him, to render justice." This showed wisdom in judgment in difficult legal cases.

"And men came from all peoples to hear the wisdom of Solomon, and from all the kings of the earth, who had heard of his wisdom." (I Kings 4:34)

The wisdom of Solomon became known far and wide so that the Queen of Sheba (South Arabia) came to test him with hard questions. "Now when the queen of Sheba heard the fame of Solomon concerning the name of the Lord, she came to test him with hard questions." (I Kings 10:1)

"Many of the world." Wisest and powerful persons made long journeys to sit in Solomon's court and to hear him speak words of wisdom.

The Ruin of Solomon

I Kings 11:4-6

"For when Solomon was old his wives turned away his heart after other gods; and his heart was not wholly true to the Lord his God, as was the heart of David his father." (Verse 4)

Moses had given warnings to rulers: "And he shall not multiply wives for himself, lest his heart turn away; nor shall he greatly multiply for himself silver and gold." (Deuteronomy 17:17)

Solomon married many foreign women to make alliances with rulers of other nations. These women wanted worship centers for their own gods to be erected. Solomon not only married many wives, but married women who did not have faith in God. When Solomon grew old, he was influenced by his pagan wives so that he "was not wholly true to the Lord, his God." At the peak of his power, he fell.

When a person is not "wholly true," there is a looseness of grip. There is the slight compromise of principle, then a little more loosening of the grip until conscience is gone with the wind.

I recently read of a device to try to prevent automobile wrecks. A buzzer sounded when the grip on the steering wheel was relaxed. We need warning signals to tighten our grip on the steering wheel of conscience.

Sometimes we are like Solomon. We try to please people, go the way of the world, and also try to serve God. We cannot do this and be "wholly true to the Lord."

"For Solomon went after Ashtoreth the goddess of the Sidonians, and after Milcom the abomination of the Ammonites." (I Kings 11:5)

Ashtoreth was the goddess of the Sidonians, the goddess of spring, and later a goddess of fertility and sexual love. She had a great temper in Sidon and was depicted on Sidonian coins as standing on the prow of a galley—thus being the original figurehead for sailing ships.

Milcom was a god of the Ammonites. He was a fire god and worshiped by being offered human sacrifices—particularly infant children.

"So Solomon did what was evil in the sight of the Lord, and did not wholly follow the Lord, as David his father had done." (Verse 6)

David was a godly father, but Solomon failed to follow his example. David's life-long example to his son should have pointed Solomon in the right direction.

God's Judgment Upon Solomon

I Kings 11:9–11

"And the Lord was angry with Solomon, because his heart had turned away from the Lord, the God of Israel, who had appeared to him twice." (Verse 9)

Here was a man who had had spiritual privileges far beyond any man of his day, and yet he turned away. Solomon failed to give complete allegiance to God.

"And had commanded him concerning this thing, that he should not go after other gods; but he did not keep what the Lord commanded." (Verse 10)

God had commanded Solomon that he should not go after other gods (I Kings 9:6), but Solomon had wandered far from God.

"Therefore the Lord said to Solomon, 'Since this has been your mind and you have not kept my covenant and my statutes which I have commanded you, I will surely tear the kingdom from you and will give it to your servant.'" (I Kings 11:11)

Because Solomon disregarded the commandments of God, the covenant had been broken. Solomon had sinned against God and he must now bear his punishment. God would strip him of his kingdom and place it in the hands of one of Solomon's servants.

LESSON IN LIFE

The promises of God to Solomon were great and wonderful. Solomon was careless with the covenant and God's promises. We, too, can be careless with God's promises.

In the New Testament, there are hundreds of promises to believers. One of these promises: "Jesus said unto her, 'I am the resurrection and the life; he that believeth in me, though he were dead, yet shall he live.'" (John 11:25)

Trust Him with your life and receive Him as your Savior. After one has accepted Christ, one should walk with Him daily.

The lesson of Solomon's rise and fall is one that all believers need to take seriously. Every Christian should live a life of self-discipline. To be a true follower of Jesus Christ, you must deny yourself. Pray daily, read the Scripture and be strong in faith.

The Two Kingdoms

Division of the kingdom occurred in 922 B.C., and we will cover the time between then and the New Testament.

David united Judah and the northern tribes of Israel into one kingdom and Solomon, his son, ruled the united kingdom for forty years. At his death, the kingdom was left to his son, Rehoboam.

Rehoboam was crowned king of Judah after Solomon died. In that the monarchy was a union of the northern and southern tribes, it was necessary for Rehoboam to go to Shechem in the northern kingdom to be crowned king of Israel by representatives of the northern tribes.

Because of heavy taxes and forced labor, there had been a growing discontent. The northern tribes met with Rehoboam at Shechem and asked him to lighten their load. Rehoboam consulted his advisors. The older men advised him to grant the request. The younger men advised him to take a stern line.

This, then, is the setting of this devotional.

Rehoboam's Fateful Decision

I Kings 12:12–15

"So Jeroboam and all the people came to Rehoboam the Third day, as the king said, 'Come to me again the third day.'" (Verse 12)

Jeroboam was a member of the northern tribe of Ephriam. At one time, he was Solomon's foreman. He rebelled against the king's cruelties to the workers and was driven into exile in Egypt. When Solomon died, Jeroboam returned to Israel.

A delegation led by Jeroboam called on Rehoboam to ask that he "lighten the hard service of your father and his heavy yoke upon us, and we will serve you." (I Kings 12:4)

Rehoboam asked for three days to think it over and get some advice.

The assembly reconvened and the people waited for his answer.

"And the king answered the people harshly, and forsaking the counsel which the old men had given him." (I Kings 12:13)

The elder statesmen had advised Rehoboam to grant the people their request. When the people returned to Shechem, Rehoboam answered them "roughly."

"He spoke to them according to the counsel of the young men, saying, 'My father made your yoke heavy, but I will add to your yoke; my father chastised you with whips; but I will chastise you with scorpions.'" (Verse 14)

One interpretation of "scorpion" is a scourge used by Romans. This was a whip made of a long bag of leather filled with sand and studded with spikes. This was called "the scorpion."

Rehoboam was faced with a bad situation. The course that he decided upon could only make this bad situation worse.

"So the king did not hearken to the people; for it was a turn of affairs brought about by the Lord that he might fulfill his word, which the Lord spoke by Ahijah the Shilonite to Jeroboam the son of Nebat." (I Kings 12:15)

Rehoboam did not seem to have any understanding of the seriousness of the situation. He took a course that could only lead to revolt.

The prophet Ahijah had previously spoken about the division of Solomon's kingdom. The writer of First Kings said that God's word spoken by Ahijah was being fulfilled.

The Revolt of the Northern Kingdom

I Kings 12:16–20

"And when all Israel saw that the king did not hearken to them, the people answered the king, 'What portion have we in David? We have no inheritance in the son of Jesse. To your tents, O Israel! Look now to your own house, David.'" (Verse 16)

The harsh reply of Rehoboam led to immediate revolt. They could stand no more. The tribes rejected the leadership of David's house. Jesse was David's father.

"To your tents" was a call for the northern tribes to go home. It could have been a battle cry.

"But Rehoboam reigned over the people of Israel who dwelt in the cities of Judah." (Verse 17)

The members of northern tribes who still lived in Judah chose to remain in Judah and to give their allegiance to Rehoboam.

"Then King Rehoboam sent Adoram, who was taskmaster over the forced labor, and all Israel stoned him to death with stones. And King Rehoboam made haste to mount his chariot, to flee to Jerusalem." (Verse 18)

Rehoboam sent Adoram to stop the rebellion. Adoram had been in charge of the laborers who had been forced to work for the king. A worse choice could not have been made. The sight of this former taskmaster so aroused the people that they stoned him to death. King Rehoboam escaped by fleeing in his chariot to Jerusalem.

"So Israel has been in rebellion against the house of David to this day." (Verse 19)

"To this day" indicates that the break in the kingdom still existed at the time this was written.

"And when all Israel heard that Jeroboam had returned, they sent and called him to the assembly and made him king over all Israel. There was none that followed the house of David, but the tribe of Judah only." (Verse 20)

The people of Israel crowned Jeroboam king of the northern kingdom. Only the tribe of Judah and the little tribe of Benjamin followed Rehoboam.

This division occurred in 922 B.C. From 922 B.C. to 722 B.C., the two kingdoms existed side by side.

Corruption of Religion

I Kings 12:26–29

"And Jeroboam said in his heart, 'Now the kingdom will turn back to the house of David; if this people go up to offer sacrifices in the house of the Lord at Jerusalem, then the heart of this people will turn again to their Lord, to Rehoboam king of Judah, and they will kill me and return to Rehoboam king of Judah.'" (Verse 26)

The Temple was in Jerusalem. Each year, three great festivals were held there. At other times, worshipers could go there for some special offering.

Jeroboam feared that if his people continued their pilgrimages to Jerusalem to worship in the Temple, they might recognize Rehoboam as their true king.

"So the king took counsel, and made two calves of gold. And he said to the people, 'You have gone up to Jerusalem long enough. Behold your gods, O Israel who brought you up out of the land of Egypt.'" (Verse 28)

Jeroboam had just returned from Egypt where the bull and cow were worshiped, and so decided on a plan to keep his people from making pilgrimages to Jerusalem. He set up two golden calves for Israel to worship.

What he did was in violation of the law of God concerning the making of graven images.

Jeroboam told the people that it was not necessary for the people to go to Jerusalem to worship. They could now worship at home.

Jeroboam's action had a religious and political aspect. He was trying to keep the people from going up regularly to worship at Jerusalem. A return to Jerusalem for worship might also lead to a political return.

"And he set one in Bethel, and the other he put in Dan." (Verse 29)

Bethel was in the southern part of Israel, and Dan in the north. Bethel, meaning "house of God," was named by Jacob in memory of a dream in which God appeared to him. It was more convenient for a worshiper to go there than to Jerusalem. Any worshiper heading for Jerusalem would have to go through or near Bethel. He could stop there and spare the rest of the journey. Jeroboam was making it easy for the people to worship gods that he had placed conveniently near at hand.

LESSON IN LIFE

Jeroboam appealed to convenience. He was placing shrines of worship conveniently close to the people. Even though it was wrong for the people to go there, it was convenient—so they went. Jeroboam was applying the principle of comfort and convenience to religion.

Are we trying to make our religion convenient? We are told that the church would succeed if it gave the people what they want. The church must serve the needs, rather than the desires, of men. The Cross is not a couch.

It is convenient to stay home and not go to church or prayer meeting. It is convenient not to teach Sunday School or work in the church.

We want Christianity without the Cross. We want to help ourselves first. It is more convenient than helping others. The Christian way shown by Christ is to lose yourself. It costs something to be a Christian. When we are joined to Christ, we are willing to go all the way. We must surrender to Him completely.

What is convenient may not always be what is Christian.

The Lord God or Baal

Jeroboam became known as "the man who made Israel sin" because he introduced pagan elements into worship. Some years later, Jezebel supported the worship of Baal. Jezebel was the wife of Ahab who was the seventh king of Israel. Ahab ruled from the city of Samaria and there built a temple to Baal. The religious life of the northern kingdom grew worse in that it had turned away from God.

Prophets are spokesmen for God, and Elijah, the prophet, came at a crucial time to try to turn the nation back to the right.

Elijah was opposed to Baal worship. He announced to Ahab that there would be no rain in Israel for three years because of the worship of idols.

After three years, the Lord commanded Elijah to return to Ahab and announce that the rain would fall again. Elijah suggested a contest between the power of God and the power of Baal. The contest was to take place on Mount Carmel.

A sacrifice was prepared by the prophets of Baal and by Elijah. There was no fire. Each side tried to produce fire. "The God who answers by fire, he is God." (I Kings 18:24)

The prophets of Baal prepared their sacrifice on their altar. They performed a ceremony to try to get their god to consume the sacrifice. Elijah taunted them. Nothing happened. It was then Elijah's turn to call upon God.

The Prophet's Preparation

I Kings 18:30-35

"Then Elijah said to all the people, 'Come near to me,' and all the people came near to him. And he repaired the altar of the Lord that had been thrown down." (Verse 30)

On Mount Carmel, then, were two large groups of people.

There were four hundred and fifty prophets of Baal and four hundred prophets of Asherah. Then, there was Elijah, and also a large number of uncommitted people. "How long will you go limping with two different opinions?" (I Kings 18:21)

The prophet was calling for a clear-cut decision. Many people today are indifferent to religious matters. Many say that it does not make any difference in what you believe, so long as you believe something. Jesus said, "I am the way, and the truth, and the life; no one comes to the Father, but by me." (I John 14:6)

Elijah called for "all the people" to come near him. The fact that Elijah "repaired" the altar suggests that it had not been used for some time.

"Elijah took twelve stones according to the number of tribes of the sons of Jacob, to whom the word of the Lord came, saying, 'Israel shall be your name.' And with the stones he built an altar in the name of the Lord. And he made a trench about the altar, as great as would contain two measures of seed." (I Kings 18: 31–32)

Elijah built an altar out of twelve stones—each one symbolizing one of the tribes of Israel. He recalled that Jacob had twelve sons from which came the twelve tribes. He also reminded them that God had changed Jacob's name to Israel. Israel and Judah were divided politically, but Elijah recognized the Lord as God of all twelve tribes.

Elijah made a trench around the altar "as great as would contain two measures of seed." Two measures of seed amount to about five gallons.

"And he put the wood in order, and cut the bull in pieces and laid it on the wood. And he said, 'Fill four jars with water, and pour it on the burnt offering, and on the wood.' And he said, 'Do it a second time;' and they did it a second time. And he said, 'Do it a third time;' and they did it a third time. And the water ran round about the altar, and filled the trench also with water. (I Kings 18:33–35)

After arrangements for the sacrifice had been completed, Elijah called for four jars of water to be poured on the sacrifice and wood. He had them do this a second and third time, the water running into the trench until it was filled.

The Prophet's Prayer

I Kings 18:36–37

"And at the time of the offering of the oblation, Elijah the prophet came near and said, 'O Lord, God of Abraham, Isaac, and Israel, let it be known this day that thou art God in Israel, and that I am thy servant, and that I have done all these things at thy word. Answer me, O Lord, answer me, that this people may know that thou, O Lord, are God, and that thou hast turned their hearts back.' " (Verses 36–37)

In calling upon the "God of Abraham, Isaac, and Israel," Elijah was reminding the people that the God of their fathers was the one true God.

The prophets of Baal had prayed long and loudly. Elijah's prayer was brief. Elijah was careful to give credit to God for what was about to happen. God was the source and Elijah, the servant. Elijah asked God to vindicate him as a true prophet, show that he was God's servant, and prove that He was the only true God. He also prayed that the hearts of the people might be turned back to Him.

It took courage to pray this prayer in this situation. If fire had not come, he could have been killed on the spot. His boldness of faith has been seldom surpassed. Elijah had faith in God and he was not afraid to put this faith to the test. Here was one courageous man standing calmly, praying quietly and with complete faith.

God's Answer

I Kings 18:38

"Then the fire of the Lord fell, and consumed the burnt offering, and the wood, and the stones and the dust, and licked up the water that was in the trench." (Verse 38)

The answer to Elijah's prayer was immediate. "The fire of the Lord" was a supernatural fire. The fire was all-consuming. It was so hot that it consumed the wood, the sacrifice, the altar stones and the water in the trench.

Elijah prayed on Mount Carmel. He was hurt by his people's attitude toward the issue between God and Baal. For his people, he saw that it was a matter of spiritual life or death. He was willing to make it a matter of physical life or death for himself. The Lord did not let his prophet down.

The People's Reaction

I Kings 18:39

"And when all the people saw it, they fell on their faces; and they said, 'The Lord, he is God; the Lord, he is God.' " (Verse 39)

The people "fell on their faces" and confessed that God was their God, the only God, and that they were His. This was a denial of Baal.

The true God is a jealous God. He will have no other gods before Him. A person chooses to be either for or against Him. The decision must be made.

LESSON IN LIFE

Every day, each of us makes many choices. We must live with the results and consequences of these choices.

Sometimes we are lulled into thinking we can get away with foolish choices. "Be not deceived; God is not mocked; for whatsoever a man soweth, that shall he also reap." (Galatians 6:7)

The true God is a jealous God who will have no other gods before Him. Every man chooses to be either for or against God—for the Lord God or for Baal. The decision must be made.

What are some of the idols that you should tear down today? How about the gods of gold, pleasure, sex?

Today, Baal is not molded in the form of a calf. It can be in the shape of a car, a house, or a dollar bill.

Some have chosen God as their only God. Others, like Israel, are indecisive. God or Baal—whom should be follow? Other gods will fail. They always will. The Lord never has failed. He is able to save to the uttermost those who come to Him.

God's Judgment on Israel

The kingdom of Israel began around 922 B.C. when the ten northern tribes revolted after the death of Solomon. The northern kingdom stood for about two hundred years. In 722 B.C., after a siege of three years, the city of Samaria fell to the Assyrians and the nation of Israel came to an end. Why and how did this come about?

Jeroboam II reigned for about forty-one years. He was a strong king. Almost all of the boundaries of David's empire were restored, except for those in the south. There was prosperity and peace, but there also was moral and spiritual decline. Jeroboam was followed by weak and incompetent kings.

While Israel was declining, Assyria was growing in strength under Tiglath-pileser III. Under his leadership and his successors, Shalmaneser V and Sargon II, the northern kingdom was finally conquered in 722 B.C. Thousands of Israelites went to upper Mesopotamia and to Media. Assyria sent people from other conquered countries to Samaria. These people intermarried with the Israelites and became the ancestors of the Samaritans. The kingdom of Israel became known as the "ten lost tribes."

The predictions of the prophets Amos and Hosea had come true. Israel's moral decay and unfaithfulness to God led to her destruction.

Their Idolatry

II Kings 17:9–12

"And the people of Israel did secretly against the Lord their God things that were not right. They built for themselves high places at all their towns, from watch tower to fortified city." (Verse 9)

The Canaanites had shrines to their gods located on high secluded places such as hill tops or mountains. Here, images to

136

their gods and altars were built. The people of Israel followed them in some of their practices. "From watch tower to fortified city" means that in all the towns from the smallest watchtower to the largest city, the people practiced pagan worship. The watchtowers were only occupied when the harvest or vintage was approaching.

"They set up for themselves pillars and Asherim on every hill and under every green tree." (Verse 10)

"Pillars" were four-sided stones or obelisks coming to a point at the top. "Asherim" were wooden idols dedicated to the pagan goddess Ashera and associated with the cult of fertility.

"And there they burned incense on all the high places, as the nations did whom the Lord carried away before them. And they did wicked things, provoking the Lord to anger." (Verse 11)

It was thought by the heathen that "burned incense" was pleasing the gods. It was linked with prayer or devotion to the god to whom the incense was burned. The worship and prayers of Israel were being directed to the gods of the nations whom Israel had subdued, and not to the one true God.

Israel adopted the heathen practices and followed after idols. This brought divine anger.

"And they served idols, of which the Lord had said to them, 'You shall not do this.'" (Verse 12)

God said, "You shall not do this," but they went right on doing it. God sent prophets to warn them, but they would not listen.

God's Warnings
II Kings 17:13

"Yet the Lord warned Israel and Judah by every prophet and every seer, saying, 'Turn from your evil ways and keep my commandments and my statutes in accordance with all the laws which I commanded your fathers, and which I sent to you by my servants the prophets.'" (Verse 13)

In the judgments of God recorded in the Old Testament, God gives a warning. To those involved in the warning, there is an opportunity to turn to Him and escape the Judgment.

Israel's sins were not done in ignorance of God's will. He had sent many prophets and seers to try to win Israel back to Him.

All to no avail. Theirs' was willful sin. A prophet was a spokesman for God. A seer was very similar to a prophet; he was one who saw visions.

Violating the Commandments of God

II Kings 17:14–17

"But they would not listen, but were stubborn, as their fathers had been, who did not believe in the Lord their God." (Verse 14)

God had made His will clear, but His people "were stubborn." They would not heed the words of His prophets. They did not really believe in God and accept His will. They persisted in their sin.

"They despised his statutes, and his covenant that he made with their fathers, and the warnings which he gave them. They went after false idols, and became false, and they followed the nations that were round about them, concerning whom the Lord had commanded them that they should not do like them." (Verse 15)

Moses had given God's Law to the people at Mount Sinai, but the people kept violating this covenant. The people worshiped false idols, and then they themselves became false. Not only did they break the laws of God, but they also hated the covenant.

"And they forsook all the commandments of the Lord their God, and made for themselves molten images of two calves; and they made an Asherah, and worshiped all the hosts of heaven, and served Baal." (Verse 16)

The people turned away from God to the gods of their pagan neighbors. Their religion had become corrupt. Jeroboam had set up two golden calves as objects of worship to prevent people from going to Jerusalem to worship at the Temple. The phrase "hosts of heaven" indicates worship of the moon, sun, planets and stars.

"And they burned their sons and their daughters as offerings, and used divination and sorcery, and sold themselves to do evil in the sight of the Lord, provoking him to anger." (Verse 17)

Israel had adopted the heathen practice of offering human sacrifices to pagan gods. Molech, a fire god, was the god of the Moabites. The first-born son was given as a burnt offering to this god. The metal idol would be heated and the children placed in its burning arms.

Their religion also became one of magic, wizardry and fortune telling.

God's Judgment of Israel

II Kings 17:18

"Therefore the Lord was very angry with Israel, and removed them out of his sight; none was left but the tribe of Judah only." (Verse 18)

Israel had wandered far from God and they showed no sign of repentance. Therefore, the kingdom of Israel came to an end. Samaria fell and many of the people were taken away to Assyria. Only the southern kingdom was left.

The judgment of God was not hasty. Two hundred years had passed from the time Jeroboam had set up the two golden calves until Israel was destroyed. God was patient with the sinful people.

LESSON IN LIFE

We are judged every day of our lives. We are judged by others in what we say and what we do. We also sit in judgment on others. Human judgment is faulty, but divine judgment is not faulty. It is also inevitable. The individual who ignores God will come to ruin. Israel could choose between the Lord's way and the idolatrous practice of Canaan. She did not choose the way of the Lord and her doom was certain.

There is a final judgment involving all mankind. God is willing to forgive the evil doer when he repents by faith. Only in Christ can one find deliverance from sin and its consequences. "Being justified by His blood we shall be saved from wrath through Him." (Romans 5:9)

Most of the time we tend to think of judgment as that which occurs on the last day when we stand before God—when we will be rewarded or punished. This will happen, but there is also judgment that falls on us while we are still alive. There is judgment that is the result of sin.

We need also to judge ourselves daily and try with God's help to be better than we were yesterday. A Christian needs "to keep going" no matter how often we trip and fall.

Some trying experience may occur, and yet, it may not be the result of sin. This makes it difficult for us to understand the reason why. We need to remember: "And we know that all things work together for good to them that love God, to them who are the called according to his purpose." (Romans 8:28)

Reforms Among God's People

Two great revivals occurred in Judah almost one hundred years apart. One revival occurred under King Hezekiah and the other under King Josiah. These were among the strongest and best kings of Judah.

The fall of Samaria and the northern kingdom occurred in 722 B.C. With the fall of the northern kingdom, "there was none left but the tribe of Judah only."

Hezekiah's Reforms

II Kings 18:1-6

"In the third year of Hoshea son of Elah, king of Israel, Hezekiah the son of Ahaz, king of Judah, began to reign." (Verse 1)

Hezekiah's father Ahaz was one of the most wicked Kings of Judah. Ahaz and Hezekiah were opposites: an evil father and a righteous son. But Hezekiah's counselor was the prophet Isaiah. He influenced the new king and a program of reform was instituted.

The name Hezekiah means, "God's strength." The king was a great reformer. He tried to eliminate all the idolatrous images and shrines.

"He was twenty-five years old when he began to reign, and he reigned twenty-nine years in Jerusalem. His mother's name was Abi the daughter of Zechariah." (Verse 2)

Hezekiah began his reign about 725 B.C. His mother's name was Abi, which is a shortened form of Abijah.

"And he did what was right in the eyes of the Lord, according to all that David his father had done." (Verse 3)

Because of his loyalty to God, and as a result of his many reforms, it was said of Hezekiah that he did what was right in the sight of the Lord. This courageous behavior also was said of Josiah. These two rulers earnestly sought to bring about a reformation in Judah.

"He removed the high places, and broke the pillars, and cut down the Asherah. And he broke in pieces the bronze serpent that Moses had made, for until those days the people of Israel had burned incense to it; it was called Nehushtan." (Verse 4)

Hezekiah began the reformation by destroying the idols and the shrines where the idols were worshiped. He removed the high places used as sacrifices for Pagan gods. "Images" were four sided stones coming to a point. "Nehushtan" can mean "Bronze god," "serpent dragon" or a "brass thing." The people were worshiping places, objects and memorials instead of the one true God.

"He trusted in the Lord the God of Israel; so that there was none like him among all the kings of Judah after him, nor among those who were before him." (Verse 5)

Hezekiah had faith and he demonstrated this faith. His prayer for deliverance in II Kings 19:15–19, when the Assyrian armies were invading his country, demonstrated that faith. At the darkest hour of his nation's history, he trusted in God.

"For he held fast to the Lord; he did not depart from following him, but kept the commandments which the Lord commanded Moses." (Verse 6)

Hezekiah followed the Lord throughout his reign. Some of the religious reforms of Hezekiah were the restoration of public worship, the Passover was observed again, and the functions of the priest were restored.

Reformation Under Josiah

II Kings 23:21–25

"And the king commanded all the people, 'Keep the passover to the Lord your God, as it is written in this book of the covenant.'" (Verse 21)

Josiah became the king of Judah in 639 B.C. at the age of eight. He reigned for about thirty-one years. Because of his age, when he began to reign, he has been called the "boy king." Both Hezekiah and Josiah had wicked fathers.

Josiah, like Hezekiah, tried to destroy idols and places of idolatrous worship, and sought to restore the true worship of Jehovah. He repaired the Temple. While this was being done, the high priest found a copy of the book of the Law which was thought to have been the book of Deuteronomy. This discovery greatly moved Josiah. Josiah called an assembly of the people. The scroll was read in their presence. The king and the people renewed their covenant with God. Josiah decided in obedience to the law, that the Passover should be observed.

"For no such passover had been kept since the days of the judges who judged Israel, or during all the days of the kings of Israel or of the kings of Judah;" (Verse 22)

Careful preparations were made for the keeping of the greatest Passover since the days of the Judges. A great crowd of people gathered for this occasion.

"But in the eighteenth year of King Josiah this passover was kept to the Lord in Jerusalem." (Verse 23)

The Passover was that great annual memorial feast. It was kept in memory of the Lord's deliverance of Israel from bondage and according to the instruction given in the Law of Moses.

In the days before Josiah, the people could observe the Passover in their homes. The law of the central sanctuary commanded worship in one central place.

"Moreover Josiah put away the mediums and the wizards and the teraphim and the idols and all the abominations that were seen in the land of Judah and in Jerusalem, that he might establish the words of the law which were written in the book that Hilkiah the priest found in the house of the Lord." (Verse 24)

Josiah abolished every kind of heathen object and custom in Judah and Jerusalem. He destroyed the household images. Josiah wanted to destroy a religion that made use of witches, wizards, images, and idols.

"Before him there was no king like him, who turned to the Lord with all his heart and with all his soul and with all his might, according to all the law of Moses; nor did any like him arise after him." (Verse 25)

This is a summary of the reign of King Josiah. With heart and soul and might, he gave himself to the Lord.

LESSON IN LIFE

The statement about Josiah reminds one of the reply of Jesus to a question, "Which commandment is the first of all?"

"Jesus answered, 'The first is, "Hear, O Israel: The Lord our God, the Lord is one; and you shall love the Lord your God with all your heart, and with all your soul, and with all your mind, and with all your strength." ' " (Mark 12:28–30)

The love God desires demands the action of the whole personality. It is not giving just a fraction of ourselves or doing certain acts. All of a man's being, his emotion, moral nature, intellect and energy must go into his love of God.

This is still the first commandment. Reforms in our own lives will follow when we love God with all that we are.

God's Judgment on Judah

In 609 B.C., King Josiah was killed while trying to halt the armies of Egypt on their way through Palestine. Josiah's son Jehoaz became king for three months. He was followed by Jehoiakim, another son of Josiah. Both were made vassals of the Egyptians. In 605 B.C., the Babylonians defeated the Egyptian army at Carchemish. Jehoiakim switched his allegiance to the Babylonians. After about three years, he rebelled against Babylon. Nebuchadnezzar, King of Babylon, then besieged Jerusalem.

The Warning by Jeremiah

Jeremiah 26:1-6

"In the beginning of the reign of Jehoiakim the son of Josiah, King of Judah, this word came from the Lord." (Verse 1)

Jeremiah delivered this sermon around 610 B.C. shortly after Jehoiakim came to the throne. The word of the Lord came to Jeremiah, instructing the prophet to warn the people of the Judgment that would come if they did not return to the Lord.

"Thus says the Lord: Stand in the court of the Lord's house, and speak to all the cities of Judah which come to worship in the house of the Lord all the words that I command you to speak to them; do not hold back a word." (Verse 2)

Jeremiah spoke in the open court surrounding the temple. His audience were people who came to the temple to worship. There was probably a large multitude from all the cities of Judah. He had a tough assignment. To speak of prediction of doom might result in his death. Because of the very real danger to his life, Jeremiah might hesitate to speak boldly, and for this reason God instructed the prophet to speak "all the words that I command you" and to "not hold back a word."

"It may be they will listen, and every one turn from his evil way, that I may repent of the evil which I intend to do to them because of their evil doings." (Verse 3)

Jeremiah was to try to get the people to repent. The Lord did

145

not want to bring judgment on Jerusalem, but He could not do otherwise if repentance was refused. Repentance means "a change of mind or attitude." This is what the prophet demanded for the people to do. God was willing to change his plans if they would turn from their evil ways. In his dealings with his people, God offered mercy and forgiveness if they would turn from their wicked ways. Unless they repented, divine judgment would strike them.

Repentance is not just an Old Testament doctrine. We also find it in the pages of the New Testament. Repentance is necessary to enter the kingdom of God. "Repent, for the kingdom of heaven is at hand." (Matthew 3:2)

"You shall say to them, 'Thus says the Lord: If you will not listen to me, to walk in my law which I have set before you, and to heed the words of my servants the prophets whom I send to you urgently, though you have not heeded.'" (Jeremiah 26:4–5)

If Judah would not heed to God and live according to God's laws, if Judah would not listen to the prophets, she must be aware of the consequences.

"Then I will make this house like Shiloh, and I will make this city a curse for all the nations of the earth." (Jeremiah 26:6)

Shiloh was a town about eighteen miles north of Jerusalem. It had been a prominent place of worship in the day of Samuel and the other judges of Israel. Shiloh had been destroyed by the Philistines around 105 B.C. The ruins were still visible in Jeremiah's time. Jerusalem would perish just as Shiloh, which previously had been the center of worship for God's people and had perished.

The people listened to Jeremiah, but there was no repentance.

The Fall of Jerusalem

Jeremiah 52:12–16

"In the fifth month, on the tenth day of the month—which was the nineteenth year of King Nebuchadnezzar, King of Babylon—Nebuzaradan, the captain of the bodyguard who served the king of Babylon, entered Jerusalem." (Verse 12)

This is the end. This is the overwhelming defeat of Judah. The date was 587 B.C., about 22 years after Jeremiah's temple sermon.

In the years preceding this date, Judah had been subject to Babylonia. Then Zedekiah, king of Judah, rebelled, and the king of Babylonia, Nebuchadnezzar, put down the revolt.

King Zedekiah watched while they killed his sons; then they blinded him and took him to Babylon where he died.

A Babylonian commander arrived for mopping up operations. He had been sent to complete the destruction of the city.

"And he burned the house of the Lord, and the king's house and all the houses of Jerusalem; every great house he burned down." (Verse 13)

The captain burned the temple, Zedekiah's palace and all the houses. Archaeologists have found evidence of a violent destruction dating from this period.

"And all the army of the Chaldeans, who were with the captain of the guard, broke down all the walls roundabout Jerusalem." (Verse 14)

The walls on every side of the city were destroyed and rendered useless as fortifications.

"And Nebuzaradan the captain of the guard carried away captive some of the poorest of the people and the rest of the people who were left in the city and the deserters who had deserted to the king of Babylon, together with the rest of the artisians." (Verse 15)

Thousands of people were deported to Babylon, joining the small group that had been deported about ten years earlier. Skilled workers and artisians were carried to Babylon. No opportunity for a future rebellion was to be permitted.

"But Nebuzaradan the captain of the guard left some of the poorest of the land to be vinedressers and plowmen." (Verse 16)

Some of the people were left in Judah because the land needed to be cared for and cultivated. These could not be a threat to Babylon.

Jeremiah chose to remain with these survivors, rather than go to Babylonia.

LESSON IN LIFE

God is telling of our sins every day. He may speak through the Bible, through worship or through the Spirit. He will not let us sin without warning us. We are given an opportunity to return to Him.

God's judgment is inevitable on the disobedient who refuse to acknowledge guilt and seek forgiveness.

With repentance, there is so need for punishment. Those who exercise faith and walk in obedience to Him will grow in their ability to exercise faith and respond to His will.

Deliverance from death and the guilt of sin is promised to you and me. What excuse can we give at the time of Judgment if we neglect God's loving offer of deliverance?

"How shall we escape, if we neglect so great salvation, which at the first began to be spoken by the Lord, and was confirmed unto us by them that heard him?" (Hebrews 2:3)

The Faith of God's Remnant

Jerusalem had fallen, the walls were destroyed, the temple was gone and the royal palace was in ruins. The leading citizens had been carried into exile in Babylon.

The beautiful five poems in the book of Lamentations expressed the sorrow of the people. The book reflects the final days of Judah, and is so-named because it is a series of poems mourning and commemorating the destruction of Jerusalem by the Babylonians.

The book has been ascribed traditionally to the prophet Jeremiah. There is much in favor of his writing this book, but there has been some disagreement among the scholars.

Chapter 3 introduces a new note of hope, faith, and encouragement.

In the first eighteen verses of this chapter, the poet laments his great affliction. In 3:19-23, we hear the note of trust and hope in God that was characteristic of the true remant of Israel.

This devotional is concerned with that remnant.

Faith Tested by Affliction

Lamentations 3:19–20

"Remember my affliction and my bitterness, the wormwood and the gall!" (Verse 19)

The prophet called upon God to remember him. The wormwood and the gall refer to a bitter substance. They are a symbol of sorrow and calamity. We might say today, "It was a bitter pill to swallow."

"My soul continually thinks of it and is bowed down within me." (Verse 20)

The prophet most certainly remembers his afflictions and his soul is bowed down in grief and repentance.

No one passes through life without having his faith tested.

Basis for Hope

Lamentations 3:21–24

"But this I call to mind, and therefore I have hope." (Verse 21)

Here we approach the depth and climax of this little book.

When the prophet remembered the mercies of God, he had faith and hope in spite of his misery.

"The steadfast love of the Lord never ceases, his mercies never come to an end." (Verse 22)

The word "steadfast love" is a great word in the Old Testament.

The word here for "love" goes far beyond the ordinary concept of love. This is a self-giving, sacrificial love as revealed in God's action in redeeming man.

God loves his people with steadfast love that never ceases. God's mercies will not end and are continually renewed.

"They are new every morning; great is thy faithfulness." (Verse 23)

From this verse comes the inspiration for the hymn, "Great is Thy Faithfulness."

The loving kindnesses of God are renewed every morning. God meets today's need with today's blessing.

" 'The Lord is my portion,' says my soul, 'therefore I will hope in him.' " (Verse 24)

This understanding of the mercy and faithfulness of God is the basis of hope on the part of the sufferer. The Bible from beginning to end is a book of hope.

The writer utterly depends on God. He had faith in God in the midst of tragedy.

No matter how great the tragedy, there is a God who cares and gives us strength. We may be unfaithful, but we have a faithful God.

A Quiet Waiting on God

Lamentations 3:25–26

"The Lord is good to those who wait for him, to the soul that seeks him." (Verse 25)

The sufferer considers how he might accept the things that have happened to him in a way that will be pleasing to God.

"Wait" means "to wait eagerly" rather than simply "to wait." It is open-eyed, watchful, expectant.

"It is good that one should wait quietly for the salvation of the Lord." (Verse 26)

Judah must wait patiently for the salvation of the Lord.

Quiet waiting is based on a faith that God will act. A right attitude is needed while waiting on God. While waiting, we are to do nothing. We still do His will.

Submission to God

Lamentations 3:27–30

"It is good for a man that he bear the yoke in his youth." (Verse 27)

Symbolically, the yoke stood for instruction, labor, trouble, or discipline. Among the ancient rabbis, the Law was often referred to as the yoke and a devout man submitted to its control. This wise author did not advise youth to "live it up." He recognized the value of discipline in youth. If he learns discipline when he is young, he will be able to maintain discipline throughout his life.

Judah was still young as a nation. Judah wore a heavy yoke, but it would turn out to be a blessing. Judah needed the loving discipline of God to become worthy of Him.

"Let him sit alone in silence when he has laid it on him;" (Verse 28)

This shows a person who is calm and trusting. This person is not complaining against the will of God when the yoke has been placed upon him.

"Let him put his mouth in the dust—there may yet be hope;" (Verse 29)

This description of the sufferer lying face down in the dust expressed absolute submission. The sufferer is humble because he is before God. When one's mouth is in the dust, he could not speak and complain. Faith helps one to suffer in silence.

"Let him give his cheek to the smiter, and be filled with insults." (Verse 30)

"Gives his cheek" means to accept insults without retaliation. When we read these words, we recall the teaching and example of Jesus. By his enduring of insults, our Lord changed man's understanding of humility. The greatest example of humility is Jesus.

Basis of the Sufferer's Submission to God

Lamentations 3:31–33

"For the Lord will not cast off for ever." (Verse 31)

Even though Judah had suffered because of her disobedience to God, God had not completely cast her off. Discipline will not last forever. After the night comes the dawn. Faith knows there will be a better tomorrow.

"But, though he cause grief, he will have compassion according to the abundance of his steadfast love;" (Verse 32)

"Compassion," is a tender word expressing God's holy love. It is a word used of mother love expressing tenderness and concern of the mother before the child is born. God lovingly and anxiously watches over His own.

God's mercies outweight His disciplines.

"For he does not willingly afflict or grieve the sons of men." (Verse 33)

God does not discipline without love. There was purpose behind His action.

LESSON IN LIFE

God's "faithful few" found hope in the midst of their suffering. Suffering is not easy and is hard to understand, but we can learn from suffering.

Are you using your sufferings or are they using and destroying you? How you react to what happens to you in a large part determines your happiness or unhappiness. Pray to God about your sufferings. It is far better to face suffering in fellowship with God, than to rely upon one's strength alone. With a confidence that God is with us in every experience of life, we can face troubles and sorrow with an inner peace.

The Christian Gospel is the Gospel of hope. God has not lost control of the world. The future belongs to Him. The Christian can pray, "Thy kingdom come. Thy will be done, on earth as it is in heaven." (Matthew 6:10).

Ours should be like the faith of God's remnant.

The Promise of Return

The exiles who lived in Babylon kept the hope that they would return to their homeland. Isaiah had prophesied that the Jews would be deported (Isaiah 39:5–7), and also that Jerusalem would be redeemed.

After Nebuchadnezzar died, around 652 B.C., Babylon began to decline. As Babylon was losing power, Cyrus the Persian was gaining power. Cyrus defeated the Babylonians and permitted the Jews to return to Palestine in 538 B.C.

God News for the Exiles

Isaiah 40:1–2

"Comfort, comfort my people, says your God." (Verse 1)

The keynote and theme of this passage is the repeated command, "comfort," which is repeated for emphasis. This repetition also indicated compassion and urgency.

The Jews had been a sorrowing and suffering people for many years. Their city was in ruins. Now they learned that God had not forsaken them.

God's tenderness toward those who have sinned against Him are greater than man can possibly know. He can offer you true comfort that comes from His restoring grace.

The other important words in this passage are "my people" and "your God." These are covenant words. Israel is the people of God and He is the God of Israel. This faith is assumed throughout the whole prophecy. The Lord would not cast off His people forever.

"Speak tenderly to Jerusalem, and cry to her that her warfare is ended, that her iniquity is pardoned, that she has received from the Lord's hand double for all her sins." (Verse 2)

To "speak tenderly" means "to speak to the heart," or "to speak consolingly, gently, kindly, tenderly." The words help dispel anxiety and inspire hope.

"Jerusalem" was in ruins, but the term is used to refer to the people of Judah.

153

"And cry to her," is one of the prophets favorite words and appears more than thirty times in Chapters 40–55. It means to call out or proclaim.

The prophet's comfort starts with the announcement that his people's period of harsh discipline is over and God has forgiven them.

Preparation for the Return
Isaiah 40:3–5

"A voice cries: 'In the wilderness prepare the way of the Lord, make straight in the desert a highway for our God.'" (Verse 3)

It was the custom in the Orient to prepare a highway for the coming of a ruler, or conquering king. This passage speaks of the King of Kings. Judah had been captive under a pagan king, but now everyone was glad that their true King, the living God, was intervening in their behalf.

This prophecy has a future application to John the Baptist as the forerunner of Christ.

"Every valley shall be lifted up, and every mountain and hill be made low; the uneven ground shall become level, and the rough places a plant." (Verse 4)

The way back to Jerusalem had many difficulties and obstacles for the exiles. There were seemingly impossible political, physical, social and psychological difficulties that needed to be overcome. These objects that hindered the return of the exile would be removed. God will bring His people out of Babylon.

"And the glory of the Lord shall be revealed, and all flesh shall see it together, for the mouth of the Lord has spoken." (Verse 5)

God was committed to bring the people home from captivity, "for the mouth of the Lord has spoken." The revelation of the Lord would be witnessed by all nations.

Contrast of Values
Isaiah 40:6–8

"A voice says, 'Cry!' And Israel, 'What shall I cry?' All flesh is grass, and all its beauty is like the flower of the fields." (Verse 6)

He is commanded to speak the divine message, but he does not know what to say.

The voice sets the message the prophet is to proclaim. Flesh is man in his weakness, and mortality contrasted with God who is spirit and eternal.

"The grass withers, the flower fades, when the breath of the Lord blows upon it; surely the people is grass." (Verse 7)

The scorching east wind from the desert blasts all vegetation so that the hills are brown and barren.

"The grass withers, the flower fades; but the word of our God will stand forever." (Verse 8)

The "Word of our God" is not of a season like the grass, but rather, it lives and abides forever.

Man knows that he will live on this earth only a short time, but "the Word of our God" has strength and lasting power; it will stand forever. Man can trust God's Word; the promises will be fulfilled. The word of our God will not fail.

"Behold, Your God"

Isaiah 40:9–10

"Get you up to a high mountain, O Zion, herald of good tidings; lift up your voice with strength, O Jerusalem, herald of good tidings, lift it up, fear not, say to the cities of Judah, 'Behold your God!'" (Verse 9)

The prophet was telling the people that in their desolation and exile they were to trust in God. Better times were ahead. They were to ascend the mountain and announce that God was going to set them free. They were to be his people and He was their God. Jerusalem was God's chosen messenger. She was to be a missionary—home missions at first, and then world missions.

"Behold, the Lord God comes with might, and his arm rules for him; behold, his reward is with him, and his recompense before him." (Verse 10)

The emphasis in this verse is God's might and His strength. God's "arm" signifies His power. By His power, God will assemble His flock and bring it again to Jerusalem.

We need to trust the promises and guidance of God, even in seemingly hopeless situations.

His Gentleness

Isaiah 40:11

"He will feed his flock like a shepherd, he will gather the lambs in his arms, he will carry them in his bosom, and gently lead those that are with young." (Verse 11)

This verse stresses God's gentleness. The picture of the Shepherd is a tender portrait of the Lord found in the Old and New Testament.

God leads His exiles home as the shepherd leads his sheep. He is the herdsman of all men. Though His herds were small, He spent the day caring for them. The young lambs that are unable to follow, the shepherd gathers to his bosom. He guides the mother ewe who requires special care.

LESSON IN LIFE

God has promised us many things. We have the promise of a release from the bondage of sin and a return to homeland.

You must first want to return. Not all of the exiles returned to Jerusalem. Some had one reason or another for not availing themselves of the promise that was made available. Some had begun to care for Babylon. Some may have lacked faith in God. Some were afraid.

One must be willing to go forward out of the Babylon of sin. Today, some seem to care more for the world than for heaven. To set out for the promised land is an act of faith.

"If we confess our sins he is faithful and just to forgive us our sins, and to cleanse us from all unrighteousness." (I John 1:9)

God is as willing to do for us what He did for the exiled people many years ago. The grace of God has been revealed in Jesus Christ. Like Judah of old, our acceptance before God is based not upon our merit, but upon God's love.

God's Remnant Rebuilds

This devotional is taken from two of the historical books of the Old Testament: Ezra and Nehemiah. The theme of these books is the return of the exiles from Babylon, and the reconstruction of the Hebrew nation.

The books known as Ezra and Nehemiah are named not for the author, but for the principal personalities encountered in each.

Ezra was a priest, a scribe, and an interpreter of the laws of God. He led a caravan of Babylonian exiles to Jerusalem with vessels of the temple.

Nehemiah had been a cupbearer to a Persian ruler. He went to Jerusalem where he made a secret inspection of the ruined city walls and rebuilt the walls. He also served as governor of Judah.

The Decree of Cyrus

Ezra 1:1–4

"In the first year of Cyrus King of Persia, that the word of the Lord by the mouth of Jeremiah might be accomplished, the Lord stirred up the spirit of Cyrus King of Persia so that he made a proclamation throughout all his kingdom and also put it in writing . . ." (Verse 1)

The "first year" was that of Cyrus as king of Babylon. He reversed the policies of the Babylonian conquerors. In 538 B.C., he allowed the exiles to return to their homelands. Jeremiah, under divine inspiration, had prophesied a return to Palestine after the period of exile. This event, then, was the fulfillment of the prophecy. Cyrus became the agent of God to accomplish his purpose in returning the exiles to Judah.

"Thus says Cyrus King of Persia: "The Lord, the God of heaven, has given me all the kingdoms of the earth, and he has charged me to build him a house at Jerusalem, which is in Judah.'" (Verse 2)

Cyrus thanked Jehovah for giving him "all the kingdoms of the earth." God had "charged" Cyrus to help rebuild His house in Jerusalem, and Cyrus obeyed.

"Whoever is among you of all his people, may his God be with him, and let him go up to Jerusalem, which is in Judah, and rebuild the house of the Lord, the God of Israel—he is the God who is in Jerusalem . . ." (Verse 3)

Any of the Hebrews of the empire of Cyrus who wished to do so were now given permission to return to Jerusalem.

"And let each survivor, in whatever place he sojourns, be assisted by the men of his place with silver and gold, with goods and with beasts, besides freewill offerings for the house of God which is in Jerusalem." (Verse 4)

Those remaining behind in Babylon, who refused to go to Judah, were expected to assist those who wished to return. They were to give supplies, money, and beasts of burden for the long trip home. They were also to make freewill offerings for the temple that was to be rebuilt in Jerusalem.

Jerusalem Fortified

Nehemiah 4:15–20

The Jews in Palestine suffered opposition from some of the people. Word reached Nehemiah, cupbearer for the Persian ruler Artaxerxes, that the people in Jerusalem were in great affliction and reproach. He fasted and prayed and went to Artaxerxes, asking permission to go to Jerusalem. Permission was granted. He served as governor and was responsible for the walls of the city being rebuilt.

"When our enemies heard that it was known to us and that God had frustrated their plan, we all returned to the wall, each to his work." (Verse 15)

Nehemiah had surveyed the walls and worked out a plan whereby each family in Jerusalem would be responsible for rebuilding a part of the wall adjacent to their home. There were enemies who opposed the building of the wall. Those enemies planned a sneak attack which failed.

"From that day on, half of my servants worked on construction, and half held the spears, shields, bows, and coats of mail; and the leaders stood behind all the house of Judah." (Verse 16)

Half the company worked on construction of the wall, and half were on guard ready to repel any attack.

"Who were building on the wall. Those who carried burdens were laden in such a way that each with one hand labored on the work and with the other held his weapon." (Verse 17)

Perhaps, because, the soldiers were few, the builders were also armed for defense. The burden bearers who carried smaller stones or baskets of debris on their heads would usually have one hand free for the missile. "Weapon" here suggests something thrown.

"And each of the builders had his sword girded at his side while he built. The man who sounded the trumpet was beside me." (Verse 18)

There seemed to be different types of laborers. The "builders" here were stone masons in contrast to the burden bearers of Verse 17. Since they needed both hands for work, a sword was worn at their side. A trumpet was to summon the workmen in time of attack. The trumpet was a curved horn of a cow or ram.

"And I said to the nobles and to the officials and to the rest of the people, 'The word is great and widely spread, and we are separated on the wall, far from one another." (Verse 19)

Because the work on the walls was widely spread, a system of alarms had to be instituted.

"In the place where you hear the sound of the trumpet, rally to us there. Our God will fight for us." (Verse 20)

When an attack was imminent, the trumpet would sound the alarm and all should rally there to repel the enemy. Nehemiah concludes his instruction with the comforting promise that the Jews would not face the enemy alone, but with the support of God.

Completion of the Wall

Nehemiah 6:15–16

"So the wall was finished on the twenty-fifth day of the month Elul, in fifty-two days." (Verse 15)

Nehemiah completed the wall in fifty-two days. According to historians, the work began on August 11, 445 B.C. and was completed on October 2 of the same year—within six months of his obtaining leave from King Artaxerxes.

"And when all our enemies heard of it, all the nations round about us were afraid and fell greatly in their own esteem; for they perceived that this work had been accomplished with the help of our God." (Verse 16)

The task of building the wall was done rapidly. The completion of the work was a blow to the confidence and pride of the enemies and they were afraid.

The marvel was accomplished not by human effort alone, but by the assistance of God. This verse is a good conclusion to the story of the building of the wall.

LESSON IN LIFE

The wall of Jerusalem was rebuilt because all the people became involved and God was with them and "the people had a mind to work." (Nehemiah 4:6)

Our attitude toward the work of the Lord may determine the success or failure of our efforts. We should be willing and enthusiastic, and motivated by a love of Christ.

No great accomplishment for God happens accidentally. It comes because somebody paid the price.

In building the wall, some of the people had different jobs. While we are all members of the same body of Christ, we have different functions. We have different gifts, talents, and abilities. We will be judged by how faithfully we use these in God's service. We need to become personally involved in some part of God's work.

God needs workers through whom He can accomplish great things. What are you willing to do?

Josephus, the historian, concludes his story of Nehemiah: "He was a man of kind and just nature and most anxious to serve his countrymen, and he left the walls of Jerusalem as his eternal monument." What you leaving as a monument?

Brengle Memorial Library
The Salvation Army
School for Officer Training
Suffern, N.Y.

God's Law Reaffirmed

The people of Judah had returned from their captivity in Babylon to Jerusalem. Many years had passed. The spiritual competition of Jerusalem was deplorable and the people needed a spiritual revival and spiritual leader. Such a leader was Ezra. Ezra was a priest and a scribe. "Scribe" means "not only a copier of the law, but a student and teacher of its meaning."

Like Nehemiah, Ezra was appointed by Artaxerxes I, king of Persia, to help the exiles in restoring Jerusalem and Judah.

The book of Nehemiah tells of three events. The first seven chapters tells of the success that Nehemiah had in rebuilding the walls of the city. Chapters 8–10 tell of the revival under Ezra. The closing chapters tell of Nehemiah's second visit to the city of Jerusalem and a description of its condition.

The Reading of the Word

Nehemiah 8:1–3

"And all the people gathered as one man into the square before the Water Gate; and they told Ezra the scribe to bring the book of the law of Moses which the Lord had given to Israel." (Verse 1)

"All the people" included both men and women. This was a situation unusual enough for comment, since women ordinarily had little share in religious meetings. The "square" was an open place where the people could assemble.

The people asked Ezra to attend the meeting to read from "the book of the law of Moses." Ezra had a very responsible position at this time, for he was the principal channel for divine truth for Judah.

"And Ezra the priest brought the law before the assembly, both men and women and all who could hear with understanding, on the first day of the seventh month." (Verse 2)

Not only were men and women present, but many of the

161

children who were old enough to understand what Ezra had to say. These people were hungry for an understanding of the Word of God.

"And he read from it facing the square before the Water Gate from early morning until midday, in the presence of the men and the women and those who could understand; and the ears of all the people were attentive to the book of the law." (Verse 3)

Reading began at daylight and continued until noon. We would probably consider this a long time, but "all the people were attentive."

The Reaction to the Word

Nehemiah 8:8–12

"And they read from the book, from the law of God, clearly, and they gave the sense, so that the people understood the reading." (Verse 8)

"They read," indicates that there were readers, probably Levites, who relieved Ezra and helped him in reading the law to the people.

The important thing was to convey the meaning of God's message to the minds and lives of the hearers. It was a message to be understood. It was important not only to hear, but also to understand the law so it could be accepted and practiced by the people.

"And Nehemiah, who was the governor, and Ezra the priest and scribe, and the Levites who taught the people, said to all the people, 'This day is holy to the Lord your God; do not mourn or weep.' For all the people wept when they heard the words of the law." (Verse 9)

Reading of the scripture had a powerful effect on the people. They were so moved that they wept. The weeping after the reading of the law is usually explained as due to repentance for past sins and fear of punishment to come.

"Then he said to them, 'Go your way, eat the fat and drink sweet wine and send portions to him for whom nothing is prepared; for this day is holy to our Lord; and do not be grieved for the joy of the Lord is your strength.'" (Verse 10)

He begins to encourage and comfort the people. Since the day is "holy" and consecrated to the worship of God, their response, then, was to be joyful. The main attitude of God's people was to be of joy and gratitude.

The people were to go and eat the choice foods and drink of the best. It was a day of rejoicing.

They were to think of others also, for they were to "send portions," gifts of food, "to him for whom nothing is prepared" because of poverty or any other reason. They were to eat and drink and share their good things with their neighbors. The sending of portions to the poor was a part of the holy day observance. Love of God is associated with love for one's neighbor.

When the people renewed their covenant with the Lord, it was a time of rejoicing. "The joy of the Lord is your strength" indicates the joy of Israel in the grace of God. The anguish they had felt when they realized their guilt gave way to rejoicing when they realized they now understood His word and could walk anew with Him. The joyous religious festivals of Israel were based on her confidence that the Lord protected her. This joy comes from fellowship with Him. This joy is not dependent upon physical circumstances.

"So the Levites stilled all the people, saying, 'Be quiet, for this day is holy; do not be grieved.' " (Verse 11)

The Levites "stilled all the people." They conveyed to the people the message that the day was holy and it was a time of rejoicing.

"And all the people went their way to eat and drink and to send portions and to make great rejoicing, because they had understood the words that were declared to them." (Verse 12)

The crowd responded and spent the rest of the day in feasting and mirth. It was a wonderful day. They rejoiced and shared their spirit of joy with others.

Many times when a sinner is converted, there are tears of remorse for his sins. This is followed with an inner peace and joy. When a revival of religion comes, people will be able to tell it by the look on the faces of Christians. There is joy that comes from walking in God's way.

In these verses, Ezra read the law of God to the people. He did his work well. He made sure the law was understood and encouraged the people to obey the law. There was a revival of religion in Jerusalem.

There is no "date line" on the Bible. It was written for the ages.

The Word of God has power to change men. The Bible is for inspiration and transformation. To help you to understand the Bible, ask His help before each reading. Use a Bible dictionary or commentary.

Dwight L. Moody said, "One day I read in the tenth chapter of Romans, 'Now faith cometh by hearing, and hearing by the word of God.' I had closed my Bible, and prayed for faith. I now opened my Bible, and began to study, and faith has been growing ever since."

Take time to read the Bible. Daily Bible reading is important for spiritual health. It will make for a happier and fuller life.

When one seriously studies the word of God, there will be a deepening of spiritual experience.

The Promise of the Messiah

All through the Old Testament, the coming of the Messiah was prophesied. A prophet named Isaiah took up the Messianic hope. He described the Deliverer in beautiful poetry and song.

God's Exalted Servant

Isaiah 52:13–15

"Behold, my servant shall prosper, he shall be exalted and lifted up, and shall be very high." (Verse 13)

This and the passages which follow are probably the most influential poem in any literature.

The prophet was speaking to a people in exile and reassuring them that all was not lost. In due time, God would send them a deliverer.

The prophet in these passages describes the Suffering Servant. The word "servant" occurs twenty times in Isaiah, Chapters 41–53. "My servant shall prosper" indicates that he shall be successful in achieving his assigned purpose. He will carry out God's purpose, and succeed in his mission. He lives in such close fellowship with God that he knows his ways and purposes, and sees the deeper meaning involved in his suffering.

The term "servant," when applied to a follower of Christ, is a title of honor. "He that is greatest among you shall be your servant." (Matthew 23:11)

"He shall be exalted and lifted up." Christ was lifted up on His cross, exalted above all other men of all time. There has been none like Him before or since.

"As many were astonished at him—his appearance was so marred, beyond human semblance, and his form beyond that of the sons of men." (Verse 14)

He had been so disfigured by ill treatment and suffering that he no longer looked like a man. People were astonished because of his humiliation. They were also astonished by His glory and victory. We are astonished when we consider how the Redeemer was mocked, crowned with thorns, scourged and crucified.

The power and influence of Christ is still cause for astonishment.

"So shall he startle many nations; kings shall shut their mouths because of him; for that which has not been told them they shall see, and that which they have not heard they shall understand." (Verse 15)

Nations will be startled by Him. Even the kings will "shut their mouths" and be silent before Him because of awe, His message and the new truth. Pilate "marvelled greatly." (Matthew 27:14)

Jesus is King and Servant. He is the lamb and the lion of the tribe of Judah.

God's Suffering Servant

Isaiah 53:1–3

"Who has believed what we have heard? And to whom has the arm of the Lord been revealed?" (Verse 1)

People would stand in awe, but not many would believe or understand. The coming of the Messiah had been announced to Israel and the message of the humility and exaltation was so unique that it was incredible. He was known as the child of a carpenter, cradled in a manger, hung up on a cross and yet was the Savior of the world! This verse pictures the general skepticism with which the announcement of the Servant's mission is received.

"The arm of the Lord" is speaking figuratively of God's power to deliver His people and His activity in history. God raised up and exalted the Servant and had revealed His actions in the Servant.

"For he grew up before him like a young plant, and like a root out of dry ground; he had no form or comeliness that we should look at him, and no beauty that we should desire him." (Verse 2)

Here begins the life story of suffering. He grew up before God like a young plant, tender and beautiful. In the eyes of man he was not a young plant, but like a "root out of dry ground."

He came from an unlikely source and from adverse circumstances. He came from humble surroundings and not from a king's palace. Dry ground suggests the religious condition of the people when the Messiah came. From this unpromising dry ground situation came one bringing new life for men. It was not his physical appearance that turned men away from Him, but His stand for righteousness. His life rebuked the hypocrisy of men. They did not "desire Him" because they did not want to face their own sins. Also, His suffering and humiliation would turn some men away from him.

"He was despised and rejected by men; a man of sorrows, and acquainted with grief; and as one from whom men hide their faces he was despised, and we esteemed him not." (Verse 3)

Is this not an amazing statement that the only holy person that ever walked this earth—the only begotten Son of God, the one who came to deliver men from the power of sin, Satan and death—should be despised and rejected of men!

John summed up the rejection of Jesus when he declared: "He came to his own home, and his own people received him not." (John 1:11)

Jesus did not come as the kind of Messiah that people were expecting. They expected a great king leading a mighty army. Instead of gathering a great army, he selected a group of unimpressive men and taught them lessons of love and service.

He Suffered For Us

Isaiah 53:4-6

"Surely he has borne our griefs and carried our sorrows; yet we esteemed him stricken smitten by God, and afflicted." (Verse 4)

This verse is quoted in Matthew 8:17. John the Baptist declared when he saw the Lord, "Behold, the Lamb of God, who takes away the sin of the world!" (John 1:29)

Why should the Son of God endure such humiliation, suffering and shame? God had to punish sin, but He wanted to let the sinner go free. The Cross is the answer to this problem.

The griefs and sorrows which the Sufferer bore were not His own, but that of the people. The Servant took these sufferings upon Himself as though they were His own. Our sins have been transferred to Him. He became our substitute.

"But he was wounded for our transgressions, he was bruised for our iniquities; upon him was the chastisement that made us whole, and with his stripes we are healed." (Isaiah 53:5)

Because he was wounded for our transgressions, we do not have to bear the punishment we deserve. By His death upon the cross, He provided the way for man to be reconciled to God, and for man to be delivered from sin.

"All we like sheep have gone astray; as have turned every one to his own way; and the Lord has laid on him the iniquity of us all." (Verse 6)

This is a moving finale. "All" begins and ends this confession. All have sinned and come short of the glory of God. There are no exceptions—all have gone astray. We were all involved in the Servant's suffering.

The climax of the act of God in this supreme epic is: "and the Lord has laid on him the iniquity of all."

The essential message of the Christian Gospel is set forth in this passage.

LESSON IN LIFE

The Savior came to earth in fulfillment of God's promise. His promises are sure and true. God provided for our salvation. God's promise of a Savior was fulfilled in Jesus Christ.

The promises of God become precious and meaningful to those who accept His promises on His terms. It was for you and me that Jesus came into the world to die, but we need to apply His promise to ourselves.

In Isaiah 53:6, substitute yourself for the plural pronoun and make it apply to yourself. You and I are sinners, but God loved us and made possible our salvation. God sent the Suffering Servant into the world to save men from their sins. It is through Jesus Christ that we have salvation from our sins. Have you really accepted Him in your heart? Accept Him as Savior and Lord.

Between the Testaments

The last book of the Old Testament, Malachi, was thought to have been written around 450 B.C. The first book of the New Testament was written around the middle of the first century A.D.

This devotional is an attempt to look at the period between the Testaments.

Historical Background

The Persians conquered the Babylonians in 538 B.C. The people of Judah were allowed to return to their homeland, and for about 200 years, the Jewish community in Palestine lived under the Persian empire. During this period, the temple was rebuilt and the walls of the city were restored. Aramaic, which was the official language of the Persian people, gradually replaced Hebrew as the common tongue of the Jews.

Another power appeared—the Greeks. Alexander the Great rose to power. Around 334 B.C., he defeated Persia. The Greek philosopher Aristotle had been a great influence on him.

Many people learned to use the Greek language. Around 250 B.C., in order that these people might have a Bible to read, the Old Testament was translated into Greek.

After Alexander died in 323 B.C. at age 33, his kingdom was divided among four of his generals. Wars and strife brought about two kingdoms: Egypt and Syria. There were wars between these kingdoms during the interbiblical period. Palestine was caught in the middle of the struggle.

The Syrians defeated the Egyptians and occupied the Holy Land. At first, the Jews were treated kindly. One of the later leaders was Antiochus Epiphanes, who became the great enemy of the Jews.

There were those who refused to yield to the demands of Antiochus. The Maccabean revolt began. As a result of this revolt, the Syrians withdrew from Jerusalem. There was partial independence until 63 B.C.

It is believed by some Bible scholars that a group covenanted together to study the law and keep the covenant no matter what happened. The members of this group came to be known later as the Pharises.

The Roman Empire soon asserted itself and Palestine was once again under the heel of a conqueror. Into this kind of world, Jesus was born.

Reverence for God's Law

Psalm 119:1–8

"Blessed are those whose way is blameless, who walk in the law of the Lord." (Verse 1)

This psalm is the longest psalm. God is addressed or referred to in every one of its verses. This psalm is distinguished also by its extraordinary tribute to the law of Israel. It stresses the blessedness of those persons who keep the law. The date is probably after Ezra.

The word "psalm" means "praise" or "song of praise." They are religious poems. In many ways, they are man's expression addressed to God.

"Blessed" here means "truly happy." Happy were those whose lives were directed by devotion to God and who walked in His way. The believer who walks with God in the way of holiness receives great benefits. Happiness of the godly is a familiar theme of the psalmist.

"Blessed are those who keep his testimonies, who seek him with their whole heart." (Verse 2)

Happy are those who keep and practice the Law of God and seek His presence and will. "Seek" means to approach God in prayer and worship. It also means trying to understand God's will.

"Who also do no wrong, but walk in his ways." (Verse 3)

The happy person is the one who refrains from doing wrong. This person received guidance from the Law of God as he walks in His ways.

"Thou hast commanded thy precepts to be kept diligently." (Verse 4)

Men should keep the laws because they have come from Him.

An important word of the Old Testament is "law." Man must obey these commandments diligently.

"O that my ways may be steadfast in keeping thy statutes!"

This is a short earnest prayer by a devout person for constant and steadfast loyalty to the divine requirements.

"Then I shall not be put to shame, having my eyes fixed on all thy commandments." (Verse 6)

The psalmist will not "be put to shame" if he succeeds in keeping all the commandments. He is to have his eyes fixed and attention centered on God's commands. He is to be continually aware of God's commandments.

"I will praise thee with an upright heart, when I learn thy righteous ordinances."

The psalmist will praise God with an "upright heart" when he learns and practices God's "righteous ordinances." The psalmist desires that his words of praise will be more than just words. He wants his praise to come from an "upright heart." He will know better how to direct his praise. He rejoices in his right relation to God. The law was studied intensively by devout Jews and much of it memorized.

"I will observe thy statutes: O forsake me not utterly!" (Verse 8)

The psalmist is determined to be faithful to God. He knows that he needs God's presence and help. If he will observe the statutes, he believes God will continue to help him. He is asking God not to forsake him.

Political Situation When Christ Was Born

Luke 2:1–4

"In those days a decree went out from Caesar Augustus that all the world should be enrolled." (Verse 1)

When this decree went out, the most powerful person on earth was Caesar Augustus, emperor of Rome. He was born in 63 B.C. and was a great nephew of Julius Caesar. Upon the assassination of Julius Caesar in 44 B.C., Augustus gradually rose to power. In 27 B.C., he became the emperor of the Roman empire and ruled to 14 A.D.

Caesar decreed that his vast empire should be enrolled for taxation.

In a small corner of this vast empire, a baby was born one night. It was in a little town where the parents had come because of this decree. Something mightier than a decree had happened. "God sent forth his son." (Galatians 4:4)

"This was the first enrollment, when Quirinius was governor of Syria." (Luke 2:2)

According to the historian Josephus, this was the first enrollment. This was protested violently.

"And all went to be enrolled, each to his own city." (Verse 3)

Each man had to return to the city of his birth, no matter how far away. Here he was placed on the tax roll.

"And Joseph also went up from Galilee, from the city of Nazareth, to Judea, to the city of David, which is called Bethlehem, because he was of the house and lineage of David." (Verse 4)

Joseph and Mary, his espoused wife, went to Bethlehem because Joseph "was of the house and lineage of David."

Such was the setting of Jesus' birth.

LESSON IN LIFE

Years ago, people did not recognize the Messiah when He came. Today, many people have their own idea about God and Christianity. As a result, they are unwilling to accept the truth of the Gospel.

Some insist on trying to earn salvation. Salvation cannot be earned. It is through repentance, faith and commitment to Him that we are saved. We are saved by God's grace.

In the first part of this devotional, the psalmist remarked on the happiness of those who walk in the law.

No matter how much we crave happiness and peace, it is not achieved through human endeavor alone. It comes from a way of life and trust and belief in God's might.

"Therefore being justified by faith, we have peace with God through our Lord Jesus Christ." (Romans 5:1)

Inner happiness grows out of a relationship with the Son of God. It is acquired by knowing God. Christianity is a way of life. Walking in it, one will enjoy life in a true way.

God With Us

This devotional concentrates on the tremendous miracle of the virgin birth of Jesus. Each Christmas season, we give thought to this story of the birth of Jesus. It is a story that never grows old. The story will never lose its meaning to the person who knows Him as the source of forgiveness, peace and salvation. He is God with us.

Matthew's Gospel emphasizes the link between the Old Testament and Christ, and begins with the genealogy of Jesus.

The Gospel is good news. A most wonderful thing has happened! God, for our salvation, came down and was made man.

Good news requires messengers, or it may be lost. Each one of us should be a messenger of the Event, with its joy and converting power. The Gospel, then, is *our* Gospel.

Genealogy of Jesus

Matthew 1:1

"The book of the genealogy of Jesus Christ, the son of David, the son of Abraham." (Verse 1)

Jesus means "Savior." Christ is the Greek form of the Hebrew word, "Messiah." In Jewish literature, the term became known as "the anointed one."

Matthew's purpose was to prove that Jesus was the rightful Messiah, according to the Jewish law. The Old Testament prophecies had told that the Messiah would be born of David's royal line. Jesus, as heir of David, is Messiah. Matthew was written by a Jew and presents Christ as the King of the Jews, a true Israelite, "the son of Abraham."

It was standard Jewish doctrine that "to Abraham and his seed were the promises made." (Galatians 3:16; Genesis 22:18)

It was through Abraham that God promised to bless all the world. The blessing would come through the Messiah, who was to be David's linear descendant.

173

Annunciation to Joseph

Matthew 1:18–21

"Now the birth of Jesus Christ took place in this way. When His mother, Mary, had been betrothed to Joseph, before they came together, she was found to be with child of the Holy Spirit." (Verse 18)

Betrothal was a contract to marry and was binding. It lasted for one year. During this time, the couple were known as man and wife—although they did not have the rights of man and wife. The marriage, then, had not taken place.

Christ was born of Mary by the act of the Holy Spirit, and not by the normal union of husband and wife.

"And her husband, Joseph, being a just man and unwilling to put her to shame, resolved to divorce her quietly." (Verse 19)

A "just man" is one who observes the Jewish law. Here, the word may also mean "one who is sympathetic and kind." If a man wanted to divorce a woman, he could do it publicly before the court, or he could divorce her privately by handing her a writ in the presence of two witnesses. His compassion would not let him have a public trial.

"But as he considered this, behold an angel of the Lord appeared to him in a dream, saying, 'Joseph, son of David, do not fear to take Mary for your wife, for that which is conceived in her is of the Holy Spirit.'" (Verse 20)

Dreams were one of the ways that God revealed himself to men in the Bible times. The "angel of the Lord" appeared to Joseph in a dream. It was told to Joseph that Mary was to bear a child, and that the child had been begotten by the Holy Spirit. This somewhat prepared him for the remarkable disclosure about to be made. Joseph was addressed as "son of David."

Not too much attention has been given to Joseph. He was "just." This implies both religious scruple and obedience to the will of God. He was sensitive to divine visitation. He must have been a man of faith in that he accepted the message of the angel as the word of God.

"She will bear a son, and you shall call his name Jesus, for he will save his people from their sins." (Verse 21)

Joseph is to name the child "Jesus." Many years before this, the psalmist had written, "He shall redeem Israel from all his iniquities." (Psalm 130:8)

Joseph was told that the child to be born would be the Saviour who would save the people from their sins. The people looked forward to a Messiah who would restore Israel from her conquerors, but the Messiah's Kingdom was to be a spiritual kingdom. He came not for His sake, but for us and our salvation.

The Incarnation of Jesus Christ
Matthew 1:22-25

"All this took place to fulfill what the Lord had spoken by the prophet." (Verse 22)

The promise of the Messiah had been made by God through the prophets in the Old Testament. His promises were beginning to be fulfilled. God's redemptive work began in the Old Testament and found its fulfillment in Christ.

Old Testament: "Behold, a young woman shall conceive and bear a son, and shall call his name Immanuel." (Isaiah 7:14)

New Testament: "Behold, a virgin shall conceive and bear a son, and his name shall be called Emmanuel." (Matthew 1:23)

The name Emmanuel, which means "God with us," is one of the grandest titles of Christ. God cares for man. Man is important in the sight of God.

"When Joseph woke from sleep, he did as the angel of the Lord commanded him." (Verse 24)

Joseph trusted God and obeyed the directions received from the angel. Joseph married Mary and took her to his own home, "but knew her not until she had borne a son; and he called his name Jesus." (Verse 25)

LESSON IN LIFE

By faith over the years, men have accepted the explanation of the birth of Jesus. The coming of God into the world in the person of his son, Jesus Christ, is known as the incarnation. This is the very heart of Christmas.

Christmas is heaven come to earth. It is another name for

love. It is God become man. It is the Word become flesh. It is
the good news that God loves you and me. This is God with us.
This is Emmanuel. When the Holy Spirit dwells in us, then
Christ is with us. What can harm us when He is with us? The
Christian can face problems and hardships because he can de-
pend on God to be with him.

God came down to take us to heaven, and also to a new life
here and now. Jesus came to help us live and find out what life
can be like. He came to offer us a second chance when we have
gone off on the wrong track. He can give us a new start. He is
our hope, joy and strength. He is the source of our forgiveness,
peace and salvation. We need to tell others about Him.

He wishes to have unbroken fellowship with us. We need to
grow in faith and knowledge of God. If we accept Him and
walk daily with Him, then he will truly be God with us.

Joy to the world, the Lord is come!

God's Beloved Son

We now proceed with a survey of the New Testament as it continues "The Story of God and His People." This will help us discover the unity of the Bible and the message it reveals.

The New Testament story of Jesus passes rather quickly from His birth to baptism. He appeared in the temple at twelve years of age. Luke records that "Jesus increased in wisdom and stature, and in favor with God and man." For thirty years, Jesus had waited in Nazareth.

When John the Baptist appeared on the scene, Jesus knew that His hour had come to begin His public ministry.

The Baptism of Jesus

Matthew 3:13–15

"Then Jesus came from Galilee to the Jordan to John to be baptized by him." (Verse 13)

Jesus came sixty or seventy miles from Nazareth to the Jordan River where John was baptizing.

The Jordan River is the largest river of Palestine. From the Sea of Galilee to the Dead Sea is sixty-five miles in a straight line, but the river, because of tortuousity, has a course of two hundred miles.

Jesus came to be baptized "by John." Accounts of Jesus' baptismal experience appear in Matthew, Mark and Luke. John was a great preacher of repentence and baptism as a sign of newness of life.

"John would have presented him, saying 'I need to be baptized by you and do you come to me?'" (Verse 14)

John's baptism was for sinners who were conscious of their sin, but had repented. The life of Jesus was absolutely sinless. The baptism did not seem applicable to Jesus, and John acknowledged that Jesus had no need to be baptized. John felt that he needed what Jesus could give, rather than Jesus needing what he, John, could give.

"But Jesus answered him 'Let it be so now; for thus it is fitting for us to fulfill all righteousness.' Then he consented." (Verse 15)

Jesus did not stand in need of repentence. Why was He baptized? "To fulfill all righteousness" states the reason. He accepted His baptism as an obligation to obey fully the will of God.

In His baptism, He identified himself with the people. He came to save. People were very much conscious of their sins and their need of God. He was announcing His involvement in the movement to bring in the Kingdom.

The Commissioning of Christ

Matthew 3:16–17

"And when Jesus was baptized, he went up immediately from the water, and behold, the heavens were opened and he saw the Spirit of God descending like a dove and alighting on him." (Verse 16)

Miraculous signs accompanied the baptism. "The heavens were opened." The "Spirit of God" descended like a dove and alighted on Jesus. Through the giving of the Spirit, God ordained Jesus for His ministry. The baptism showing His divine appointment by water and Spirit. In this baptism was the realization that He was the chosen one of God, and that the way in front of Him was the way of the Cross. The baptism was the first step in the unfolding Messiahship. Jesus was the Messiah.

"And lo, a voice from heaven saying, 'This is my beloved Son, with whom I am well pleased.'" (Verse 17)

A voice came from heaven concerning Jesus. "This is my . . . . Son" is a quotation from Psalm 2:17. "The beloved" is a messianic title. "With Him I am well pleased" is from Isaiah and is a description of the Suffering Servant.

The Coming of the Spirit

John 1:32–36

"And John bore witness, 'I saw the Spirit descend as a dove from heaven, and it remained on him.'" (Verse 32).

Something happened at the baptism of Jesus that convinced John that Jesus was the Son of God. John saw the Spirit descend on Jesus. The Spirit remained in Jesus.

"I myself did not know him; but he who sent me to baptize with water said to me, 'He on whom you see the Spirit descend and remain, this is He who baptizes with the Holy Spirit.'" (Verse 33)

At first, John did not recognize Jesus. The One who sent Him to baptize said that he would see the Spirit descend and remain on Jesus. He would then know Him.

"And I have seen and have borne witness that this is the Son of God." (Verse 34)

John testified that Jesus baptized with the Holy Spirit. He is the "Son of God" in whom God's Spirit remains. The "Son of God" implies a perfect revelation of the divine nature.

"The next day again John was standing with two of his disciples; and he looked at Jesus as He walked, and said 'Behold, the Lamb of God!'" (Verses 35–36)

The fourth Gospel abounds in titles and symbolic names for Jesus.

In the days of the Old Testament, lambs were sacrificed in the temple. The lamb symbolized innocence and gentleness.

The "Lamb of God" referred to Jesus' innocence, suffering and sacrificed redemption. One day, He would be sacrificed for the sins of the world.

LESSON IN LIFE

"He has put his seal upon us and given us his spirit in our hearts as a guarantee," (II Corinthians 1:22)

Christians believe in the Holy Spirit. The Holy Spirit is the living Christ present within us which continues the work and ministry of Jesus. It guides us and gives us comfort and strength.

The Holy Spirit makes a difference in the life of a Christian. The fellowship of the Holy Spirit is needed today in these troubled times. A summary of the gifts and graces imparted by the Spirit is found in Galatians 5:22.

"But the fruit of the Spirit is love, joy, peace, patience, kindness, goodness, faithfulness, gentleness, self-control; against such there is no law." We may have such fruit if we will let the Spirit have His way within us!

Jesus Confronted Evil

The English word "tempt" usually has a bad meaning, such as "to seduce a person into sin" or "persuade or entice someone to do wrong." The meaning of the words "to tempt" in the Bible is "to test," "to try" or "put to the proof." It means "to test" more than "to tempt" in our sense of the word.

Temptation is a part of life. We are tested daily in both our business and social life. We have to make many decisions. If we truly wish to do God's will, this decision-making will be made easier. God first, others second and ourselves third. The strength of God comes upon the victor. We need to remember the example that Christ gave us in the wilderness. He obeyed fully the will of God. Jesus faced temptation and overcame it because of his complete abandonment to the will of God.

Jesus has "in every respect" been tempted as we are (Hebrews 4:15), and this enables Him to help us in our temptations (Hebrews 2:18).

Temptation is not to make us sin, but to enable us to conquer sin. It is not meant to make us bad; it is meant to make us good. It is not to weaken us, but to make us stronger. We should think of this Scripture passage as the testing, rather than the temptation, of Jesus.

Time and Place of Temptation
Matthew 4:1–2

"Then Jesus was led up by the Spirit into the wilderness to be tempted by the devil." (Verse 1)

The temptation occurred immediately after His baptism. The wilderness between Jerusalem and the Dead Sea, where there is a precipitous drop of some twelve hundred feet. It measures about thirty-five by fifteen miles. It is an area of yellow sand, crumbling limestone and scattered shingle. The hills look like

180

dust heaps. The rocks are bare and jagged. Historically, the wilderness had been the scene of testing and training for Israel.

Led and empowered by the Spirit, which had come at baptism, Jesus faced his adversary in solitude. From the height of assurance, He went to the pit of trial.

Temptation is a fork in the road: the choices are the leading of the Spirit or the opportunity of the devil. We must choose. It is a chance to rise as much as a chance to fall.

The devil or Satan means the adversary or accuser. The devil is the supernatural creature who tried to defeat the Son of God before He began his public work. The whole future activity of Jesus depended on the outcome. Jesus won this contest against evil. He won all through his life.

The devil may seem so real to us that we can almost see him. One can still see the ink stain on the wall of Luther's room when he threw his ink pot at the devil as he tempted him.

Sometimes, Christians become worried because they think they should reach a stage at which the power of the tempter is broken. We need to remember that although Jesus conquered the tempter in the wilderness, the tempter did not give up.

"And He fasted forty days and forty nights, and afterward He was hungry." (Verse 2)

Jesus fasted forty days. The number frequently recurs in the Scriptures. Moses fasted forty days on Sinai. The Jews were forty years in the wilderness. Noah was in the ark for forty days and nights. The temptation came to Jesus at the end of forty days. His temptation and struggle were real. Jesus is divine, but He was also human. He fasted and was hungry. He may not have eaten because the region was mostly without food. The spiritual struggle was so intense that He seemed not to be concerned with food.

The First Temptation

Matthew 4:3–4

"And the tempter came and said to Him, 'If you are the Son of God, command these stones to become loaves of bread.'" (Verse 3)

The first words of the tempter tried to cast doubt on the

reality of the baptismal experience by the use of the word "if." "Son of God" calls attention to Jesus' unique relation to God and His superhuman powers.

There was the temptation to turn the stones into bread. This was a temptation to Jesus to use His powers selfishly and for His own use. He could turn the bread-shaped stones of the desert into bread and satisfy the physical needs of Himself and mankind.

"But He answered, 'It is written, "Man shall not live by bread alone, but by every word that proceeds from the mouth of God."'" (Verse 4)

To give men bread would be persuading them to follow Him for the sake of what they could get out of it. Jesus came to call men to a life of giving, not getting. He offered a cross. He did not minimize this basic need of man, but He knew there was a greater need.

He answered, using a quotation from the Old Testament. Man lives by more than bread. There is a greater need. Soul hunger was deeper than body hunger. This longing can only be satisfied through complete dependence on God.

The Second Temptation

Matthew 4:5–7

"Then the devil took him to the holy city, and set him on the pinnacle of the temple, and said to Him, "If you are the son of God, throw thyself down; for it is written, "He will give His angels charge of you," and "On their hands they will bear you up, lest you strike your foot against a stone."'" (Verses 5–6)

The second temptation was the suggestion that Christ win the applause and loyalty of the multitude by performing a spectacular miracle. The tempter suggested that our Lord cast himself down from the pinnacle of the temple. The tempter quoted a psalm to prove his point that God would give His angels to save Him. Jesus is tempted to put God's promise of protection to the test.

"Jesus said to him, 'Again it is written, "You shall not tempt the Lord your God."'" (Verse 7)

Jesus met this use of Scripture with a verse from Deuteronomy.

God may test the faith and loyalty of man, but man has no ground to test God. Testing God is an assertion of unbelief. This was at the core of the temptation which Jesus resisted.

A faith that depends on signs and wonders is not faith. It is doubt looking for proof. Jesus would not base his ministry on sensationalism. God's power is not to be experimented with, but rather, quietly trusted every day. Jesus would live His life and fulfill His ministry waiting upon God and trusting Him.

The Third Temptation

Matthew 4:8–11

"Again the devil took Him to a very high mountain and showed Him all the kingdoms of the world and the glory of them, and said to Him, 'All these I will give you if you will fall down and worship me.'" (Verses 8–9)

The tempter offered political leadership. Satan offered the kingdoms of the world if Jesus would "fall down and worship" him. The tempter was telling Jesus to compromise.

"Then Jesus said to him, 'Begone, Satan! As it is written, "You shall worship the Lord your God and Him only shall you serve."'" (Verse 10)

Jesus refused to compromise with God. He demands all. Christianity can not stoop to the world; it must lift the world.

"Then the devil left him and behold, angels came and ministered to him." (Verse 11)

The devil left Jesus. Temptation, however, did not end in the wilderness. Temptation recurred, but Jesus had chosen His path. "Not my will, but thine be done." (Luke 22:42)

The choice of Jesus meant the Cross, but the Cross meant the final victory.

LESSON IN LIFE

Every day we are tested, tried and tempted. Someone said that we are tempted to either whine, shine or recline. Every day we should make a decision for God.

We need to overcome temptation. We need to make wise use of the Word of the Lord and to recognize the fact that our chief needs are spiritual. Prosperity sometimes may tend to make us forget God. Our greatest source of power is in the living presence of Jesus. There is no substitute for this power that comes through fellowship with Him. Dedication to God will result in a victorious life.

Jesus Announces God's Kingdom

Matthew uses "kingdom of heaven" thirty-three times. It is important to understand that the "kingdom of God" or "kingdom of heaven" means the reign or kingly rule of God.

Jesus proclaimed that the time had come to prepare men for it by repentance and changed lives. The truth He preached proclaimed God's rule and man's opportunity to accept it. However, man is first obligated to seek it. It is God's gift and the eternal fact of his salvation.

He taught men to pray "thy kingdom come, thy will be done." We should seek to do His will in every relationship, between man and God, and between man and man.

The following Scripture deals with the beginning of Jesus' ministry of preaching, teaching and healing in Galilee.

The Prophetic Setting

Matthew 4:12–16

"Now when he heard that John had been arrested, he withdrew into Galilee." (Verse 12)

The arrest of John the Baptist was the sign for Jesus to go forth to His work.

"He withdrew into Galilee." The name Galilee comes from the Hebrew word meaning "circle." The full name of the area was Galilee of the Gentiles, so-named because Galilee was surrounded by Gentiles. It was densely populated and fertile, and because frequent invasions had taken place, the population was of mixed races.

"And leaving Nazareth he went and dwelt in Capernaum by the sea, in the territory of Zebulun and Naphtali." (Verse 13)

Capernaum was a town situated at the north end of the Sea of Galilee. It was a busy city along the main Roman roads of commerce. It had a flourishing trade in fruit and fish. The center

185

of the community life was the synagogue. In the city today are the ruins of a synagogue.

Matthew says "the territory of Zebulun and Naphtali" in order to prepare for the quotation which follows. "That what was spoken by the prophet Isaiah might be fulfilled: 'The land of Zebulun and the land of Naphtali, toward the sea, across the Jordan, Galilee of the Gentiles—the people who sat in darkness, have seen a great light and for those who sat in the region and shadow of death, light was dawned.'" (Verses 14–16)

This prophecy concerned the northern parts of Palestine, including Galilee, which had been invaded and despoiled by the Assyrians. The original point of the prophecy was that even these regions would share in the coming bliss and messianic blessings. This explained why Jesus worked in despised Galilee, rather than Judea.

Matthew constantly pointed out how the Old Testament prophesies were fulfilled in the life, ministry, death and resurrection of Jesus.

Jesus' Proclamation
Matthew 4:17

"From that time Jesus began to preach, saying, 'Repent, for the kingdom of heaven is at hand.'" (Verse 17)

The word used by Matthew for preaching means "to herald." Jesus came as a Herald of the Kingdom of God. This was accompanied by an appeal for repentance. Man's decision does not determine the fact of God's being King, but it does determine man's relation to the Kingdom. Man decides to be a rebel (who must still answer to God), or a willing subject who participates in God's rule. The Greek word "repent" means "a change of mind." In Jewish doctrine, it involved profound sorrow for sin, restitution so far as possible, and a steadfast resolution not to commit the particular sin again. It means to stop walking away from God and begin walking toward God. Closely linked with repentance is faith. To have faith in Christ is to know Him as an actual presence.

The terms "kingdom of heaven" and "kingdom of God" are used interchangeably in the synoptic Gospels. The Kingdom of

God begins with an inner experience in the heart of an individual. It is spiritual in that men's hearts are changed.

The Methods of the Master

Matthew 4:23–25

"And he went about all Galilee, teaching in their synagogues and preaching the gospel of the kingdom and healing every disease and every infirmity among the people." (Verse 23)

Jesus began His mission in the synagogues. Jesus taught. He preached and He healed the sick. The manifold activity of Jesus is seen in this one verse. He was concerned with the whole person. People were made whole in body and spirit. True Christian belief results in concern for others and Christian action.

The temple was in Jerusalem, but wherever there was the smallest colony of Jews, there was a synagogue. The synagogue service consisted of three parts: prayers, readings from the Law and from prophets, and finally, an address.

"So his fame spread throughout all Syria, and they brought him all the sick, those afflicted with various diseases, and pains, demoniacs, epileptics, and paralytics, and he healed them." (Verse 24)

The people came crowding to hear Him, to see Him, and to be healed. "Crowds followed Him" from Galilee, from across Jordan, Jerusalem and Judea. They came from Syria. Syria was the great province of which Palestine was only a part. They also came from Decapolis. The Decapolis was a federation of ten independent Greek cities. Not only the Jews, but the Gentiles were coming to Jesus Christ.

The Divine Companion

Matthew 9:36–38

"When he saw the crowds, he had compassion for them, because they were harassed and helpless, like sheep without a shepherd." (Verse 36)

Our English word "compassion" comes from two Latin words. The first word, *passio*, means "to suffer." We speak of the passion of our Lord or Passion Week. The other part of "compassion" is *com*, which means "along with." The word "compassion" then means "to suffer with" or "enter into the sorrow and pain of others."

Jesus saw the people as sherpherdless people. He was moved to compassion by the pain, sorrow, hunger, loneliness and bewilderment of the people. This compassion was not costless. This compassion took Him to the Cross. Jesus is the true Shepherd. He laid down His life for the sheep. Jesus came to feed them, to heal them and to save that which was lost.

"Then he said to his disciples, 'The harvest is plentiful, but the laborers are few; pray therefore the Lord of the harvest to send out laborers into his harvest.'" (Verse 37–38)

The figure of speech now changes. In Verse 36, humanity is pictured as scattered sheep, but in Verses 37 and 38, humanity is pictured as ripened wheat. Jesus compares the gathering of people to the harvesting of a crop. He saw the people as a harvest to be reaped and saved.

Notice the word "laborers." The wheat does not harvest itself. Harvesters are needed. Every Christian should be a harvester. There is someone whom each one of us could and should bring to God. Men are made for life with Him, since He is the "Lord of the harvest."

LESSON IN LIFE

Most of us at one time or another think of heaven. We all want to go to heaven.

The joy of Christianity is an anticipation of heaven while we are living here on earth. Every prayer is an anticipation of heaven. Every act of selfless love is an anticipation of heaven because in doing this, we admit we are nothing and God is all.

To enter the Kingdom of God is not only to become a willing subject under the reign of God, but to participate in the reign! Man reigns with Christ when he gives up all notion of reigning. When the Christian seems the least likely to reign, as when he is persecuted, he is assured of his present and continuing reign in Christ. Those persecuted for the sake of righteousness and who, by the world's standards, seem to be defeated, are the ones to reign.

Jesus Interprets the Law

This text is taken from the Sermon on the Mount. The Sermon on the Mount is the core and essence of the teaching of Jesus to the inner circle of His chosen men. It is heart to heart communion between the disciples and their master.

The Sermon may be taken as an outline of the ideal Christian life. It tells of the nature of our Lord's Kingdom and the qualifications of its citizens.

The Sermon on the Mount was delivered in Galilee.

Completion of the Old Law
Matthew 5:17–20

"Think not that I have come to abolish the law and the prophets; I have come not to abolish them, but to fulfill them." (Verse 17)

"Think not that I have come to abolish the law" tells us of the reaction to Jesus in the religious community of that day. He seemed to threaten the Mosaic law.

He said that he had come not to destroy, but to "fulfill" the law and the prophets. "To fulfill" means "to enforce" or "to press it into its full significance." He came to confirm the true meaning of the law and to give to it the highest expression.

At this time, to the orthodox Jew, serving God was a matter of keeping many rules and regulations. This is not what Jesus meant by the Law. It consisted not of sacrifice and legalism, but of mercy and love.

"For truly, I say to you, till heaven and earth pass away, not an iota, not a dot, will pass from the law until all is accomplished." (Verse 18)

Jesus viewed the law as eternal. There are some things that do not change.

"Truly" and "Verily" are the nearest English equivalent of

"Amen." "Amen I say to you" is one of Jesus' characteristic phrases, and marks a solemn assertion of divine truth.

"Not an iota" (iota is the smallest Greek letter and corresponds to the smallest character of the Hebrew alphabet), "not a dot" will pass away from this law. The law will not lose a single dot until its purpose is completed.

"Whoever then relaxes one of the least of these commandments and teaches men so, shall be called least in the kingdom of heaven; but he who does them and teaches them shall be called great in the kingdom of heaven." (Verse 19)

Those who have taken the will of God seriously in small things will be great. The right kind of faith produces obedience to the will of God. Greatness in the Kingdom is based on lowly service.

"For I tell you, unless your righteousness exceeds that of the scribes and pharisees, you will never enter the kingdom of heaven." (Verse 20)

Here, Jesus hints that the religious leaders of his time may be barred from the gates of heaven. They were meticulous in religious obedience. There was no finer outward example of righteousness in the ancient world than the Pharisees. Yet, Jesus here says that His followers should exceed the righteousness of those groups. What did He mean by that?

Jesus set before men the love of God. When we realize how God loved us, then we want to answer that love. This is the greatest task in the world. It is an obligation more binding than the obligation to any law. The claims of love have no limit.

Retaliation

Matthew 5:38–42

"You have heard that it was said, 'An eye for an eye and a tooth for a tooth.'" (Verse 38)

The law of retaliation was practiced in Jesus' day. It is the oldest law in the world and appeared in the earliest known code of laws: the code of Hammurabi, who reigned in Babylon from 2285 to 2242 B.C. The principle is clear: if a man has inflicted an injury on any person, an equivalent injury shall be inflicted on him.

"But I say to you, do not resist one who is evil. But if any one

strikes you on the right cheek, turn to him the other also."
(Verse 39)

"Do not resist one who is evil" means that we should not oppose evil with more evil, or oppose it in a spirit of vengeance.
His point is that if wrong has been done to us, this does not give
us the license to do wrong. Christians have learned from Jesus
to accept any insult and not to retaliate or resent it. A Christian's conduct and attitude should be of this kind.

"And if any one would sue you and take your coat, let him
have your cloak as well." (Verse 40)

The "coat" is the long undergarment made with sleeves. The
"cloak" was the blanket-like outer garment. A man used it as a
blanket at night. Jesus said that if anyone takes your coat, "let
him have your cloak as well." Jesus is saying that the Christian
does not stand for his rights. The Christian thinks not of his
rights or his privileges, but of his duties and responsibilities.

"And if any one forces you to go one mile, go with him two
miles." (Verse 41)

Jesus is saying here that if your masters compel you to be a
porter for a mile, do not go one mile bitterly, but go two miles
with cheerfulness. Think of your privilege of being of service to
others.

"Give to him who begs from you, and do not refuse him who
would borrow from you." (Verse 42)

It is Jesus' demand that we should give to all who ask and not
refuse anyone who wants to "borrow from you."

The Meaning of Christian Love
Matthew 5:43–48

"You have heard that it was said, 'You shall love your neighbor
and hate your enemy.' But I say to you, love your enemies and
pray for those who persecute you." (Verses 43–44)

Jesus said "Love your enemies." This love is God-like. It is an
active love. It is love for people who do not love us. There are
no limits to this love. No matter what a person does to us, there
will not be bitterness towards him. In addition, we are to do
something for him. We are to pray for him. It is only when
Christ lives in our lives that we can have this love.

"So that you may be sons of your father who is in heaven, for he makes his sun rise on the evil and on the good, and sends the rain on the just and on the unjust." (Verse 45)

Such a love as this makes man like God—"sons of your father." God's love is universal. He poured out His sunshine and His love on good and bad alike. His love knew no boundaries and neither should ours.

"For if you love those who love you, what reward have you? Do not even the tax collectors do the same? (Verse 46)

When we only love those who love us, then we should not expect any reward from God since even the "tax collectors do the same."

"And if you salute only your brethern, what more are you doing than others? Do not even the Gentiles do the same?" (Verse 47)

The righteousness of Jesus' followers must exceed that of others.

"You, therefore, must be perfect, as your heavenly Father is perfect." (Verse 48)

Man's attitude toward other men must be like that of God: sincere, constant and merciful.

When Jesus says that his followers must be perfect, He doesn't expect that they will be completely flawless. We have the ideal toward which we must keep striving. We will never be perfect in our own strength. We have a source of power in Christ. We must commit our lives to Him.

LESSON IN LIFE

So many times we use human standards to measure ourselves. We say that we are as good as anyone. God is not interested in human standards. The true standard is found in God.

Jesus set a very high standard for His people. He lived up to His divine standard. He lived much more than the law required. If a Christian intends to do no more than absolutely required, he has missed the Spirit of Christ. As growing Christians, we shall do as much as we can, rather than as much as we have to do.

Jesus Teaches God's Judgment

A parable is intended to highlight one particular truth. It is an earthly story with a heavenly meaning. It is drawn from every day life and makes use of things that people understand. Its purpose is to help man discover truth.

The sermon in parables was delivered by the Sea of Galilee. The crowd was so large that Jesus had to get in a boat to separate Himself from the people so that all could see and hear Him.

The Parable of the Tares

Matthew 13:24–30

"Another parable he put before them, saying, 'The kingdom of heaven may be compared to a man who sowed good seed in his field.'" (Verse 24)

In this parable we have a picture of Jesus as the sower going about preparing his harvest fields. The good seed are the people of God. The field in which they are sown is the world which is "His field." The Biblical writers saw God as the personal God of action. He invaded history to work in the lives of men.

"But while men were sleeping, his enemy came and sowed weeds among the wheat, and went away." (Verse 25)

The picture in this parable would be clear to a Palestinian. The picture of a man sowing darnel in someone else's field was actually sometimes done. This crime has even been mentioned in Roman law.

This weed, like evil, represented an insidious invasion of the good field. Jesus is the sower of the good seed of the Gospel, which is sometimes choked by evil. There is evil in the world. God is at work in this world, but the adversary, Satan, labors to destroy the kingdom of righteousness. This is a world mixed with good and evil. The rabbis regarded darnel as a perverted kind of wheat. It very closely resembled the wheat plant in its early stage.

This parable teaches us how hard it is to distinguish between those who are in the Kingdom and those who are not. We are often too quick to classify people as good or bad without knowing all the facts.

"So when the plants came up and bore grain, then the weeds appeared also." (Verse 26)

When the wheat and darnel matured, it was not difficult to distinguish between them.

"And the servant of the householder came and said to him, 'Sir, did you not sow good seed in your field? How, then, has it weeds.'" (Verse 27)

Why is there evil in the world? A common human question with no easy answer.

"He said to them, 'An enemy has done this.' The servants said to him, 'Then do you want us to go and gather them?'" (Verse 28) When the servants of the householder recognized that weeds had been sown in the field, they wanted to root them out.

The "servants" are disciples of Jesus, who wish to purge the church of the unfaithful.

"But he said, 'No, lest in gathering the weeds you root up the wheat along with them.'" (Verse 29)

He advised his servants to be patient in the presence of evil. It teaches us not to be so quick with our judgments. It is sometimes hard to distinguish the wheat from the weeds and good men from bad men. Judgment is difficult. We had better not judge at all.

"Let both grow together until the harvest; and at harvest time I will tell the reapers, 'Gather the weeds first and bind them in bundles to be burned, but gather the wheat into my barn." (Verse 30)

It is disastrous to try to achieve a "pure" church in which there are no sinners.

Interpretation of the Parable of the Tares
Matthew 13:36–43

"Then he left the crowds and went into the house, and his disciples came to him saying, 'Explain to us the parables of the field.'" (Verse 36)

The disciples wanted Jesus to interpret the Parable of the Tares to them.

"He answered, 'He who sows the good seed is the son of man.'" (Verse 37) Jesus is the sower in this parable.

"The field is the world, and the good seed means the sons of the kingdom; the weeds are the sons of the evil one." (Verse 38)

This seems to me to be a great missionary passage. The Christian faith is a universal one. The Word of God is meant for every one. The "good seed" are God's people—regenerated men and women. The disciples of Jesus must work to make disciples of all nations and bring about a new kind of world.

"And the enemy who sowed them is the devil; the harvest is the close of the age, and the reapers are angels." (Verse 39)

"The close of the age" is a frequent expression of Matthew. In fact, these are the last words in the Gospel. Matthews always looked forward to the great day when Jesus will be visibly present in His celestial form and to say once more, "Come O blessed of my Father, inherit the kingdom prepared for you from the foundation of the world." (Matthew 25:34)

To the early Christians, this promise meant that when the curtain fell on human history, Christ would remain as friend and Lord.

"Just as the weeds are gathered and burned with fire, so will it be at the close of the age." (Matthew 13:40)

There will be a time in history in which evil will forever be banished from God's world. The wicked cannot defy God forever.

"The Son of man will send his angels, and they will gather out of his kingdom all causes of sin and all evil-doers." (Verse 41)

The deity of Jesus is emphasized. The angels belong to the "Son of man." The world is His.

"And throw them into the furnace of fire; then men will weep and gnash their teeth." (Verse 42)

In the end, there is terrible pain and grief for those who have defied God.

"Then the righteous will shine like the sun in the kingdom of their father. He who has ears, let him hear." (Verse 43)

For a while, the wicked may seem to have the upper hand,

but the righteous will finally prevail in the time of judgment. The parable closes with a solemn warning to repent while there is time. "He who has ears, let him hear."

In this parable is a warning to us not to judge other people. There is also a warning to us that in the end, there comes the judgment of God.

LESSON IN LIFE

Good and evil exist side by side. It is a fact of life. Each one of us should think of things we can do to oppose evil.

Judgment will come. This is a sobering biblical truth. Repent while there is yet time. "He who has ears, let him hear." (Matthew 13:43)

Memory Selection: "Salvation and glory and power belong to our God, for his judgments are true and just." (Revelations 19: 1–2)

Jesus Offers God's Forgiveness

Sin and its results are a real problem today. Feelings of guilt cause much mental anguish. We all need the forgiveness that only Jesus can give.

In this devotional, we want to discuss the meaning of forgiveness, conditions and results of forgiveness, and who needs to be forgiven.

The printed text is taken from the Gospel of Luke. Some distinctive characteristics of this Gospel are an interest in social relationships, a deep concern for outcasts and sinners, and an interest in stories about women. There is an emphasis on joy, prayer and the Holy Spirit.

Jesus And A Penitent Sinner
Luke 7:36–38

"One of the Pharisees asked him to eat with him, and he went into the Pharisee's house and sat at the table. And behold, a woman of the city, who was a sinner, when she learned that he was sitting at the table in the Pharisee's house, brought an alabaster flask of ointment." (Verses 36–37)

St. Luke is the only evangelist who tells us that Jesus was sometimes invited to dinner by the Pharisees.

The houses were often built around an open courtyard, and here in the warm weather meals were eaten. When a rabbi was at a meal in such a house, the doors were left open so people could come in and listen to the teaching of the rabbi. To this meal came a woman "who was a sinner." A sinner probably meant a prostitute. She brought an alabaster flask of ointment. This was very costly.

The Pharisee was of the strictest sect of the Jews who adhered to the laws of his religion. He probably was a man of some wealth. In contrast, the woman was a woman of the streets. These are the chief characters in the divine drama.

Jesus came to minister to all people, all classes and all races. He came to the down-and-out, but also to the up-and-out.

"And standing behind him at his feet, weeping, she began to wet his feet with her tears, and wiped them with the hair of her head and kissed his feet, and annointed them with the ointment." (Verse 38)

As the woman saw Him, the tears came and fell upon His feet. She wiped them off with her long hair. She then kissed His feet and "annointed them with the ointment." Kissing a person's foot was a sign of the most humble gratitude, such as a man might show to someone who had saved his life.

The woman here was penitent. Her acts of devotion and tears expressed love and gratitude.

Penitence preceeds forgiveness. Love and gratitude follows. The love that follows forgiveness involves penitence which is a continued awareness of unworthiness. Our penitence is an expression of love.

A Different Viewpoint

Luke 7:39-50

"Now when the Pharisee who had invited him saw it, he said to himself, 'If this man were a prophet, he would have known who and what sort of woman this is who is touching him, for she is a sinner.'" (Verse 39)

The Pharisee, Simon, had invited Jesus in the belief that He was a prophet. The Pharisee felt that a prophet would have known what type of woman she was, and would have refused to let this woman touch Him.

The Pharisee did not realize that Jesus was expressing a wisdom and virtue far beyond his own. The Pharisee had classified the woman as a sinner and had decided how she should be treated. Simon was influenced by prejudice. Jesus was more interested in what a person might become, rather than what one was at the moment.

"And Jesus answering said to him, 'Simon, I have something to say to you,' and he answered, 'What is it, Teacher?'" (Verse 40)

The unspoken criticism of the Pharisee was known by Jesus and He responded to it.

"A certain creditor had two debtors; one owed five hundred denarii, and the other fifty. When they could not pay he forgave them both. Now which of them will love him more?" (Verses 41–42)

Jesus tells a parable about a creditor and two debtors. "One owed five hundred denarii," which was approximately $100 in United States currency. The other owed 50 denarii. The creditor forgave them both and cancelled the debts.

"When they could not pay" is a picture of a man's helpless, hopeless condition in sin. The position is not whether a man has sinned a lot or a little, but whether he has sinned at all. Simon and the woman were both sinners, even though their sins may have been different.

When the two debtors stood in the presence of God, the Lord of Mercy forgave them. We see here a picture of God's grace, which is not dependent on man's merit. Both persons were equally helpless. Their hope lay in the forgiveness offered by God.

"Simon answered, 'The one, I suppose, to whom he forgave the more.' And he said to him, 'You have judged rightly.'" (Verse 43)

The woman's love was the proof of His forgiveness.

"Then turning toward the woman, he said to Simon, 'Do you see this woman? I entered your house, you gave no water for my feet, but she has wet my feet with her tears and wiped them with her hair. You gave me no kiss, but from the time I came in she has not ceased to kiss my feet. You did not annoint my head with oil but she has annointed my feet with ointment.'" (Verses 44–46)

"Do you see this woman?" is a searching question. The Pharisee was preoccupied with what sort of a woman she was. He could not really see the woman. There is a distinction here. Often, we are so blinded by our prejudices that we cannot really see the person as he is, or what he can become. How do we see people and react to them?

In Jesus' time, when a guest entered a house, three things

were usually done. The host gave the guest a kiss of welcome, water was poured over a guest's feet to cleanse and comfort them, and the head was annointed. The host had failed to extend these special courtesies.

There was a sharp contrast between the reception given Jesus by the Pharisee, and the reception given by the woman.

"Therefore I tell you, her sins, which are many, are forgiven, for she loved much; but he who is forgiven little, loves little." (Verse 47)

In this story is a contrast between two attitudes. Simon was conscious of no need, felt no love, and therefore, received no forgiveness. The woman realized the reality of her sin. Those who know that they are unworthy of forgiveness can receive it.

Self-sufficing shuts a man off from God. A sense of need will open the door to the forgiveness of God.

Where there is a great sense of sin that has been forgiven, there will be great love. In order to have this profound feeling about sin, it is not necessary to sin greatly. Great saints have been sensitive about their imperfections. Paul could speak of sinners "of whom I am chief." (I Timothy 1:15)

"Then those who were at table with him, began to say among themselves, 'Who is this, who even forgives sins?' And he said to the woman, 'Your faith has saved you, go in peace.'" (Luke 7:49–50)

Jesus forgave the woman. This aroused the critics who knew that only God could forgive sins. They were right. Jesus Christ was God in human flesh.

The woman's faith had saved her. Forgiveness is the consequence of faith.

LESSON IN LIFE

All are in need of God's forgiving love. God's forgiving love is offered to all. We canont pay for our forgiveness. All men depend on the mercy of God for forgiveness. Jesus forgave the sins of an outcast woman. Jesus offers forgiveness when by faith, repentence, confession, and baptism, we give ourselves to Him.

God's forgiving love should result in devotion to Christ, a

desire that others may know Him, and a forgiving spirit toward others.

Some people say that they may forgive a person, but cannot forget. This means that they do not really forgive. One must forget.

God forgives our sins and remembers them no more. Do we?

God's Mighty Acts Through Jesus

These passages emphasizes the power of God as revealed in the ministry of Jesus Christ.

By a series of healings, Jesus is set forth as the Lord of life and death. These miracles of Jesus were a sign of his compassion. They also were a sign of Jesus' power over nature.

God did mighty acts through Jesus while He lived here on earth, and today, through Jesus, is still doing so.

The King James version of the Bible uses the word "miracle" no fewer than thirty-seven times. Five of these are in the Old Testament and thirty-two are in the New Testament.

Words frequently used in other English versions are "sign," "wonder," "work," and "mighty work." I think that the tendency to avoid the word "miracle" has been unfortunate.

There has been a great deal of discussion over "miracles." If one believes in God, that God created the universe, sustains and controls it, then most of the difficulties of miracle have truly been dealt with.

A miracle is any event in which one sees a revelation of God. Religious faith is grounded in the sense and possibility of miracle.

Miracles were not done with the main purpose to produce faith. Faith helped to create conditions that called forth miracles.

The Healing of a Centurian's Servant

Matthew 8:5–13

"As he entered Capernaum, a centurian came forward to him, beseeching him." (Verse 5)

Jesus returned to Capernaum and a centurian came to Him. A centurian was an officer in the Roman Army who commanded one hundred men. It is interesting to note that every centurian mentioned in the New Testament is mentioned with honor.

202

A second century synagogue has been excavated in Capernaum which probably took the place of the one which, according to Luke 7:5, was built by the centurian.

"And saying, 'Lord, my servant is lying paralyzed at home, in terrible distress.'" (Matthew 8:6)

A servant was suffering greatly because of his paralysis. This centurian was grieved that his servant was ill, and was determined to do everything to save him. This concern for a slave was unusual in that time. This centurian was an extraordinary man in that he loved his slave. He was compassionate.

"And he said to him, 'I will come and heal him.'" (Verse 7)

The response of Jesus was instant: "I will come and heal him."

"But the centurian answered him, 'Lord I am not worthy to have you come under my roof; but only say the word, and my servant will be healed.'" (Verse 8)

The centurian said that he was "not worthy" to have Jesus come into his home. This reply shows humility on the part of the centurian.

The centurian may have feared that Jesus had scruples against entering a Gentile house or he may have been trying to relieve Jesus of taking such a step to help Him. Our Lord was willing to break social customs in order to minister to man. The centurian had confidence in Jesus' word alone. He completely trusted Jesus. The emphasis of this story is on the centurian's faith. The centurian staked all his hope on Jesus' power.

It was here that the centurian's faith reached its peak.

"For I am a man under authority, with soldiers under me; and I say to one 'Go,' and he goes, and to another, 'Come,' and he comes, and to my slave, 'Do this,' and he does it." (Verse 9)

This man had insight into the life and ministry of Jesus. The centurian was a man of authority and knew how to command his soldiers to do his bidding. The centurian knew that when there was authority, commands are obeyed. He recognized that Jesus had authority over everything.

"When Jesus heard him, he marveled, and said to those who followed him, 'Truly, I say to you, not even in Israel have I found such faith.'" (Verse 10)

The centurian believed and Jesus rejoiced in his faith. Jesus said that nowhere had He found such faith, not even among the faithful in Israel.

"I tell you, many will come from east and west and sit at table with Abraham, Isaac, and Jacob in the kingdom of heaven." (Verse 11)

Here is the promise of Christ that the Gospel offers redemption to all men.

"While the sons of the kingdom will be thrown into the outer darkness; there men will weep and gnash their teeth." (Verse 12)

This was a warning of doom to those who did not believe. Each person has to learn that the passport to God's presence is not citizenship in any nation; it is faith. Faith is the passport to the blessedness of God.

Jesus Christ is not the possession of any race of men. He may be possessed by every man in every race—if there is faith.

Faith is ultimately heaven; lack of faith is darkness and gnashing of teeth.

The outer darkness and gnashing of teeth were part of the usual description of Gehenna.

"And to the centurion Jesus said, 'Go, be it done for you as you have believed.' And the servant was healed at that very moment." (Verse 13)

Jesus spoke the word and the servant of the centurion was healed.

A Miracle In A Cottage

Matthew 8:14–15

"And when Jesus entered Peter's house, he saw his mother-in-law lying sick with a fever." (Verse 14)

The home of Peter is the scene. The mother of Peter's wife was ill with a fever. The fever may have been malaria, but we do not know for sure.

"He touched her hand, and the fever left her, and she rose and served him." (Verse 15)

Here, He was in a modest little cottage, and a poor woman was tossing with a fever. Here was no crowd. In a crowd or cottage, Jesus was ready and able to help. "He touched her hand,

and the fever left her." Jesus' presence, as always, had healing power. The touch of Jesus' hand must have been unforgettable on every occasion.

She was completely restored so much so that she began to help Peter's wife in serving a meal to the guests.

Miracles In A Crowd
Matthew 8:16–17

"That evening they brought to him many who were possessed with demons; and he cast out the spirits with a word, and healed all who were sick." (Verse 16)

It was considered work to carry a sick person on the Sabbath. It was also illegal to heal on the Sabbath unless a person's life was in danger. The crowd therefore waited until evening to come to Jesus for the healing, which they knew that He could give.

"This was to fulfill what was spoken by the prophet, Isaiah, 'He took our infirmities and bore our diseases.'" (Verse 17)

Matthew refers to the healing ministry of Jesus Christ as a fulfillment of the prophecy of Isaiah 53:4.

"He took our infirmities." Redemption is given if we turn believingly to Christ.

LESSON IN LIFE

God came to earth in the person of Jesus Christ. Once we get this fixed in our mind, then miracles will fall into their proper place. The whole Gospel of Christ proclaims the miraculous.

The Son of God came into this world in the fullness of time. He was born in a miraculous way. He performed miracles. He died on the cross. He was buried and on the third day He rose again and ascended into heaven.

God is the author of life. God loves us. We must believe in the power of God.

"He that cometh to God must believe that he is, and that he is a rewarder of them that diligently seek him." (Hebrews 11:6)

If we ask, we shall receive; if we seek, we shall find; if we knock, it shall be opened to us.

Jesus Calls for Decision

Life seems to be made up of decisions. There seems to be the need of making one decision after another. Peter made an important decision concerning Jesus at Caesarea Philippi.

The most important decision that one can make is the one concerning Jesus Christ and one's relationship to Him.

Caesarea Philippi marked the turning point in the ministry of Jesus. Where previously Jesus had been ministering, chiefly to the multitudes, now He would devote most of His time to His innermost disciples.

The Crucial Question

Matthew 16:13–15

"Now when Jesus came into the district of Caesarea Philippi, he asked his disciples, 'Who do men say that the Son of man is?'" (Verse 13)

Caesarea Philippi was an ancient city. It received its name from Caesar. Philip, the son of Herod, added his own name, Philippi, to distinguish it from the Caesarea on the coast of the Mediterranean.

Jesus Christ was determined to know, before He set out for Jerusalem and the Cross, if His disciples knew who He was. He led up to the question by first asking what people were saying about Him.

"And they said. 'Some say John the Baptist, others say Elijah, and others Jeremiah or one of the prophets.'" (Verse 14)

Some said that He was John the Baptist. Elijah is mentioned in Malachi as returning to act as a forerunner of the Messiah. Jeremiah, whose suffering was outstanding, was one of the greatest of the prophets.

The people thought Jesus to be an outstanding leader and spokesman for God. He had impressed them as being an outstanding religious personality. The world had many opinions about Jesus.

"He said to them, 'But who do you say that I am?' " (Verse 15) Christ wanted to know what the disciples thought about Him. The question now became personal. The answer to this question cannot be evaded. This was, and still is, the most important question.

Peter's Great Confession

Matthew 16:16–17

"Simon Peter replied, 'You are the Christ, the Son of the living God.' " (Verse 16)

Peter made his great confession. Jesus was not just a good man, not just a prophet, but "Christ, the Son of the living God." The word, Messiah and Christ are the same. One is Hebrew and the other is Greek, meaning "the anointed one." Kings were ordained to office by being anointed. As spokesman of the group, Peter was declaring that Jesus was the expected Messiah and not the forerunner. He had come on a special mission of redemption. He is the Messiah, the Christ and the Anointed One. He is God's Divine King over men. He is the eternal Son of God.

I take my stand with Peter and affirm, "You are the Christ, the Son of the living God."

"And Jesus answered him, 'Blessed are you, Simon Bar-Jona! For flesh and blood has not revealed this to you, but my Father who is in heaven." (Verse 17)

Bar-Jona means son of Jonah. "Flesh and blood" is often used in Jewish writings to mean "humanity," as contrasted with divinity. This knowledge about Jesus had not come through human reasoning, but by spiritual insight that came from God.

The Great Promise

Matthew 16:18–19

"And I tell you, you are Peter, and on this rock I will build my church, and the powers of death shall not prevail against it." (Verse 18)

There are several possible interpretations to this passage. The "rock" may mean Jesus Himself. A second explanation is that the rock is the truth that Jesus Christ is the Son of the living God. A third explanation is that the rock is Peter's faith. Another interpretation is that Peter is the rock in the sense that he was the first man to make the leap of faith in recognizing Jesus Christ as the Son of the living God.

Everyone who makes the same discovery as Peter is another stone added to the edifice of the church of Christ. God is the rock on which the church is founded.

Many people think of a building when the word church is used. A church is a fellowship of believers. Peter was the first of the fellowship of believers in Christ. Jesus is represented here as the builder responsible for the church. Death itself will not be able to destroy this church.

"I will give you the keys of the kingdom of heaven, and whatever you bind on earth shall be bound in heaven, and whatever you loose on earth shall be loosed in heaven." (Verse 19)

It is the steward who carries the keys of the house. This promise meant that Peter would be the means of giving the door to God to thousands of people in the days to come. At the council of Jerusalem, Peter's witness made it possible to open the door for the Gentiles. At Penticost, Peter again opened the door. Every Christian has the keys of the Kingdom. The method of using the keys is that of witnessing personally to someone else of Jesus Christ.

In Jewish thinking, to bind or loose meant to declare an action forbidden or permissable. This meant that in the days to come, the administration of the infant church would fall upon him.

The Great Rebuke

Matthew 16:20-23

"Then he strictly charged the disciples to tell no one that he was the Christ." (Verse 20)

The people were looking for a worldly conquering Messiah. If the disciples preached to the people that Jesus was the Messiah, there may have been a revolt.

"From that time, Jesus began to show his disciples that he must go to Jerusalem and suffer many things from the elders and chief priests and scribes, and be killed, and on the third day be raised." (Verse 21)

Jesus began to reveal to the disciples the suffering and death that awaited in Jerusalem. He opened their eyes to the fact that for Him, there was no way but the way of the Cross.

Jesus predicted His suffering, death and resurrection "on the third day."

"And Peter took him and began to rebuke him, saying, 'God forbid, Lord! This shall never happen to you.' " (Verse 22)

Peter reacted to this announcement with horror and in love. Peter tried to restrain Jesus from his journey to Jerusalem.

"But he turned and said to Peter, 'Get behind me Satan! You are a hindrance to me; for you are not on the side of God, but of men.' " (Verse 23)

Jesus reminded Simon that he was to be a follower, and not one who dictated the course to be followed. "Satan" means "adversary." Peter loved Jesus, but he spoke the words of Satan in offering a way of escape from the cross.

The way of the Cross was the way of God, and Satan's way was any influence which tried to turn Him from this way.

LESSON IN LIFE

"But who do you say that I am?" This is a very personal question. It is a question that must be answered.

The discovery of Jesus Christ must be a personal discovery. Christianity is not knowing about Jesus; it consists of knowing Jesus.

Jesus demands a personal decision. To decide for Jesus Christ as the Son of God, and to surrender our lives to Him, will take us toward God and eternal life. This decision is a leap of faith. A person does not make an adequate decision for Christ unless there is a willingness to obey.

"But who do you say that I am?" Upon the answer to this question rests your eternal destiny. Decide now.

God Calls A New People

These verses describe the new people of God. They deal with the church. Many think that the church is a building. Others think that the church is the activity which takes place inside the building, such as the worship service. Some look on a church as a club or social agency. Finally, some think of the church as a place to hear a sermon. What really is a church?

The word "church" means "that which belongs to the Lord." This is the people of God. The church is the people who respond to Christ and follow Him. They are a community of believers. The church is that community that Jesus established to meet man's deepest need.

The Reach of The Church

Matthew 18:10–14

"See that you do not despise one of the little ones; for I tell you that in heaven their angels always behold the face of my Father who is in heaven." (Verses 10–11)

"These little ones" are probably children. "Their angels" may be guardian angels. This saying emphasizes the supreme value which God places on a child. A great deal depends on how a child is taught and trained. We need to help these children, and should set a good example because they are very susceptible to influence.

Children often stumble when they are learning to walk. New Christians in their development may stumble and fall. When this happens, we should give help to this "young" and struggling Christian. Give him the same type of help that you would want if you stumbled.

We all are as God's "little ones" in that we are in need of, and dependent on, Him. We need to have childlike faith in God—humble, trusting and loving.

"What do you think? If a man has a hundred sheep and one

210

of them has gone astray, does he leave the ninety-nine on the hills and go in search of the one that went astray?" (Verse 12)

In Judea, it was easy for sheep to go astray. There were usually two or three shepherds with the sheep so that one shepherd could leave the other ninety-nine. The great love of the shepherd causes him to endure all kinds of hardships to save the one that was lost.

This parable of the lost sheep shows that God was concerned about every man who was in need of spiritual help. Again and again in the Gospels, there is the emphasis on the value of an individual, his soul and his relationship to God and to others.

The love of God is a seeking love. The Messiah came to seek and save the lost. He went the way of the cross for those lost ones.

"And if he finds it, truly, I say to you, he rejoices over it more than over the ninety-nine that never went astray." (Verse 13)

The straying one is in danger. "He rejoices over it" because the one has been rescued from deadly peril.

"So it is not the will of my Father who is in heaven that one of these little ones should perish." (Verse 14)

God is interested in each individual. His love knows no limits. "It is not the will of my father . . . that one of these little ones should perish."

Every sinful man is dear to the Shepherd's love.

A Rule For Church Discipline

Matthew 18:15–17

"If your brother sins against you, go and tell him his fault, between you and him alone. If he listens to you, you have gained your brother." (Verse 15)

Here is a principle to be followed when a brother sins against another in the faith. If we have been wronged or sinned against by our brother, we should go see him personally and talk to him about it. We should not brood about it. This brooding can poison our mind so that all we can think about is our personal injury. It is not psychologically good to brood about something. Get it out in the open. Face it with your brother. Try to bring about reconciliation privately.

Note also that the one who has been wronged is the one to make the initiative. This is the spirit of Christian love. A friend is to go to the offender and privately point out the fault. The one who has been wronged is to go alone the first time. His purpose is not to humiliate or condemn him, but to gain a brother.

"But if he does not listen, take one or two others along with you, that every word may be confirmed by the evidence of two or three witnesses." (Verse 16)

If this private plea fails, then one or two men of Christian grace are to be taken with you. They may have wisdom enough to bring about reconciliation.

"If he refuses to listen to them, tell it to the church; and if he refuses to listen even to the church, let him be to you as a Gentile and a tax collector." (Verse 17)

As a last step, let the offender be brought before the Christian fellowship. If all these means fail, then he is "as a Gentile and a tax collector." The offender has made himself an outsider. This does not mean to abandon the person. It is a challenge to win him with love. Jesus has found no man hopeless and neither should we.

The Resources of the Church
Matthew 18:18–20

"Truly, I say to you, whatever you bind on earth shall be bound in heaven, and whatever you loose on earth shall be loosed in heaven." (Verse 18)

The promise is made to Christians assembled together. The church can proclaim to all that anyone who receives Christ as Lord and Savior shall be loosed from his sins, and those who reject Him will be bound in their sins.

"Again I say to you if two of you agree on earth about any thing they ask, it will be done for them by my Father in heaven." (Verse 19)

The emphasis here is on fellowship in prayer. Christians need to take counsel together and agree what they will ask in prayer. Even two people's agreement is enough to be sure of the promise. This promise should make us bold. Those who are willing to seek, know and do His will can claim this promise. There is a great resource of power in the consecrated prayer of a few. When prayer is unselfish, it is answered. God sends His answer, but it is not necessarily the answer which we desire. God in His wisdom and love knows what is best.

"For where two or three are gathered in my name, there am I in the midst of them." (Verse 20)

In the rabbinical tradition, there is a saying that the Shekinah, the glory of God's presence, is among them when two sit together and study the word of the Torah. Now it is the exalted Lord who is present among His disciples. Jesus, as the exalted Lord, lives in the midst of His believers as closely as He once lived as man among men. When two or three are gathered in His name, it is a meaningful, joyful, and great occasion.

LESSON IN LIFE

I recently wrote a book on insect allergy. The bee family was one of my subjects. There are workers and non-workers in the bee colony. The worker bees minister to the drone bees by bringing them food.

The idea of drones or non-working Christians is foreign to the New Testament idea of the church. To be in the body of Christ is to be a part of his working body. Christians need to take this seriously. This would transform the church.

Christians who insist on being waited on have missed the meaning of the Christian calling. Christians who sit back, waiting to be ministered to, should realize that this contradicts their calling to be the ministering body of Christ.

In a sense, each Christian is a minister.

What Jesus said of Himself holds true for the Christian. "For the Son of man also came not to be served but to serve, and to give his life as a ransom for many." (Mark 10:48)

Demands of Discipleship

The Greek word translated as "disciple," occurs about 275 times in the Gospels and the Book of Acts. The word means "a learner or pupil: one who accepts and follows a given doctrine."

Jesus did not lower His standards to get the multitude to follow Him. The demands that Jesus placed on His first disciples have not been relaxed for today's disciples.

This devotional should make each one of us examine ourselves in the light of what Jesus said about those who would be His disciples.

The Cost of True Discipleship

Mark 8:34–35

"And he called to him the multitude with his disciples, and said to them, 'If any man would come after me, let him deny himself and take up his cross and follow me.'" (Verse 34)

Each person must decide whether he is prepared to accept Christ's spiritual kingdom and pay the price of discipleship.

Here are two of the hardest words that one can face—"deny" and "cross." The word "deny" as used here means more than refusing to give things to ourselves. It is denying ourselves for Christ's sake. It is losing of one's life for His sake. Self is cast out and Christ enters in. Such a person, then, does not follow his own will, but rather does the will of Christ.

The people that heard Jesus knew what a cross meant. His hearers had seen Romans execute people on a cross.

Some people speak of an illness, disappointment, misfortune or sorrow as a cross. In the truest sense of the word, this is not a cross. A cross is that which a man assumes in committing himself to Christ and serving Him. It is the suffering we take on ourselves for the sake of Christ. This is a choice that we make.

Jesus wanted followers, but not on just any basis. He was on

214

His way to Jerusalem and the Cross. He was reminding His
disciples that being loyal to Him would be costly.

We are under no compulsion to take up the cross except the
compulsion of God's love for Christ. We should rejoice that we
are permitted to suffer with Him.

"For whoever would save his life will lose it; and whoever
loses his life for my sake and the gospel's will save it." (Verse 35)

This passage had special meaning to the Christians of the
time the Gospel of Mark was written. These Christians faced
great persecution.

The word "save" here means "preserve," "safeguard," "keep in
health." Many people go through life concerned only about
themselves. They try to preserve their looks, their money and
health. If a person spends all of his time and energy in trying to
preserve his physical life, he may end up as a spiritual mummy.
One of the best physically preserved things in history is an
Egyptian mummy, but it is spiritually dead.

The greatest art and the greatest music has never come from
concern for reputation. We get by giving, we live by dying and
we gain by losing. God meant for us to spend our life in serving
Him and our fellowman. To really save our life, we need to put
Christ first.

Values

Mark 8:36-38

"For what does it profit a man to gain the whole world and
forfeit his life?" (Verse 36)

Our age is one of materialism. By various advertisements, appeals are made for us to satisfy our earthly appetites. Men put
emphasis upon things which God places little significance. We
need to face the fact that life's choices are eternal choices. We
need to think of these choices in relation to eternity. To gain a
world of things and miss the fellowship with Christ is life's
biggest blunder.

"For what can a man give in return for his life?" (Verse 37)

Where do we place our values in life? We need not be concerned of what men think of the things we do, but of what God
thinks. We should try to see things as God sees them.

"For whoever is ashamed of me and of my words in this adulterous and sinful generation, of him will the Son of man be ashamed, when he comes in the glory of his Father with the holy angels." (Verse 38)

Christianity is not a creed of philosophy. It is Jesus Christ. One who has been ashamed to acknowledge Jesus as Lord before men would not be recognized as a disciple in the Judgment.

These words have a pertinence to our day. This is not a day for apology, but for affirmation of His words.

Jesus' prediction of His death is followed by the revelation that He is to come again in glory, surrounded by the holy angels, to summon all men to judgment.

The Conditions of Discipleship

Luke 14:25–33

"Now great multitudes accompanied him; and he turned and said to them," (Verse 25)

The "great multitudes" that accompanied Jesus on His journey are warned of the condition of discipleship.

"If any one comes to me and does not hate his own father and mother and wife and children and brothers and sisters, yes and even his own life, he cannot be my disciple." (Verse 26)

These words of Jesus sound harsh. He does not require hatred of family. Jesus and His claims must have first place. Remember that these words were spoken to multitudes who thought they wanted to follow Jesus. Many may have had shallow understanding or unworthy motives.

The man who would follow Him must be ready for a loyalty which would sacrifice the dearest things in life. The love for Jesus must outweigh all other love.

"Whoever does not bear his own cross and come after me, cannot be my disciple." (Verse 27)

Jesus wanted followers, but not on just any basis. The cross stood for death. We must die in self when surrendering to Christ. It is new life and death of self love and self assertion.

The parable of building the tower and going to war stress the importance of counting the cost of an undertaking before committing oneself to it. There are high demands of being a disciple of Him, but He will walk every step of the way with the Christian. He never asks anything of you or demands anything of you that He has not first demanded of Himself.

LESSON IN LIFE

True discipleship to Christ is as costly today as when Luke wrote. The world changes only superficially. There are new inventions but the same greed, lust, hatreds and prejudices exist. Dedication to Christ may mean a loss of job or physical life. Discipleship is costly, but not to follow the Christ is more costly. A commitment to Christ brings us into a daily living relationship with the living Christ. It delivers us from sin and delivers us to Christ with whom we shall live for eternity.

Some questions we should consider are: What is of supreme value in my life? Do I really love Jesus Christ? Is there anything I would not give up if He asked me to do it?

Jesus Promises the Spirit

For many Christian people, the Gospel of John is the most precious book in the New Testament. It is the simplest, and at the same time, the most profound New Testament book. The evangelist declares his purpose in the words "that you may believe that Jesus is the Christ, the son of God, and that believing you may have life in his name." (John 20:31)

In Chapter 14, Jesus promises help for the disciples after His death. This concerns the Holy Spirit.

The Promised Helper

John 14:15–17

"If you love me, you will keep my commandments." (Verse 15)

By our obedience, we show our love to Jesus. Real love is shown in true obedience.

"And I will pray the Father, and he will give you another Counselor, to be with you forever." (Verse 16)

Jesus does not leave us to struggle with the Christian life alone. For those who exhibit this obedience of love, Jesus will pray to the Father, who will give another Counselor.

In Chapters 14–16, there are a group of sayings about the promised presence of the Holy Spirit. Four of these use the word "paralete" or "counselor." The Greek word *parakletos* means "someone who is called in." The Holy Spirit comes to our side to help us, strengthen us, encourage us and support us in our weak moments and difficulties of life. The word "comforter" is sometimes used. This is a good translation if one remembers that "to comfort" means "to strengthen" as well as "to counsel."

"Even the Spirit of truth, whom the world cannot receive, because it neither sees him nor knows him; you know him, for he dwells with you, and will be in you." (Verse 17)

The Holy Spirit is here referred to as the "Spirit of truth." If we know Him, we know the truth and the truth will set us free

218

in Him. Jesus said, "I am the way, and the truth, and the life." (John 14:6)

Jesus went on to say that the world cannot recognize the Spirit. The world is too busy to give the Holy Spirit a chance to enter in. A knowledge of Jesus involves the welcome of His Spirit. We do not face life alone "for He dwells with you." No believer walks alone.

Who Receives the Holy Spirit

John 14:18-21

"I will not leave you desolate; I will come to you." (Verse 18) Christ further assures His disciples that He will come to them.

"Yet a little while, and the world will see me no more but you will see me; because I live, you will live also." (Verse 19) He is talking of His Resurrection and His risen presence. Christ was to be crucified, but there will be the Resurrection when Jesus will manifest Himself to His disciples—but not to the unbelieving world. They will see Him because He will be alive. Death could never conquer Him. At the moment, they are numb with the sense of impending tragedy. However, the day will come when their minds will understand and they will really see Him and seeing Him, be alive spiritually. The disciples would experience spiritual life through His living presence. Through faith in Him, they enter into the life of God.

"In that day you will know that I am in my Father, and you in me, and I in you." (Verse 20)

"In that day" is an eschatological term for "the doctrine of last things." It first means the period of the Easter appearances. Jesus would come to His disciples and they would see Him. This is a foretaste of the new era of the reign of God. God dwells in the believing disciple who enters into mystic communion with Christ. Christ and the Father are one. We are in Christ and He is in us by His Spirit. With the guidance of the Spirit, the disciples would understand the perfect unity of the Father and Christ.

"He who has my commandments and keeps them, he it is who loves me; and he who loves me will be loved by my Father, and I will love him and manifest myself to him." (Verse 21)

Foremost, there is love. Men love God through Jesus. Jesus reveals Himself to the man who loves Him and keeps His commandments. The revelation of God is dependent on love, and love is dependent on obedience.

Our Heart Is God's Home
John 14:22–27

"Judas (not Iscariot) said to him, 'Lord, how is it that you will manifest yourself to us, and not to the world?' " (Verse 22)

Judas (not Iscariot) asks why this manifestation is not to be given to the unbelieving world.

"Jesus answered him, 'If a man loves me, he will keep my word, and my Father will love him, and we will come to him and make our home with him.' " (Verse 23)

By love was the way by which the Father and Jesus Christ would come to live in the one who observed Jesus' teaching. Our heart will be the home of God!

"He who does not love me does not keep my words; and the word which you hear is not mine but the Father's who sent me." (Verse 24)

He who does not love Jesus disregards His words, which are indeed the words of God.

"These things I have spoken to you, while I am still with you. But the Counselor, the Holy Spirit, whom the Father will send in my name, he will teach you all things, and bring to you remembrance all that I have said to you." (Verses 25–26)

The Holy Spirit will teach us all things. The Christian must be a learner. The Holy Spirit will lead him deeper into the truth of God. The Holy Spirit will remind us of what Jesus said. He will bring back to us the things Jesus said and the meaning of the truth.

"Peace I leave with you; my peace I give you; not as the world gives do I give to you. Let not your hearts be troubled, neither let them be afraid." (Verse 27)

Jesus' gift is peace. This peace is independent of outward circumstances. When a person places himself at His disposal, holding back nothing and making no reservations, he will have that peace that passes understanding. A Christian has a peace which comes from the abiding presence of Christ in the Holy Spirit.

LESSON IN LIFE

This devotional concerns a doctrine that needs to be experienced as well as understood by the believer.

The Holy Spirit is the living Christ, present with us through all time. The supreme gift of the Holy Spirit, to any who will receive it, is a fellowship of God. The Holy Spirit means God present with us and active for us. He brings us the experience of God's presence, the life of Christ to be believer, help from God, divine truth and the peace of God.

The Holy Spirit comes to those who love God and keep His commandments. Only those who are Jesus' followers can experience the presence of the Spirit.

If we allow Him to dominate our lives, the result is love, joy, peace, long suffering, gentleness, goodness, faith and meekness (Galatians 5:22–23).

God Gave His Son

It is in the Cross that God has acted on behalf of man to make possible reconciliation and redemption. In the Cross and Resurrection, we see both God's limitless love and power.

The Scripture chosen helps us think on the meaning of the Cross.

The Crucifiers

Matthew 27:35–38

"And when they had crucified him, they divided his garments among them by casting lots." (Verse 35)

The story of the Crucifixion does not need commentary. It has its power in the telling by itself. It has more weight than any sentence should bear. All we can do to make the picture clearer is to give some of the background.

Matthew 27:33 tells of the arrival of Jesus and the others at Golgotha (which means the place of a skull). "Calvary" is the Latin word with the same meaning.

Jesus had undergone terrible scourging and the mockery of the soldiers.

They then divided among themselves the few possessions. They gambled beneath the Cross for the garments of Jesus.

"Then they sat down and kept watch over him there." (Verse 36)

When the soldiers had divided the clothes, they sat down on guard until the end should come.

"And over his head they put the charge against him, which read, 'This is Jesus the King of the Jews.'" (Verse 37)

It was a Roman custom to place a titulus or notice around the neck of a criminal stating his crime for which he was condemned. "The charge" in this case was high treason. The titulus was a warning to the Jews—that this is what would happen to any "King of the Jews."

"Then two robbers were crucified with him, one on the right and one on the left." (Verse 38)

Jesus was crucified between two robbers. "Bandits" is a better term for these two men. They may have been revolutionaries.

In His life, Jesus had eaten "with tax collectors and sinners." (Verses 9–11)

In His death, He was "numbered with the transgressors." (Isaiah 53:12)

The Third Mocking

Matthew 27:39–44

"And those who passed by derided him, wagging their heads." (Verse 39)

The servants of the high priest had mocked Him before He was condemned. The soldiers mocked Him after He had been sentenced to die. The crowd mocked Him in His agony of death. "Wagging their heads" is an oriental gesture of scorn.

"And saying, 'You who would destroy the temple and build it in three days, save yourself! If you are the Son of God, come down from the cross.'" (Verse 40)

This is cynicism. It reminds one of Satan tempting Jesus in the wilderness: "If you are the son of God, throw yourself down . . ." (Matthew 4:6)

From the beginning, the great temptation of Satan was offering Him another way besides the way of the Cross.

"So also the chief priests, with the scribes and elders mocked him, saying, 'He saved others; he cannot save himself. He is the King of Israel; let him come down now from the cross, and we will believe him.'" (Verses 41–42)

The patience, mercy and gentleness that Jesus showed toward these people revealed that He did not yield to the final assaults of Satan.

"He trusts in God; let God deliver him now, if he desires him; for he said, 'I am the Son of God.'" (Verse 43)

If Jesus were His Son, would not He save His Son? This was the question and the taunt. God is power, but He is also wisdom, righteousness, justice, mercy and love. Jesus showed men that God is sacrificed love. God could have used His power to save

His Son, but He chose to use His Son to save mankind. We must remember that Jesus was both God and man. His humanity was real. His temptations were real. Jesus could have saved Himself, and this fact made the temptations powerful ones. But He refused to do so. The nails did not hold Him to the cross; rather, it was His love for mankind.

"And the robbers who were crucified with him also reviled him in the same way." (Verse 44)

The "two robbers who were crucified with Him" also mocked Jesus. One of these dying thieves turned to Him for salvation. "Jesus, remember me when you come into your kingly power." (Luke 23:42)

Jesus' Death

Matthew 27:45–50

"Now from the sixth hour there was darkness over all the land until the ninth hour." (Verse 45)

The sixth hour is noon. This darkness lasted until 3:00 P.M., the ninth hour. The darkness that came upon the land was miraculous. This darkness also symbolized the greatest crime ever committed on earth. Many times, people minimize sin. A visit to calvary will change this attitude.

"And about the ninth hour Jesus cried with a loud voice, 'Eli, Eli, lama sabachthani?' that is, 'My God, my God, why hast thou forsaken me?'" (Verse 46)

This is a quotation from Psalm 22:1. It is interesting to notice how Psalm 22 runs through the Crucifixion narration. Read Psalm 22, and especially verses 1–2, 7–9, 12, 18, and 25–31. The twenty-second Psalm is a hymn of victory. This was victory for Jesus and the Father. The great act of redemption was accomplished. The suffering of Jesus on the Cross was real.

Jesus' cry was a profound expression of suffering. The meaning of the cry is a mystery. These words are almost too sacred for interpretation.

God did not desert Jesus. Others had deserted Him, but God was with Him. God heard the prayer.

"And some of the bystanders hearing it said, 'This man is calling Elijah.'" (Verse 47)

The "bystanders" misunderstood Jesus and thought that He was calling Elijah. They did not understand.

"And one of them at once ran and took a sponge, filled it with vinegar, and put it on a reed, and gave it to him to drink." (Verse 48)

One of the soldiers offered a "sponge filled" with vinegar. "And for my thirst they gave me vinegar to drink." (Psalms 69:21b)

"But the others said, 'Wait, let us see whether Elijah will come to save him.'" (Matthew 27:49)

"And Jesus cried again with a loud voice and yielded up his spirit.'" (Verse 50)

Jesus dies with a loud cry. Jesus "yielded up his spirit." This tells us that His death was a voluntary act.

John tells us that Jesus died with a shout: "It is finished!" (John 19:30)

This word is the victor's shout. It is the cry of the man who has completed his task, of the one who has won through the struggle and has grasped the crown. Jesus died with a shout of triumph on His lips.

LESSON IN LIFE

At times, things seem impossible. There may be times when we have about given up all hope. It may seem there is no where to turn.

If we will just hold on to God and keep our faith—as little as it is sometimes—the dawn will finally break and we will triumph.

The one who triumphs is the one who refuses to believe that God has forgotten him. This person is the one who will not let go of his faith. The victor is the one who still keeps his faith, even when he is at the end of his rope. God loves you and He will hear your prayers.

Victory Over Sin and Death

No book ever had such a triumph and joy as that recorded in each of the Gospels, for there is only one Christ and one Easter.

The Easter Dawn

Matthew 28:1-8

"Now after the sabbath, toward the dawn of the first day of the week, Mary Magdalene and the other Mary went to see the sepulchre." (Verse 1)

"Mary Magdalene and the other Mary went to see the sepulchre" early Sunday morning. The Sabbath ran from sunset Friday until sunset Saturday. These women had been present both at the Cross and when He was laid in the tomb. It is fitting that they are the first to know the joy of the Resurrection.

"And behold there was a great earthquake; for an angel of the Lord descended from heaven and came and rolled back the stone, and sat upon it." (Verse 2)

In ancient times, there was a groove in the ground in front of the tomb. A circular stone, like a cart wheel, ran in the groove to form a door.

The stone was not rolled away to allow Christ to come out of the tomb, but to allow the women to go into it. "And sat upon it;" this seems to be a gesture of divine victory.

"His appearance was like lightening, and his raiment white as snow." (Verse 3)

The angel was a messenger of purity.

"But the angel said to the women, 'Do not be afraid; for I know that you seek Jesus who was crucified.'" (Verse 5)

The angel spoke in tenderness to the women. He also spoke with concern and understanding. The angel understood the sadness of the friends of Jesus.

"He is not here; for he has risen, as he said. Come, see the place where he lay." (Verse 6)

The angel spoke in hope and assurance. "He is not here, for he is risen." How tenderly and simply the news is told!

"As he said" refers to the predictions of Jesus concerning his Passion and Resurrection. The angel reminded them of the promise of Jesus and comforted them with the empty tomb.

From God comes the message to man: "He is risen." Death has been swallowed up in victory. The new age had dawned.

"Then go quickly and tell his disciples, that he has risen from the dead, and behold, he is going before you to Galilee; there you will see him. Lo, I have told you." (Verse 7)

The second part of the angel's message was a command to be given to the disciples. They had scattered. Their faith had been shaken, but it would soon be restored by the words: "He is risen from the dead." What a great message these women were commissioned to tell.

"So they departed quickly from the tomb with fear and great joy, and ran to tell his disciples." (Verse 8)

The women heard the message and hurried off. Fear had seized them at the sight of the angel, but at the same time they were filled with overwhelming joy since all was changed. The sepulchre was no longer a place of mourning for the dead. It had become a place of joy and praise. This is why Easter Sunday is the happiest day of the year.

We worship a living, risen Christ. There is resurrection for all who believe.

Jesus Appearance To The Women

Matthew 28:9–11

"And behold, Jesus met them and said, 'Hail'! And they came up and took hold of his feet and worshiped him." (Verse 9)

Jesus met the women while they were on their way to the disciples. Jesus greeted them with the word "Hail!" This was the normal word of greeting. Its literal meaning is "Be glad!" or "Rejoice."

The women recognized Him and fell on their knees and worshiped Him.

"Then Jesus said to them, 'Do not be afraid; go and tell my brethern to go to Galilee, and there they will see me.'" (Verse 10)

It was like Jesus to quiet their fears.

Final Appearance to the Eleven

Matthew 28:16–20

"Now the eleven disciples went to Galilee, to the mountain to which Jesus had directed them." (Verse 16)

Jesus "had directed" the disciples to a certain mountain in Galilee. As He had foretold, they are reunited once more.

"And when they saw him they worshiped him; but some doubted." (Verse 17)

"They worshiped him" as they had not done before the Crucifixion. "Worshiped is a strong word. They prostrated themselves before Him in the act of worship.

The fact that some of the disciples "doubted" and were not quick to believe until all their doubts were removed is one of the convincing proofs that Jesus did arise.

Our life is also a mixture of faith and doubt. This describes us so many times. Doubt can be overcome by sincere prayer to God. Thomas brought his doubts directly to Christ and was answered.

"And Jesus came and said to them, 'All authority in heaven and on earth has been given to me.'" (Verse 18)

This Gospel ends with a claim (Verse 18), a commission (Verse 19), and a great promise (Verse 20).

"All authority" in heaven and earth has been given Him by the Father. He has the authority over the souls of men and the eternal destiny of all souls is determined by their relationship to Christ.

"Go therefore and make disciples of all nations, baptizing them in the name of the Father and of the Son and of the Holy Spirit." (Verse 19)

The disciples were to win men to Him. They were sent out to make all the world His disciples. It must have been a staggering thing for eleven humble men to be sent forth on the greatest task in the world.

Jesus commissioned His disciples to baptize in the name of the Father, the Son and the Holy Spirit.

"Teaching them to observe all that I have commanded you; and lo, I am with you always, to the close of the age." (Verse 20)

The mission of the disciple included two elements—baptizing and teaching. Jesus emphasized the teaching ministry. To teach others, we must know the truth ourselves.

Jesus is "with" His church always, "to the close of the age." It is fitting that the Gospel should end with this phrase since Matthew looked forward to the great day when Jesus will be present in celestial glory to judge the world and to say once more, "Come, O blessed of my Father, inherit the kingdom prepared for you from the foundation of the world." (Matthew 25:34)

The evidence for the Resurrection is overwhelming. We have the testimony of witnesses of the highest-type character. There were over 500 eyewitnesses. There is the growth of the church. There is the transformation of the disciples from despair and cowardice to sacrificial love and willingness to face hardships and even death for their faith.

The Gospel of Matthew comes to a conclusion. It began in the Spirit of the Old Testament with the genealogy of the true Messiah and ends with the universal Savior and Lord of heaven and earth. This gospel gives to Christians the vision of a worldwide church sending them to all nations, bearing the message of salvation through Christ.

LESSON IN LIFE

We have Matthew's story of the empty tomb. The people who were confronted with the empty tomb were urged to believe, to share and to rejoice.

These imperatives apply to us today. We must repent of our sins, and believe in Him if we will share eternity with Him. When we have committed ourselves to Him, we must tell others about Him. "Go quickly and tell."

God's Gift of the Holy Spirit

Luke wrote the Book of Acts and the Gospel of Luke. These two books are the longest contribution made by any one author in the New Testament, and constitute more than one quarter of it.

The Book of Acts tells of the growth of the Christian church in the first century A.D. The book emphasizes the work of the Holy Spirit.

These passages tells of the beginning of the early church. Jesus had promised the gift of the Holy Spirit to His disciples. The Holy Spirit would make real the spiritual presence of Jesus to His followers.

The Day of Pentecost

Acts 2:1–6

"When the day of Pentecost had come, they were all together in one place." (Verse 1)

These disciples of Jesus were "all together in one place" on this day of Pentecost. These people probably had nothing else in common except their love of Jesus. Christ draws men together. The place has been thought by many to be the "Upper Room."

The name Pentecost means "The Fiftieth." A great Jewish festival, the Feast of Weeks, occurred on the fiftieth day of the Passover and was referred to as the Pentecost. Every male Jew who lived within twenty miles of Jerusalem was required to come to this festival. The feast had historical and agricultural significance. It commemorated the giving of the Law to Moses on Mount Sinai. Also, two loaves were offered in gratitude for the ingathered harvest. This day was a holiday.

"And suddenly a sound came from heaven like the rush of a mighty wind, and it filled all the house where they were sitting." (Verse 2)

This was a mysterious time when the presence of God was coming in the midst of His disciples.

"And there appeared to them tongues as of fire, distributed and resting on each one of them." (Verse 3)

Fire is sometimes used in the Bible as reference to the presence of God. The disciples in the upper room probably were as conscious of God being in their midst as was Moses when he stood at the burning bush.

"And they were all filled with the Holy Spirit and began to speak in other tongues, as the Spirit gave them utterance." (Verse 4)

The disciples had an experience of the power of the spirit such as they never had before.

They began to speak "in other tongues." The Greek word for "tongue" is *glossais*, from which comes our word used in reference to speaking with tongues, *glossalia*.

The gift of tongues allowed the disciples to give the Word of God and the message of Christ to all of those present.

"Now there were dwelling in Jerusalem Jews, devout men from every nation under heaven." (Verse 5)

The crowd at Pentecost represented the whole world. This is the beginning of the world-wide mission entrusted to the disciples.

"And at this sound the multitude came together, and they were bewildered, because each one heard them speaking in his own language." (Verse 6)

Each man was able to understand "in his own language" what the disciples were saying. The people were amazed at what they heard.

Pentecost is a climatic moment in God's ministry to men. At this time, a group met together and received a gift destined to make that group a living church.

In the following passages, the Holy Spirit was revealed in three ways: the sound of wind, appearance of fire, and the miracle of tongues.

Peter's First Sermon

Acts 2:14,36

"But Peter, standing with the eleven, lifted up his voice and addressed them, 'Men of Judea and all who dwell in Jerusalem, let this be known to you, and give ear to my words.' " (Verse 14)

Acts 2:14–42 is an account of the first Christian sermon ever preached. Peter proceeded to preach. The way of salvation through Jesus Christ was made known.

"Let all the house of Israel therefore know assuredly that God has made him both Lord and Christ, this Jesus whom you crucified." (Verse 36)

Peter, in his sermon, declared that the gift of the Spirit fulfills the promise of Joel 2:28–32. He tell us of the ministry, death, resurrection and ascension of Jesus and the gift of the Spirit. All of this which Peter says supports the witness that the crucified Jesus is the risen Lord and Christ. Jesus was their Messiah and Lord.

Acts stresses the Resurrection as the final proof that Jesus was God's Chosen One. A Christian is a man who never forgets that He lives and walks with a Risen Lord.

Results of Pentecost
                                                              Acts 2:37–42

"Now when they heard this they were cut to the heart and said to Peter and the rest of the apostles, 'Brethern, what shall we do?' " (Verse 37)

Verses 37–42 describes the immediate results of Pentecost, Peter's speech, and summarize the requirements for membership in the new community.

When the sermon of Peter was finished, it had struck home to the consciences of the hearers. Their hearts were broken. In great anguish of spirit they appealed for help—"What shall we do?" A convicted sinner will ask the same question.

"And Peter said to them, 'Repent, and be baptized every one of you in the name of Jesus Christ for the forgiveness of your sins; and you shall receive the gift of the Holy Spirit.' " (Verse 38)

Peter demanded sincere repentance. A complete change of heart, mind and life was needed. Closely linked with repentance is baptism "in the name of Jesus Christ." Then, it was promised that they would receive the gift of the Holy Spirit.

"For the promise is to you and to your children and to all that are far off, every one whom the Lord our God calls to him." (Verse 39)

Forgiveness and the gift of the Holy Spirit is promised to all who repent and are baptized in the name of Jesus Christ.

"And he testified with many other words and exhorted them saying, 'Save yourselves from this crooked generation.'" (Verse 40)

They were to save themselves from the Judgment by complying with the conditions Peter gave.

"So those who received his word were baptized, and there were added that day about three thousand souls." (Verse 41)

The response to Peter's sermon was overwhelming. The effectiveness of Peter's ministry was seen in that "about three thousand souls" responded and were baptized.

"And they devoted themselves to the apostles' testimony and fellowship, to the breaking of bread and the prayers." (Verse 42)

That they were genuine conversions is shown by their dedication to instruction, fellowship, the Lord's Supper and prayer.

This was a learning church. They listened to the apostles as they taught. All of us need to grow daily in the wisdom and grace of God.

LESSON IN LIFE

A sermon that was preached almost two thousand years ago at Pentecost still applies today.

When this sermon was preached, the people cried out, "What shall we do?" Peter told the people to repent of their sins and be baptized in the name of Christ.

What must one do to be saved today? He must repent. "Repent" means "to be so sorry for one's sins" and "to turn from sin and toward God."

A person must accept Jesus Christ by faith. He must be the Lord of a person's life—in his home, business and social life. Baptism is a symbol of the inner change.

When all of this is done, the Holy Spirit will enter into the Christian. God gives the Holy Spirit to every obedient believer.

The universal outpouring of the Holy Spirit upon all believers is the striking feature of the New Testament. Every Christian should make his life a temple fit for the Spirit. The Holy Spirit will strengthen the believer, intercede for him, and give him assurance.

The Early Church's Life and Witness

The response to Peter's sermon on the day of Pentecost had been overwhelming. A new community of believers was established which made a positive witness for Christ.

The enthusiasm of this early church made it an example of what any church ought to be.

Characteristics of the Church

Acts 2:43–47

"And fear came upon every soul; and many wonders and signs were done through the apostles." (Verse 43)

From Verse 42 we learned in the previous lesson that this church was a church of fellowship, a learning church and a praying church.

The word "fear" in Verse 43 has the idea of awe and reverence in it. This little group of believers had a feeling that God was at work in their group. There was a religious awe over the miraculous events which had happened. "Wonders and signs were done." They were called "wonders" because they were so striking and amazing. They were called "signs" because they pointed to God's presence and work in the apostles. If we expect great things from God, things will happen.

"And all who believed were together and had all things in common." (Verse 44)

These early Christians had a feeling of responsibility for each other. The fellowship was a community of sharing. This was a voluntary expression of the concern of Christians for one another.

"And they sold their possessions and goods and distributed them to all, as any had need." (Verse 45)

These early Christians sold as the need arose. They sold their possessions and divided the proceeds according to individual need. This was a voluntary sharing of goods to keep fellow Christians from starving.

"And day by day, attending the temple together and breaking bread in their homes, they partook of food with glad and generous hearts." (Verse 46)

This was a worshiping church. "They attended the temple together" for worship. They also had common worship in their homes, breaking bread together as Christians.

This early church also was a happy church. Gladness was there. Christian faith did not make them gloomy. They lived in the presence of Jesus. The dominant mood of these gatherings was joy.

"Praising God and having favor with all the people. And the Lord added to their number day by day those who were being saved." (Verse 47)

Wherever the people were, they proclaimed their devotion to God. They praised God for the blessings they had received.

Their worship, their daily work, and their care for one another earned for the Christian the respect of the people. It was a church of people whom others could not help liking. Real Christianity is a wonderful thing.

The number of believers grew. Growth in the church came from those "who were being saved."

Attack of Authorities

Acts 4:13–22

"Now when they saw the boldness of Peter and John, and perceived that they were uneducated, common men, they wondered; and they recognized that they had been with Jesus." (Verse 13)

After the healing of a lame man, Peter preached a sermon. Peter and John were arrested and, on the next day, brought before the Sanhedrin. Once again, Peter seized the opportunity to preach Christ. Upon being asked by what power they had been able to heal the lame man, Peter boldly declared that it was "by the name of Jesus Christ of Nazareth, whom you crucified." (Acts 4:10)

Here was something from which the authorities could not get away. This was the undeniable influence of Christ in the lives of these men.

"But seeing the man that had been healed standing beside them, they had nothing to say in opposition." (Acts 4:14)

There was the lame man standing in front of them. They could not get away from the undeniable evidence that he had been healed. Apparently the man was well-known to many of the people.

"But when they had commanded them to go aside out of the council, they conferred with one another." (Verse 15)

The council had a private conference.

"Saying, 'What shall we do with these men? For that a notable sign has been performed through them is manifest to all the inhabitants of Jerusalem, and we cannot deny it.'" (Verse 16)

These rulers found themselves in a perplexing situation. The council recognized that the healing had occurred, and that this was known to all the inhabitants of Jerusalem.

"But in order that it may spread no further among the people, let us warn them to speak no more to any one in this name." (Verse 17)

They decided to forbid Peter and John to preach in "this name" of Jesus.

"But Peter and John answered them, 'Whether it is right in the sight of God to listen to you rather than to God, you must judge.'" (Verse 19)

It was a question of choosing between obeying man and obeying God. Peter and John were in no doubt as to what course to take.

"For we cannot but speak of what we have seen and heard." (Verse 20)

Peter and John said they were unable to stop speaking of those things which they had personally seen and heard. They had defense of personal experience. They knew it was true. They were so sure of it that they were willing to stake their lives upon it. They would not deny their Christ.

Peter and John had been with Jesus. He was living in them through His Holy Spirit. These men were spirit-filled men. They had a personal experience with the living Lord. All true courage of a Christian is born out of this conviction.

"And when they had further threatened them, they let them

go, finding no way to punish them, because of the people; for all men praised God for what had happened." (Verse 21)

Because the apostles had no crime and being afraid of what the people might do, the leaders "further threatened them" and let them go. They added more threats to those threats made previously.

"For the man on whom this sign of healing was performed was more than forty years old." (Verse 22)

A man who had been a cripple for some forty years now stood and walked like a normal person. This strong evidence prevented the Sanhedrin from punishing the apostles. Luke was a physician. This was indeed a miracle!

LESSON IN LIFE

"For we cannot but speak of what we have seen and heard." (Verse 20)

A man talks about the weather because he has nothing else to talk about. He talks about Jesus because nothing else is worth talking about. This compulsion comes only to those who have felt the power of Jesus at first-hand.

We Christians need a fresh experience with our Lord. Each of us can have that experience if we forsake those things displeasing to Him and seek to walk in close fellowship with Him day by day. When we yield to the power of the Holy Spirit, we will be a more powerful witness. We can witness through word and deed.

When we walk with Him, we will be able to be a successful witness. We can witness in word and share our faith. We can witness through our life, compassion and worship.

Good News for All

The letters of Paul are an interesting part of the New Testament. This is because of all the forms of literature, a letter is most personal. One of the best ways to know about a person is by the letter he writes. It is because he left us so many letters that we feel we know Paul so well.

In the letters that Paul wrote, he opened his heart and mind to the folk he loved so much.

Galatians is Paul's declaration of religious independence from men, and dependence on God. He repudiated all authorities, institutions, customs, and laws that interfered with the direct access of the individual to God.

The next six devotionals consider the expansion of the Christian movement across geographical, cultural, ethnic, and religious barriers.

Children of Abraham
Galatians 3:7–9

"So you see that it is men of faith who are the sons of Abraham." (Verse 7)

How did Abraham please God? It was not by doing the works of the law, because at that time the law did not exist. It was by taking God at His word, by trusting God entirely and surrendering himself in one great act of faith. The real descendant of Abraham is the man who makes the same act of faith.

Abraham's faith, Paul insists, made him acceptable to God; and it is faith like Abraham's that will do the same for any person.

Justification by faith is one truth that makes Christianity different from all other religions. It alone offers to man salvation as a gift. The other religions teach that man must earn his way to salvation by good works or by rites and ceremonies.

Christianity proclaims that salvation has been provided by the sacrifices of Christ on the Cross.

"And the scripture, foreseeing that God would justify the

Gentiles by faith, preached the gospel beforehand to Abraham, saying, 'In you shall all the nations be blessed.'" (Verse 8)

Scripture foresaw that God would make the Gentiles righteous. Paul saw Scripture as something living and active. He saw that history was not aimless, but rather, God's action whereby sons and heirs in Christ are produced.

"So then, those who are men of faith are blessed with Abraham who had faith." (Verse 9)

All "men of faith" will share God's blessing along "with Abraham." This blessing, Paul testifies, is for all nations. It is for all men of faith. All share a common experience with Abraham. They have joined the fellowship of believers with its privileges and responsibilities.

The Nature of the Law Versus Faith

Galatians 3:10–12

"For all who rely on the works of the law are under a curse; for it is written, 'Cursed be every one who does not abide by all things written in the book of the law, and do them.'" (Verse 10)

"It is written" is a reference to Deuteronomy 27:36. It is impossible to completely keep all the laws. If one fails in any one commandment, he is placed under a curse because he should fulfill the whole law.

One cannot profess his faith in the law and at the same time profess his faith in Christ. One must choose. The way of law or the way of faith are direct opposites.

If a person thinks that living the law can lead to righteousness, then he is renouncing the grace which comes from Christ.

"Now it is evident that no man is justified before God by the law; for 'He who through faith is righteous shall live.'" (Verse 11)

Scripture has another saying: "It is the man who is right with God by faith who will really live." (Habakkuk 2:4)

Paul is not opposing moral obedience to God's will. It is good discipline for the religious life. Faith in Christ is the basis for justification.

"But the law does not rest on faith, for 'He who does them shall live by them.'" (Galatians 3:12)

Here, Paul turns the law against the legalists. He says that since no one can obey the commandments well enough for eternal life, then salvation by law is impossible. The ruling principle of the law is not on faith, but works. It has nothing in common with faith. The law is in a different world where what counts is what men do and achieve. It is a merit system.

Redeemed Through Christ
Galatians 3:13–14

"Christ redeemed us from the curse of the law, having become a curse for us—for it is written, 'Cursed be every one who hangs on a tree.'" (Verse 13)

Christ came into the world to take man's sins upon Himself so that He might set men free from the curse. He took the Cross and made it the only way to bring people out of death into life. By His death on behalf of men, Christ has redeemed them.

"That in Christ Jesus the blessing of Abraham might come upon the Gentiles, that we might receive the promise of the Spirit through faith." (Verse 14)

By faith in Jesus Christ, all men may receive the same blessing Abraham received, and may be given the Holy Spirit, whom God gives to all believers.

Salvation comes by faith in Jesus Christ; it is not by good works. It does not mean that good works have no place in the Christian life. Good works are the result of faith. We do good works because we have been justified, not in order to be justified.

New Status of Men of Faith
Galatians 3:26–29

"For in Christ Jesus you are all sons of God, through faith." (Verse 26)

In living fellowship with Christ Jesus, all believers are sons of God. If we are one with Christ, then we, too, inherit the promises. This privilege comes to us by the act of faith in the generous and free grace of God.

"For as many of you as were baptized into Christ have put on Christ." (Verse 27)

To be baptized into Christ was to be immersed in His character, to take up His Cross, and to produce the fruit of His Spirit.

"There is neither Jew nor Greek, there is neither slave nor free, there is neither male nor female; for you are all one in Christ Jesus." (Verse 28)

In the fellowship of believers, there is no longer any place for the old difference of rank and privilege between Greek and Jew, slave and free, man and woman. In Christ Jesus, they are all one. Union with Christ obliterates all racial, sexual, and social inequalities.

There is something of interest here. In the Jewish form of morning prayer, in the days of Paul, there was a thanksgiving in which the Jews thanked God that "Thou hast not made me a Gentile, a slave or a woman." Paul says that these old distinctions are gone.

"And if you are Christ's, then you are Abraham's offspring, heirs according to promise." (Verse 29)

Every true believer, Paul said, belonged to Christ and therefore was a spiritual descendant of Abraham and the heir to the promises of Abraham. Only those who believe, accept and follow Him, belong to Him.

LESSON IN LIFE

Someone has said that the ground is level at the foot of the cross. Do we really feel this deep within us? Do we cling to ideas of class, status and race?

We are all brothers and sisters, members of the same family, children of God. We should, as a family, love one another and bear one another's burdens.

There is only one thing which can wipe out the differences between men. When we are all in Christ, all will be one. The love of God alone can unite a disunited world.

Do we hate anyone? Do we dare hate?

"For God so loved the world that he gave his only son, that whoever believes in him should not perish but have eternal life." (John 3:16)

Jerusalem and Beyond

The early Christians recognized the duty and privilege of proclaiming the Gospel to all men everywhere. The Book of Acts tells of the story of the progress of the Gospel—from the Upper Room experience on the day of Pentecost until the apostle Paul carried the message to Rome.

As the number of believers multiplied, seven deacons were chosen to assist the apostles in administering the practical affairs of the church. One of these deacons was Stephen.

Stephen preached Christ with such fervor that the authorities killed him for it. He became the first martyr in the Christian Church.

The death of Stephen and the persecution which followed helped to spread the Gospel. Persecution scattered the Church abroad—and where the members went, they took their Gospel.

The Church Reaches Out

Acts 8:1-5

"And Saul was consenting to his death. And on that day a great persecution arose against the church in Jerusalem; and they were all scattered throughout the region of Judea and Samaria, except the apostles." (Verse 1)

The man who was to become the apostle to the Gentiles is the man who "was consenting" to the execution of Stephen. The spectacle of Stephen not losing his faith or courage, but rather, abounding more in spiritual power as he was stoned to death, must have been a strong influence on Saul. Saul could never forget the way in which Stephen had died. The blood of the martyr had begun to be the seed of the church.

"Devout men buried Stephen, and made great lamentation over him." (Verse 2)

"Devout men" who "buried Stephen" were probably pious

Jews who were impressed by the character of Christians like Stephen.

They "made great lamentation over him." A Jewish custom was to beat one's own breast with the fists as a sign of great grief.

"But Saul laid waste to the church, and entering house after house he dragged off men and women and committed them to the prison." (Verse 3)

The word translated "laid waste" is sometimes used for "scourging," "torturing" or "violent mistreatment." It was extreme persecution. The word denotes a brutal cruelty.

"Now those who were scattered went about preaching the word." (Verse 4)

The fleeing Christians used the opportunity to preach where the Gospel had not been heard before. If the Christians could not preach Christ in Jerusalem, they would preach Him in some other place.

If a person has a living relationship to Jesus, he will speak of Christ wherever he finds himself. It is tragic that many professing Christians leave Christ at home as they travel from place to place.

"Philip went down to a city of Samaria, and proclaimed to them the Christ." (Verse 5)

Like an Old Testament prophet, Philip wandered about with sudden and spontaneous movements under the immediate impulse of the Spirit. His mission to Samaria is chiefly important as marking the first movement into non-Jewish territory.

The love of God through Christ in Philip's heart had given him a love for all men. Prejudice disappeared. We need this today as it was needed then.

The Prejudiced Disciple

Acts 11:11–18

"At that very moment three men arrived at the house in which we were, sent to me from Caesarea." (Verse 11)

Peter took the Gospel into the Gentile's world. He answered those who criticized him for entering the home of Gentiles and eating with them. He told of his vision on a housetop in Joppa while he was praying. It was at that moment that three men called at the house to extend to Peter an invitation from Cornelius to come to Caesarea.

"And the Spirit told me to go with them, making no distinction. These six brethren also accompanied me, and we entered the man's house." (Verse 12)

Peter did not argue. He stated facts and insisted that he was led by the Spirit.

"And he told us how he had seen the angel standing in his house and saying, 'Send to Joppa and bring Simon called Peter.'" (Verse 13)

Peter told how Cornelius had been instructed by an angel to send for Peter.

"He will declare to you a message by which you will be saved, you and all your household." (Verse 14)

Peter was to tell Cornelius how he and his house could be saved.

"As I began to speak, the Holy Spirit fell on them just as on us at the beginning." (Verse 15)

When Peter "began to speak," the Holy Spirit came on the Gentiles just as the disciples had experienced at Pentecost.

"And I remembered the words of the Lord, how he had said, 'John baptized with water, but you shall be baptized with the Holy Spirit.'" (Verse 16)

Peter "remembered the word of the Lord." The reference is to Christ's promise in Acts 1:8.

"If then God gave the same gift to them as he gave to us when we believed in the Lord Jesus Christ, who was I that I could withstand God?" (Verse 17)

Peter continued by saying that God gave them the same gift He had given the disciples.

If the Spirit had marked these men as belonging to Christ, then to refuse to acknowledge them as brothers in the church was to withstand God.

Peter began to get a glimpse of what God was doing in the world. We all need to try to find out what God is doing, and what His will is in our lives and in the world. We need to move in His direction. Changes are taking place in the world. We must try to determine which changes are in accordance with His will, and let God direct our paths.

"When they heard this they were silenced. And they glorified God, saying, 'Then to the Gentiles also God has granted repentance unto life.'" (Verse 18)

The door was open for further spreading of the Gospel in other parts of the world.

LESSON IN LIFE

Individuals are important to Jesus. We should try to see people as Jesus sees them. All men are accepted by God on an equal basis. "I perceive that God shows no partiality." (Acts 10:34)

Peter had to unlearn the habits of traditions of a lifetime. In the first days, it was characteristic of Christianity that it break down the barriers. Christianity can still do so when it gets the chance.

The proof of Christianity is that it works. It *does* change men. It *does* bring in men the Spirit of God. The duty of the Christian is to demonstrate his faith.

When we become a member of the church, we need to remember that this is not the end, but rather, the beginning of the road. There still remains the duty of learning and penetrating more deeply every day into the unsearchable wishes of Christ.

From Persecution to Missionary

After the death of Stephen, Saul led a persecution of believers in Christ. On the road to Damascus he experienced a life-changing revelation. In a blinding vision he saw the Risen Lord. The experience changed Saul the persecutor into Paul the Apostle, the great Christian missionary. From that time on, he could not stop telling the story of the marvelous, unlimited, undying love of God.

Paul's Commission As An Apostle
Galatians 1:11–17

"For I would have you know, brethren, that the gospel which was preached by me is not man's gospel." (Verse 11)

Paul insisted that the Gospel he preached had not come from any human authority. He addressed the Galatians as brothers. The apostle appeals to the fellowship which demands that each should be ready to listen to the other as a brother.

"For I did not receive it from man, nor was I taught it, but it came through a revelation of Jesus Christ." (Verse 12)

Paul, just as did the first apostles, received this Gospel from Christ by direct revelation. He was not afraid to use "I" because he was trying to explain the impact Christ had made upon his life.

"For you have heard of my former life in Judaism, how I persecuted the church of God violently and tried to destroy it." (Verse 13)

Undoubtedly, the Galatians had heard of Paul's activities before his conversion. Paul violently persecuted the followers of Jesus.

"And I advanced in Judaism beyond many of my own age among my people, so extremely zealous was I for the tradition of my fathers." (Verse 14).

Paul acquired the best education of his day. His knowledge of the law far surpassed many of his own age. He was a true Pharisee who was devoted to the traditions of his forefathers.

"But when he who had set me apart before I was born, and had called me through his grace . . ." (Verse 15)

Paul was convinced that God had set him apart for Christian service before he was born. It was in the eternal plan of God. He did not think of himself as chosen for honor, but for service.

The call of Paul is a work of divine grace. "Grace," meaning "undeserved favor," was the secret of Paul's new life. Grace brought him a new conception of religion and God. It brought also a new conception of himself. Paul never found his sense of worth, dignity and adequacy until he experienced the grace of Christ. The assurance of the psalmist, "He restoreth my soul" (Psalms 23:3), was fulfilled for Paul only in Jesus.

"Was pleased to reveal his Son to me, in order that I might preach him among the Gentiles, I did not confer with flesh and blood." (Verse 16)

God was pleased to reveal His Son to the persecutor of the church. Paul was commissioned. The salvation experience is always personal. Christ wants us to become an instrument of His blessing to others. God calls each of us for some great purpose.

"Nor did I go up to Jerusalem to those who were apostles before me, but I went away into Arabia; and again I returned to Damascus." (Verse 17)

Paul did not seek consultations with other Christians after his conversion. He went away to be alone. He had to think out this tremendous thing that had happened to him. He also had to speak to God before he spoke to man. We all need time by ourselves to face ourselves and God.

A Missionary Career Begun

Acts 11:19–21

"Now those who were scattered because of the persecution that arose over Stephen traveled as far as Phoenicia and Cyprus and Antioch speaking the word to none except Jews." (Verse 19)

Antioch ranked as capital of the East. It was the third largest city of the Roman Empire and second only to Rome and Alexandria. Most of the population was Gentile, along with a large Jewish colony. Its culture was chiefly Greek.

"But there were some of them, men of Cyprus and Cyrene, who on coming to Antioch spoke to the Greeks also, preaching the Lord Jesus." (Verse 20)

These few words tell of one of the greatest events in history. The Gospel was deliberately preached to the Gentiles.

We do not know the name of these people who took this step. All we know is that they came from Cyprus and Cyrene. They are nameless pioneers for Christ. The first Christian community of any size outside of Jerusalem was the one in Antioch.

The church needs people who will do the work and never care who gets the credit for it.

Antioch was a very immoral city. In a city like this, Christianity took a great step forward to becoming the religion of the world.

"And the hand of the Lord was with them, and a great number that believed turned to the Lord." (Verse 21)

"The hand of the Lord" is a Hebrew expression which refers to the manifestation of God's miraculous power.

Visit of Barnabas
Acts 11:22-24

"News of this came to the ears of the church in Jerusalem, and they sent Barnabas to Antioch." (Verse 22)

When the Jerusalem leaders heard of what was going on at Antioch, they sent Barnabas to investigate the situation. The name Barnabas means "son of consolation" or "son of encouragement."

"When he came and saw the grace of God, he was glad; and he exhorted them all to remain faithful to the Lord with steadfast purpose." (Verse 23)

Barnabas rejoiced over what he found in Antioch. He found these Gentiles really converted. Barnabas lived up to his name "son of encouragement."

"For he was a good man, full of the Holy Spirit and of faith. And a large company was added to the Lord." (Verse 24)

Barnabas had been described as one who had the rare gift of discerning merit in others. He seems to have been without jealousy, eager to excuse the faults of others and quick to recognize merit. He was a man of generosity and big-heartedness. He was sympathetic and full of faith. The church leaders sent the best man they could lay their hands on to lead the new church in Antioch.

Barnabas' personal qualities of goodness and faith are described as due to possession of the Spirit.

Paul Comes to Antioch

Galatians 11:25-26

"So Barnabas went to Tarsus to look for Saul." (Verse 25)

Barnabas remembered Paul. He knew that he needed help. He went to Tarsus to "look for Paul." A lesser man may have been tempted to run the whole show for himself.

"And when he found him, he brought him to Antioch. For a whole year they met with the church, and taught a large company of people; and in Antioch the disciples were for the first time called Christians." (Verse 26)

Barnabas brought Paul back to Antioch. There, they worked together—teaching, instructing, and preaching.

It was in Antioch that the Christians were called "Christians." There never has been a better name by which to describe the followers of Christ. The word "Christian" began by being a nickname. The Christian made it a name which all the world was to know. By their lives, they made it a name of courage and love of which all men were to wonder.

LESSON IN LIFE

Every Christian can be an effective servant of the Lord regardless of his past conduct. We can all be challenged by Paul's example of service. The conversion experience leads to a life of useful service in the church.

As Christians, we have no choice but to be missionaries. We are saved to serve. Christ commands us to try to bring each person to Him.

We do not need to go to Africa. There are people next door who need to know Christ.

You are only one, but you *are* one. You cannot do everything, but you *can* do something. God *can* use you if you will let Him.

Sent Out by the Holy Spirit

It is estimated that the Apostle Paul, on his three missionary journeys, traveled approximately 15,000 miles on land. This was in addition to his travel by boat. Chapters 13 and 14 of Acts tell the story of the first missionary journey.

The Mission Is Launched

Acts 13:1–3

"Now in the church at Antioch there were prophets and teachers, Barnabas, Symeon, who was called Niger, Lucius of Cyrene, Manaen, a member of the court of Herod the tetrarch, and Saul." (Verse 1)

The passage speaks of prophets and teachers. The prophets were not attached to any one church. They were wandering preachers who listened for the word of God and then took that word to their fellowmen.

The teachers were the men in the local churches whose duty it was to instruct those who came into Christianity in the faith.

Barnabas was a Jew from Cyprus. Lucius came from Cyrene in North Africa. Symeon was also a Jew, but his other name was Niger; "black" suggests an African origin. He could conceivably be the "Symeon" who carried Jesus' cross. It would be a wonderful thing if this same man was the one responsible for sending out the story of the cross to all the world. Many scholars believe that he was one of the first Negroes in the church. Manaen was a man with aristocratic connections. He was a companion of Herod Antipas. Paul was a Jew from Tarsus. This list is a symbolic of the universal appeal of the Gospel. These men were from all walks of life. These dedicated men of God gave outstanding leadership to the church. No church ever rises higher than its spiritual leadership.

The important thing was not their social or national background, but rather, that they were dedicated men. God has all kinds of men to do His work. He only requires that they be faithful to their task.

"While they were worshiping the Lord and fasting, the Holy Spirit said, 'Set apart for me Barnabas and Saul for the work to which I have called them.'" (Verse 2)

The Christian church was ready to take a great step—that of taking the message of the Gospel to all the world. This step was taken under the guidance of the Holy Spirit. The Holy Spirit could communicate with these sensitive men whose hearts and minds were open to divine guidance. The Spirit came upon them as they were fasting and worshiping, and said, "Set apart for me Barnabas and Saul for a special mission." These men of the early church never did what they wanted to do, but always what God wanted them to do.

"Then after fasting and praying they laid their hands on them and sent them off." (Verse 3)

The laying on of hands is a formal sign of an appointment. Here, it is an act of recognition of these men to a new work of world evangelism.

Mission To Cyprus

Acts 13:4-5

"So, being sent out by the Holy Spirit, they went down to Seleucia; and from there they sailed to Cyprus." (Verse 4)

This is usually called Paul's "first missionary journey." This tour was not just a private enterprise undertaken by Barnabas and Paul. The church was standing behind this work, had commissioned them, and was sending them out as its representatives.

"When they arrived at Salamis, they proclaimed the word of God in the synagogues of the Jews. And they had John to assist them." (Verse 5).

Salamis, on the eastern end of Cyprus, was the island's largest town, and upon their arrival, the missionaries went first to the synagogues.

The third person in the missionary party was John Mark, who assisted them. Before the journey was well under way, however, Mark left Paul and Barnabas.

Committed To The Lord

". . . They returned to Lystra and to Iconium and to Antioch . . ." (Verse 21)

At the conclusion of the first missionary journey, Barnabas and Paul retraced their steps and revisited the new churches.

"Strengthening the souls of the disciples, exhorting them to continue in the faith, and saying that through many tribulations we must enter the kingdom of God." (Verse 22)

The Christian was not any easy way. Barnabas and Saul made clear that tribulations would accompany discipleship. Paul and Barnabas acted on the principle that Jesus had come "not to make life easy, but to make men great." They warned them of suffering and persecution.

"And when they had appointed elders for them in every church, with prayer and fasting, they committed them to the Lord in whom they believed." (Verse 23)

On the return journey, Paul set apart the elders in little groups of newly made Christians. Much dependence was placed on the power of prayer. No decision was made until there had been a seeking to know the will of God. The center of the Christian life is communication with God.

I read somewhere that you could tell how much the people thought of their church by the attendance on Sunday morning, how much they thought of their pastor by their attendance on Sunday evening, and how much they thought of their Lord by their attendance on Wednesday evening.

Meaningful Missionary Report

"And from there they sailed to Antioch, where they had been commanded to the grace of God for the work which they had fulfilled." (Verse 26)

The first missionary journey had ended. Paul returned with Barnabas to Antioch, from which they originally sailed. The missionaries had been entrusted to God's care and protection while carrying out their missionary work.

"And when they arrived, they gathered the church together and declared all that God had done with them, and how he had opened a door of faith to the Gentiles." (Verse 27)

The same grace which supported Paul and Barnabas is still effective in anyone who acts in obedience to God's will.

Barnabas and Saul returned to give the church a report of their missionary efforts. The missionaries did not claim any credit for the work done; they were only the agents through whom God worked.

The "open door" suggests continuing obligation and opportunity. The door had been opened. The work was not finished. The Holy Spirit calls people to His work. Are we "ready and willing to go?"

"And they remained no little time with the disciples." (Verse 28)

For an undefined time, Barnabas and Saul remained at Antioch, worshiping with the Christians there.

LESSON IN LIFE

It was to a praying church that God first revealed His will for an outreach into the Gentile world. The total membership was involved. Every Christian needs to realize that he is a missionary commissioned by the Spirit as surely as those who bear the formal title.

Whether we admit it or not, we are all missionaries. We walk through life and leave our influence for good or bad.

All of us need to be missionaries wherever we are—in the home, in the office, the shop, the school room, the social circle. Missions do not necessarily mean Christian work done at a distance from our place. God intends every Christian to be a witness for Jesus Christ.

The story is told of a man who came rushing late to church. "Is the service over?" he asked the usher. "The worship hour is over, but the service is only beginning" was the reply.

We need to support world missions. "God so loved the world . . ." Do we love it enough to support the representatives of the church who work everywhere in it? After centuries of missionary endeavors, the world is still waiting to be evangelized.

Law Versus Grace

It is normal to want to be accepted by others. In this devotional, we will discuss how to find acceptance by God.

The central idea is that justification is not by the law, but by grace through faith.

A Problem Becomes Acute

Acts 15:1–6

"But some men came down from Judea and were teaching the brethren, 'Unless you are circumcised according to the custom of Moses, you cannot be saved.'" (Verse 1)

Some men, probably Pharisees, came to Antioch from Jerusalem and insisted that every Gentile man in the church be circumcized by the Law of Moses. Keeping of the Mosiac law was to be a condition of salvation.

"And when Paul and Barnabas had no small discussion and debate with them, Paul and Barnabas and some of the others were appointed to go up to Jerusalem to the apostles and the elders about this question." (Verse 2)

If Gentiles are to become Christians, must they first become Jews? The answer could not be postponed. Hence, the council was called. Paul, Barnabas and other Antioch leaders were delegated to go to Jerusalem and consult the elders.

"So, being sent on their way by the church, they passed through both Phoenicia and Samaria, reporting the conversion of the Gentiles, and they gave great joy to all the brethren." (Verse 3)

They visited with Christians and told about the conversion of many Gentiles. The Christians they visited heard this news gladly.

"When they came to Jerusalem, they were welcomed by the church and the apostles and the elders and they declared all that God had done with them." (Verse 4)

255

When the messengers arrived in Jerusalem, the church gathered to meet them. Barnabas and Paul told what God "had done with them."

"But some believers who belonged to the party of the Pharisees rose up, and said, 'It is necessary to circumcize them, and to charge them to keep the law of Moses.'" (Verse 5)

The name Pharisee means "the separated one." They had separated themselves from all men in an attempt to keep the law.

"The apostle and the elders were gathered together to consider this matter." (Verse 6)

The church heard the discussion.

Justification By Faith

Galatians 2:15–16

"We ourselves, who are Jews by birth and not Gentile sinners," (Verse 15)

Paul is identifying himself with the Jews "by birth." When he used the word "sinners" for Gentiles, he was thinking of the observance of the law.

"Yet who know that a man is not justified by works of the law but through faith in Jesus Christ, even we have believed in Christ Jesus, in order to be justified by faith in Christ, and not by works of the law, because by works of the law shall no one be justified." (Verse 16)

Paul concludes that law observance is not the basis of right relationship with God, but this relationship is "only through faith in Christ."

The word "justified" comes from the law court. The word points to a standard to which a person must conform to be right. In Hebrew, a wall is "righteous" when it conforms to the plumb line; a man is righteous when he does God's will. Paul found that there was not law that could force man's unruly nature to fit God's form. Man had to admit he was a criminal and throw himself upon the mercy of the court. When he did, God, the Judge, not only acquitted him, but accepted him as a son and fellow heir with Christ. The sinner is acquitted, accepted, set right with God and saved despite his crimes. Justification is not simply an escape from sin; it is deliverance from sin. It means not only remission of punishment, but also, a new standing of the believer with God.

No amount of observance of the law can make a man right with God. That is a matter of grace. A man cannot earn, he must accept, the generous offer of the love of God. Men are saved by God's grace through faith in Christ. The question is not, "What do you believe?" Rather, it is "To whom do you belong?" A Christian is one who belongs to Christ. "Believe in Christ Jesus" means absolute surrender to Him.

Living By Faith
Galatians 2:17–18, 20–21

"But if, in our endeavor to be justified in Christ, we ourselves also were found to be sinners, is Christ then an agent of sin? Certainly not!" (Verse 17)

The opponents of Paul accused him and his doctrine of promoting loose morality. They maintained that he made faith and forgiveness so simple that men sin again and again, turning each time to Christ for forgiveness which is always available. They argued that salvation, as the free gift of God, would encourage people to sin. Paul replied: "Certainly not." He did not want his Christians to even think of such a thing.

Forgiveness is not that simple, and faith is not that superficial. Faith is utter commitment to Christ and though man stumbles daily, forgiveness brings healing, strengthening and renewal. Forgiveness is not invitation to sin, but rather, a deterrent. Paul rejected any salvation that did not produce actual righteousness in life.

"But if I build up again those things which I tore down, then I prove myself a transgressor." (Verse 18)

Paul had tried the way of the law. He had tried to put himself right with God by a life that sought to obey every item of the law. Such an attempt failed. The law had showed him his own helplessness. Paul had cast himself on the mercy of God. If Paul went back to salvation by law and works, he would be destroying the very truth he had been proclaiming.

"I have been crucified with Christ; it is no longer I who live, but Christ who lives in me; and the life I now live in the flesh I live by faith in the Son of God, who loved me and gave himself for me." (Verse 20)

So great was the change that the only way to describe it was to say that he had been crucified with Christ, and that the man he used to be was dead.

Christ was at the center of Paul's life. Christ was living in him. What Paul set forth is true in every believer in Christ.

To be crucified with Christ is to share the motives, purposes and the way of life that led Jesus to the Cross. It is to take up burdens of others while forgiving and loving, instead of condemning.

"I do not nullify the grace of God; for if justification were through the law, then Christ died to no puropse." (Verse 21)

Paul closes the first part of his letter with a statement that Christ's death cannot have been wasted. If the law had been capable of bringing about righteousness, Christ would not have needed to die.

Jesus gave himself to men as Savior. He gave himself fully and completely at the Cross. That Cross is the fullest expression of His grace.

LESSON IN LIFE

To bear His Cross is to be like Him, to make His cause our cause, and to be willing to live in His service.

Let your religion be seen. Lamps do not talk—they shine. If your religion does not shine in your works, you have pretty poor religious oil in your lamp!

The value of religion is judged by the fruit it produces, the character it develops, the actions it motivates. True religion is known by its fruits.

You can show your religious convictions by the way you react to people, by the things you do and say each day, and by how you live. You never show them by argument. To get along with people, we must first find God.

Someone said, "I would give nothing for that man's religion whose very dog and cat are not the better for it."

Salvation is not a matter of faith *or* works, but rather, as James points out, faith *and* works.

Confronting the Pagan World

How should Christians approach a pagan world with the message of the Gospel? A different approach is needed for different people. The early church disturbed its society with its Gospel. Are we disturbing ours?

Paul Confronts Intellectuals

Acts 17:16–17

"Now while Paul was waiting for them at Athens, his spirit was provoked within him as he saw that the city was full of idols." (Verse 16)

"Paul was waiting" for Silas and Timothy to come from Macedonia to join him "at Athens." As he walked around the streets of Athens, he could not help but be "provoked" when "he saw that the city was full of idols." Someone has estimated that there were around thirty thousand statues to gods. Athens was famed for the number of religious cults. It was the seat of a famous university and was the world's intellectual mecca also.

"So he argued in the synagogue with the Jews and the devout persons, and in the market place every day with those who chanced to be there." (Verse 17)

Paul was stirred to action by what he saw. He felt that a city with so much false religion must be given the Gospel.

Paul was alone in Athens. But with comrades or alone, Paul never stopped preaching Christ.

Christianity Confronting Philosophy

Acts 17:18–19,32

"Some also of the Epicurean and Stoic philosophers met him. And some said, "What would this babbler say?' Others said, 'He seems to be a preacher of a foreign divinities'—because he preached Jesus and the resurrection." (Verse 18).

These were the two most influential schools of philosophy at the time. The Epicureans had happiness as its main aim. The Stoics believed that God was a Spirit and a part of everything. When they died, the Spirit returned to God. They believed in fate and whatever happened was the will of God. Therefore, whatever happened, we must not care.

"Babble" literally means "seed-picker." The term seems to have been used first of birds that picked up grain, then of men who picked up odds and ends in the market. A "babbler," then, was someone who dealt in second-hand scraps of philosophy.

"And they took hold of him and brought him to the Areopagus, saying, 'May we know what this new teaching is which you present?'" (Verse 19)

They took Paul to the Areopagus, which is Greek for "Mars Hill." It was the name of both the hill and the court that met on it.

The court was very select. Before this exclusive court in the most learned city in the world, Paul had to state his faith. It might have frightened anyone, but Paul was never ashamed of the Gospel of Christ. To him, it was another God-given opportunity to witness for Jesus.

"Now when they heard of the resurrection of the dead, some mocked, but others said, 'We will hear you again about this.'" (Verse 32)

This verse and the two that follow tells of the reaction to Paul's sermon. Some of the hearers "mocked," others suggested that they would hear more of the apostle's teaching at a later time.

Christianity Against Culture

Acts 19:23–29

"About that time there arose no little stir concerning the Way." (Verse 23)

Paul was now at Ephesus, the chief city of western Asia Minor. "The Way" was a term to describe the Christian fellowship and life—"The Way" of Christ, the way of salvation, the Christian way. Jesus had called Himself "The Way." Paul's Ephesus experience was much like that which he had in other cities. He preached Christ, people were converted, then opposition would arise.

"For a man named Demetrius, a silversmith, who made silver shrines of Artemis, brought no little business to the craftsmen." (Verse 24)

At Ephesus was the world-famous temple of the goddess, Artemis, (Latin, *Diana*). When pilgrims came to Ephesus, they liked to take a little souvenir home. Demetrius, a silversmith, was a maker of model silver shrines which were bought and sold as souvenirs. Images of the goddess could be seen in many homes and the making of the images kept scores of silversmiths busy and rich.

"There he gathered together, with the workmen of like occupation, and said, 'Men, you know that from this business we have our wealth.'" (Verse 25)

Demetrius gathered together his fellow craftsmen and told them that their prosperity depended upon this work.

"And you see and hear that not only at Ephesus but almost throughout all Asia this Paul has persuaded and turned away a considerable company of people, saying that gods made with hands are not gods. And there is danger not only that this trade of ours may come into disrepute but also that the temple of the great goddess Artemis may count for nothing, and that she may even be deposed from her magnificence, she whom all Asia and the world worship." (Verses 26–27)

As Paul converted people to the Christian faith, they gave up idolatry. As a result, the sale of silver shrines fell off and the silversmiths business was hurt.

Demetrius, in a clever speech, turned his fellow craftsmen to anger by an appeal to their business instincts and their religious loyalty to Artemis. Not only was their livelihood at stake, but also, the validity of their religion.

"When they heard this they were enraged, and cried out, 'Great is Artemis of the Ephesians.'" (Verse 28)

There is nothing that so stirs people into frenzy as a religious battle cry based upon sound business principles.

"So the city was filled with the confusion; and they rushed together into the theater, dragging with them Gaius and Aris-

tarchus, Macedonians who were Paul's companions in travel."
(Verse 29)

It is interesting and frightening to see how quickly a mob can gather. They rushed to the great open air theaters whose impressive ruins still stand. They took with them two of Paul's helpers.

LESSON IN LIFE

The silversmiths of Ephesus believed Paul was wrong when he interferred with their business.

"Silversmiths" in our church shut their eyes to the teachings of the Bible if these teachings encroach on their economic interests.

A business that will not stand religion is a business to be afraid of and avoided. Religion and business should mix if it is the right kind of business and the right kind of religion.

God's New Covenant

We now will consider what God had to say to His new covenant people and what they are to be and do in the world.

A human covenant is a solemn and binding promise and relationship between individuals and groups. The Bible mentions covenants between God and individuals, and especially between God and His people, Israel. In the New Testament, the word is also used to describe the relationship between God and man.

The letter to the Hebrews was written to Hebrew Christians living in Rome. These people had come out of Judaism into the Christian faith. In the New Testament, the name "Hebrews" meant Aramaic-speaking Jewish Christians, or those who had been born Jews.

It was written to a scholarly group who were probably preparing themselves to become teachers of the Christian faith. Understanding the Book of Hebrews demands such a knowledge of the Old Testament that it must have been a book written by a scholar for scholars.

Hebrews exalted Christ. He is shown to be superior to all others—the prophets, angels, Moses and Aaron. The book gives us a glorious picture of Jesus Christ, in all the splendor of His manhood and in all the majesty of His deity.

The letter to the Hebrews is a difficult book to read. However, I believe there is no book in the New Testament which is more worth the effort to understand.

The Better Covenant

Hebrews 8:6–9

"But as it is, Christ has obtained a ministry which is as much more excellent than the old as the covenant he mediates is better, since it is enacted on better promises." (Verse 6)

Christ established the better covenant, based on better promises, providing a ministry that is more excellent. The writer to the Hebrews calls Jesus a "mediator." This word comes from the Greek word "mesites," which means "one who stands in the middle between two people and brings them together."

Jesus is our Mediator. He stands between us and God. He can bring about this union and reconciliation between men and God.

"For if that first covenant had been faultless, there would have been no occasion for a second." (Verse 7)

The ancient covenant was the covenant made with the people after the giving of the Law.

The idea of a new covenant was mentioned in Jeremiah hundreds of years ago. The fact that Scripture itself speaks of the new covenant shows that the old covenant was not fully satisfactory because had it been so, a new covenant would never need to have been mentioned.

"For he finds fault with them when he says: 'The days will come, says the Lord, when I will establish a new covenant with the house of Israel and with the house of Judah.'" (Verse 8)

The author quotes Jeremiah, one of the prophets. It was Jeremiah who predicted the establishment of the new covenant. The covenant which Jesus brings is new.

"Not like the covenant that I made with their fathers on the day when I took them by the hand to lead them out of the land of Egypt; for they did not continue in my covenant, and so I paid no heed to them, says the Lord." (Verse 9)

Throughout the Old Testament, the bondage in "the land of Egypt" is given high significance. It was dramatic evidence of Israel's dependence upon the mercy of God.

God led and provided for the people of Israel throughout the journey from Egypt, and through the wilderness. He led them by hand, as a parent leads a child.

When the people departed from Egypt under the leadership of Moses, they came to Mount Sinai, where God gave them the Law.

The new covenant was necessary because "they continued not in my covenant." The old covenant had been broken.

The Nature of The New Covenant

Hebrews 8:10

"This is the covenant that I will make with the house of Israel after those days, says the Lord: I will put my laws into their minds and unto them on their hearts and I will be their God and they shall be my people." (Verse 10)

Under the old covenant, the Israelites were educated in the Law. The people could not live up to the terms of the old covenant. The old law was written upon tablets of stone. It was legal and external. The new covenant was to be written upon man's heart and mind. Men would obey God not because the law ordered them to do so, but because the desire to obey Him was written on their hearts. The desire to obey would be in a man's own heart. Only when men find their joy in doing the will of God has the Law of God been written on their hearts. Those who come under the new covenant experience an inward change. They will worship Him "in spirit and in truth." (John 4:24)

God will love, guide, and keep this people. "I will be their God, and they shall be my people." This is the fulfillment of the covenant and the purpose of the Gospel. When this comes to pass, salvation is complete, man is redeemed, and evil is overcome. This is the answer to our prayers.

The Knowledge of The New Covenant

Hebrews 8:11–12

"And they shall not teach every one his fellow or every one his brother, saying, 'Know the Lord; for all shall know me, from the least of them to the greatest.'" (Verse 11)

What is described here is the doctrine of the priesthood of all believers. All believers will enjoy this personal knowledge of God. God speaks directly through His words by the Holy Spirit to every believer's heart.

"For I will be merciful toward their iniquities, and I will remember their sins no more." (Verse 12)

Men carry a burden of guilt. The new covenant offers complete forgiveness for all sins. Jesus Christ is the world's only Savior.

There will now be real fellowship between God and man—no longer disrupted by the remembrance of sin.

The new relationship is based on the love of God. Under the old covenant, a man could keep this relationship to God only by obeying the law. Now, everything is dependent not on man's efforts, but on the love, mercy and grace of God. When one is saved, God forgives and forgets. The believer's sins are put away.

The Old Is Obsolete

Hebrews 8:13

"In speaking of a new covenant he treats the first as obsolete. And what is becoming obsolete and growing old is ready to vanish away." (Verse 13)

Now, in Christ, the old order has ended and the new order, the new convenant in Christ, has taken its place.

LESSON IN LIFE

God is not way out there somewhere. His Kingdom is within the heart of the believer. That was part of the new covenant— one of the great blessings of the personal presence of Christ. We become His people and He our God. He says to us, "I will be with you always."

It is God present in our hearts that inspires us to be like Him. This makes us people of the new covenant.

As a believer, we are not only promised that the Lord will be our God, but we are to be to Him a people. We shall reflect Him. We shall share His work. We shall praise His name. We shall spread His word.

The Nature of the Church

Ephesians deals with the spiritual unity which exists between Christ and His Church. The Epistle of the Ephesians has been called the Epistle of the Church. The theme is the Church which is the body of Christ—a new and spiritual community created by God.

Jew And Gentile United In The Church

Ephesians 2:11-12

"Therefore remember that at one time you Gentiles in the flesh, called the uncircumcision by what is called the circumcision, which is made in the flesh by hands . . ." (Verse 11)

The letter was written to Gentile Christians. In the church, the Jew and Gentile are united in a single worshiping community.

The writer calls the Gentile believers to remember their former state of their religious condition as seen from the Jewish point of view. They were to remember what they were before becoming Christians, and what they were now by the grace of God.

"Remember that you were at that time separated from Christ, alienated from the commonwealth of Israel, and strangers to the covenants of promise, having no hope and without God in the world." (Verse 12)

Here is one of the great phrases of the Bible. Here is a description of the Gentile converts before they had been reborn into the new life with God. They were "separated from Christ." They had no deliverer. They were without the hope of the Messiah. They did not know God and had no promise of future blessings.

They were also "alienated from the commonwealth of Israel." The word "commonwealth" means "the sum total of what makes up the full life of a citizen." Israel was the commonwealth of

God in the Old Testament. The people of Israel were different from other peoples in that, in the realest sense, their only king was God.

New Relationship

"But now in Christ Jesus you who once were far off have been brought near in the blood of Christ." (Verse 13)

The Gentiles were "far off" and in need of redemption. They had been without Christ, without citizenship, without promise, without hope, and without God in the world.

"For He is our peace, who has made us both one, and has broken down the dividing wall of hostility . . ." (Verse 14)

In the Jerusalem temple, there was a wall between the outer court into which the Gentiles could enter and the inner courts, into which only Jews could go. That dividing wall that separated Jews from Gentiles was broken down in Christ. Gentiles and Jews alike were able to share their spiritual faith.

"By abolishing in His flesh the law of commandments and ordinances, that he might create in himself one new man in place of the two, so making peace . . ." (Verse 15)

The Law given to the Jews marked them off from the Gentiles. The Law came from God. He abolished the Law, causing His Son to fulfill it once for all—to fulfill it far and away beyond its claims. Christ "in His flesh" on the Cross abolished the Law—not its meaning, but the Law with its rules and regulations. Salvation is of grace by faith, and not through obeying laws.

Christ brings together Jew and Gentile. Jesus does not make the Gentiles into Jews or Jews into Gentiles. He produces a "new" kind of person, thus bringing peace. This unity is not achieved by blotting out racial and national characteristics. It is achieved by making all men of all nations Christians.

Sometimes, we try to win others to be externally like ourselves. We try to produce people who wear the same clothes, speak the same language, and act as we do.

It is not Jesus' purpose to turn all men into one nation, but rather, that there should be Christian Indians and Christian

Africans whose unity lies in their Christianity. The oneness in Christ is in Christ and not necessarily in any external change. The "new man" is the creation of Christ.

"And might reconcile us both to God in one body through the Cross, thereby bringing the hostility to an end." (Verse 16)

He took Jew and Gentile and formed them into one body to make up His Church. Reconciliation with God involves reconciliation with man. Jesus died for all men.

"And He came and preached peace to you who were far off and peace to those who were near." (Verse 17)

The peace Christ has established is preached to all men everywhere. At Jesus' birth, the angels sang of peace on earth, good will toward men.

"For through him we both have access in one Spirit to the Father." (Verse 18)

The unity in Christ produces men who are friends with each other. It produces men who are one because they met in the presence of God to whom they have access.

Fellow Citizens With The Saints

Ephesians 2:19–20

"So then you are no longer strangers and sojourners, but you are fellow citizens with the saints and members of the household of God." (Verse 19)

In ancient times, the stranger in the land was without rights and protection. A sojourner was a person who had come to stay in a place, but had never become a naturalized citizen. The stranger and sojourner were always on the fringe. Before Christ came, the Gentiles seemed to be outside of God's people. Paul says that the Gentiles are now real citizens of the society of God. Through Jesus, we are at home with God.

"Built upon the foundation of the apostles and prophets, Christ Jesus himself being the chief cornerstone . . ." (Verse 20)

Paul changes his picture again to help his readers realize their new position. Not only are the Gentiles at home in the House of God, but they make up this House. Every Christian is as a stone built into a church.

Dwelling Place of God

Ephesians 2:21-22

"In whom the whole structure is joined together and grows into a holy temple in the Lord . . ." (Verse 21)

The words suggest the growth of a living organism. Christians are the living stones. New stones (Christians) are constantly being added—and the building grows. The suggestion is of a building consisting of many parts. The goal of the building is "a holy temple in the Lord."

"In whom you also are built into it for a dwelling place of God in the Spirit." (Verse 22)

God's Spirit dwells in this spiritual building. God "does not dwell in houses made with hands." His true habitation is the community of the redeemed. Jews and Gentiles are stones built into God's dwelling place, the Church.

LESSON IN LIFE

Passages from Ephesians tell us something of the nature of the church.

The church is Christ-centered. The church exists where men are in union with Christ and peace with one another. Christ is the head and power of the church. The church is the people of God. It is a people of privilege and responsibility. Many want the privileges, but not the responsibilities of church membership.

The unity of the church comes from Christ. The church exists to give a home and dwelling place where the Spirit of Christ can dwell, and where all men who love Christ can meet in that Spirit.

Unredeemed man can build towers of Babel, pyramids of Egypt, and skyscrapers of New York, but only the Holy Spirit can build a Christian church. "Know ye not that ye are the temple of God, and that the Spirit of God dwelleth in you?" (I Corinthians 3:16)

Meaningful Worship

One of the nurses in my office was late to work. When she turned the starter of her car, nothing happened. Someone had cut the wires to the engine. The connection was broken. There was no power.

Until a person comes in contact with the living Christ, he is spiritually dead. When he accepts Christ, he is spiritually alive with power given by the Holy Spirit.

The Lord's Supper

I Corinthians 11:23–26

"For I received from the Lord what I also delivered to you, that the Lord Jesus on the night when he was betrayed took bread." (Verse 23)

Upon leaving the Upper Room, Jesus went to the garden where He was betrayed by Judas. This was a solemn night for Jesus, but He was thinking of His disciples. This sacred rite was instituted on the last night of our Redeemer's life, even though He knew what tomorrow would bring.

"And when he had given thanks, he broke it, and said, 'This is my body which is for you. Do this in remembrance of me.'" (Verse 24)

In any true observance of the Supper, one is in communion with Christ and is in living contact with Him. It is a joyful celebration of the presence of the living Christ in the midst of His Church.

The Master has given to His Church for all time this sacred rite as a reminder of His willing sacrifice. The breaking of the bread is a symbol of the sufferings Christ endured for His people. His body was bruised and wounded for our salvation.

Men everywhere may be assured that the love and power revealed in the Lord's sacrifice are available for them. This Sacrament has become the most sacred and priceless element of our heritage in Christ.

"In the same way also the cup, after supper, saying 'This is the new covenant in my blood. Do this, as often as you drink it, in remembrance of me.'" (Verse 25)

There was an old covenant between God and man based on law. With Jesus, a new relationship is opened to man which is dependent on love. It depends on the free grace of the love of God offered to man. It cost the life of Jesus to make that new relationship possible. "The blood is the life," says the law. (Deuteronomy 12:23)

It cost Jesus' life, Jesus' blood, to make that relationship possible. The wine of the sacrament stands for the very life-blood of Christ without which the new covenant, the new relationship to God, could never have been possible.

"In remembrance of me" calls for a serious recollection of His life, death, spiritual presence, and fellowship with believers. We remember who God is and what He has done for us through Christ. It is a reminder of the Lord's death till He comes again to claim His church.

"For as often as you eat this bread and drink the cup, you proclaim the Lord's death until he comes." (I Corinthians 11:26)

We may note that the frequency of the Supper is not indicated, but that its significance is emphasized. In the Supper, there is both a backward and forward look. The sacrifice of forgiveness is remembered, and the Lord's return proclaimed. The Christian Church worships not a dead Christ, but rather, a living Lord. The Sacrament is observed not only for the redemptive sacrifice made, but also for a living Christ—to wait upon Him and His manifestation in final, complete triumph. This memorial meal was to be kept until the end of history, when Christ would establish His perfect Kingdom.

Speaking With Tongues

I Corinthians 14:23–26,40

"If, therefore, the whole church assembles and all speak in tongues, and outsiders or unbelievers enter, will they not say that you are mad?" (Verse 23)

The spiritual gifts (Charisma) were bestowed upon the apostles. They were also given to others. These spiritual gifts were given to further the work of the Lord, or to edify the church. In using them, the Christian must consider the effects on the "outsiders or unbelievers." A mass confusion of babble could not bring inspiration or conviction to the unbelievers. Those who do not possess the Spirit get an impression of insanity from the speaking of tongues. These frenzied utterances would, Paul felt, make outsiders think the Christians were crazy. Worship should build up the faith and life of the Christian who takes part in it.

"But if all prophesy, and an unbeliever or outsider enters, he is convicted by all, he is called to account and by all." (Verse 24)

Speaking in tongues, if not interpreted, can do little to edify the unbeliever.

The first thing that the message of God does is to make man realize that he is a sinner. It makes a man see that he must answer for what he has done. Great preaching has, as its purpose, the bringing of those who hear into the very presence of God.

"The secrets of his heart are disclosed; and so, falling on his face, he will worship God and declare that God is really among you." (Verse 25)

The Christian message compels a man to face himself. It also brings a man to his knees before God. When a man has faced both God and himself, all that is left is to kneel and pray. "God be merciful to me a sinner."

"When then, brethren? When you come together, each one has a hymn, a lesson, a revelation, a tongue, or an interpretation. Let all things be done for edification." (Verse 26)

This is an interesting section in the letter, for it sheds light on what a church service was like in the early church. The Corinthians' worship does not strike us as very formal. The service had no set pattern. Each person took part as he felt led to do so. The service resembled the Quaker form more nearly than any in existence today.

Paul gave some practical advice. He was determined that anyone who possessed a gift should receive every chance to exercise that gift, but everything should be done for mutual edification.

"But all things should be done decently and in order." (Verse 40).

He made it clear that he had no wish to quench anyone's gift. Paul was interested in a proper and orderly worship. The church should be conducted in an orderly manner, but to remain open for the exercise of spiritual gifts. Worship services should avoid those things which contribute to disorder and confusion.

The spirit of Paul shines through all that he wrote. He was the "man in Christ" who bore upon his loving heart a great concern for the life and well-being of the church.

LESSON IN LIFE

It does not matter if the place of worship is a lofty cathedral or a plain room with four walls, so long as the act of worship brings us into the presence of God. It will affect the work and play of the days that follow.

One day, a married couple was driving down the road. The wife turned to her husband, who was driving, and said, "Do you remember how close together we used to sit in the car?" The husband replied, "I haven't moved."

If God seems far off, distant and remote to you, remember that He has not moved. He will draw near to us as we draw near to Him.

When we go to our worship service, let us present ourselves to the Lord in prayer. Every Christian has a responsibility for making the worship services of his church more meaningful for himself and others. Christ stands at the heart of all Christian worship.

Worship is a spiritual experience. We need to achieve this spiritual quality by participating in the worship service—singing the hymns of praise, joining in the prayers, listening to the Word as it is preached, and meditating. We should also be willing to use our time, talents and money.

True worship brings an awareness of God, the peace of cleansing, inspiration for service, and transformation of life.

If we worship the living God, we shall be like Him!

The Christian in the World

Paul wrote the Epistle to the Romans from Corinth while on his third missionary journey. This book comes nearest to being a statement of Paul's faith.

These verses deal with some of the practical admonitions concerning how to live in Christ and offer inspired guidance for everyday Christian living. These are some of the most basic practical truths that are preserved in the Word of God. Paul taught that Christianity is more than a system of doctrine. It is a life lived in right relationship with God and man.

Finding And Doing The Will Of God

Romans 12:1–2

"I appeal to you therefore, brethren, by the mercies of God, to present your bodies as a living sacrifice, holy and acceptable to God, which is your spiritual worship." (Verse 1)

"Present your bodies as a living sacrifice" is a giving of one's whole life and all its abilities to God in grateful service. The body is the temple of the Holy Spirit. The Christian believes that his body belongs to God. The total man, body, soul and spirit must be dedicated to the Glory of God.

The true worship is the offering of one's body and all that one does every day with it, to God. We cease to live to ourselves in order that we may live to Him.

The word "holy" means "consecrated," "set apart." "Acceptable" means "well-pleasing."

Consecrated obedient living is the spiritual worship God wants. In many passages, Jesus made it clear that He wanted His disciples to understand the terms of following Him. He never lowered His standards to get disciples. Are we willing to pay the price to follow Jesus?

"Do not be conformed to this world but be transformed by

the renewal of your mind, that you may prove what is the will of God, what is good and acceptable and perfect." (Verse 2)

The Christian is not to let his life be shaped and molded by the world. The world is that area from which God is excluded. The Christian is not to adopt its customs and ways. A threat to the dedicated life is the pull of the environment in which one lives. So many church members accept without question the intellectual and social atmosphere of the age.

"Prove" here means "know surely." One cannot have such knowledge of God's will unless one's mind has been renewed and one's life reoriented. With a new insight, we discover what God would have us do.

When a person is transformed, he is able to realize what is the perfect will of God. Such a person demonstrates commitment to the will of God.

Formula For Christian Behavior
Romans 12:14-21

"Bless those who persecute you; bless and do not curse them." (Verse 14)

There can be little doubt that Paul is thinking of persons outside the church when he speaks of "those who persecute you." Christian behavior outside the church is of great importance. "Bless" means "to speak well of" or "to praise" or "to pray for."

The Christian must meet persecution with a prayer for those who persecute him. When the Christian is hurt and insulted, he has the example of His master before him. Love must govern our behavior. Paul said that blessing is the right attitude, but he did not suggest it is natural or easy. Many a persecutor has become a follower of the faith because he has seen how a Christian can forgive.

"Rejoice with those who rejoice, weep with those who weep." (Verse 15)

To rejoice with others calls for complete absence of any envy or jealousy of another's success. We are apt to envy those who rejoice, rather than share in their happiness. Someone said that it requires more Christian love to rejoice with the joyful than it does to weep with someone who suffered calamity. Christians should live in sympathy and helpfulness with persons in all kinds of situations.

"Live in harmony with one another; do not be haughty but associate with the lowly; never be conceited." (Verse 16)

Christians should bring harmony, rather than discord. It is easy to magnify differences and overlook things that unite us.

We are to avoid pride and snobbishness. It is wrong to have respect of persons because of wealth, fame or position.

"Repay no one evil for evil, but take thought for what is noble in the sight of all." (Verse 17)

Nothing can justify revenge to anyone. The spirit of getting even is contrary to the Christ-way of life. What happens if we suffer evil? We are not to repay in like manner. Christians should be noble and honorable in all things.

"If possible, so far as it depends upon you, live peacefully with all." (Verse 18)

Not only does this mean that one must do one's utmost to avoid arousing another's anger or resentment, but also that one must not be angry in return. The true Christian will not rest until he has tried in every way to bring about reconciliation.

"Beloved, never avenge yourselves, but leave it to the wrath of God; for it is written, 'Vengeance is mine, I will repay, says the Lord.'" (Verse 19)

The Christian is not to take the law into his own hands to vindicate himself. Vengeance does not belong to us; it belongs to God. In the last analysis, no human being has the right to judge another; only God can do that.

"No, 'If your enemy is hungry, feed him; if he is thirsty, give him drink; for by so doing you will heap burning coals upon his head.'" (Verse 20)

"You will heap burning coals upon his head" means that this kindness will move him to shame. Love for enemies will fill those enemies with the burning pain of shame and remorse. No doubt, Paul hoped these "coals of fire" would strengthen the heart and bring them to a faith in Christ.

"Do not be overcome by evil but overcome evil with good." (Verse 21)

To stoop to vengeance is to be overcome by evil. Evil can

never be conquered by evil. We are not to hate our enemies. To do so is to be overcome by the very evil which conquered Him.

Love Is The Road

"Owe no one anything, except to love one another; for he who loves his neighbor has fulfilled the law." (Verse 8)

Paul goes on to speak of the debt that a man must pay every day. That is the debt to love one another. It is Paul's claim that if a man does this, he will have kept the commandment and fufilled the law. In the deepest sense, one should live in the attitude of love. Love is the gift of the Spirit. When one truly loves God and his neighbor, he has fulfilled the law. Christianity cannot be reduced to laws and regulations. Love is the road Christians should follow.

LESSON IN LIFE

Christians live in the world, but are not like the world. They are responsive to the world and its needs, but responsible and accountable to God.

The Christian must always love even his enemies. He must show good will toward all. He must do this for the sake of others, but also for his own sake. The spiritual life is sapped by hatred. It costs to hold a grudge. Such a person is committing spiritual suicide.

To be like others, return good for good. To be like the devil, return evil for good. To be like God, return good for evil.

Christian love is a positive contribution to the world. It may bring a knowledge of God to others.

The Christian Hope

The passages from the Book of Revelation present the Christian hope.

The Book of Revelation is sometimes called the Apocalypse, which means "an unveiling," "a revealing," "a disclosure of that which is hidden and secret."

Apocalypticism is the belief that the power of evil (Satan), who is now in control, is soon to be overcome by God. He will create a new perfect and eternal age under His control for His righteous followers from the living and resurrected dead.

It is helpful to know the historical background. The Book of Revelation was written to churches that had known persecution. The message was intended to encourage and strengthen the faith of fellow Christians who were in danger of their lives. They were being persecuted by Roman officials for their refusal to worship the emperor. Against this background, John wrote the magnificent message of hope and triumph found in the Revelations.

Man's Hope—The New Creation

Revelation 21:1–4

"Then I saw a new heaven and a new earth; for the first heaven and the first earth had passed away, and the sea was no more." (Verse 1)

The dream of a new heaven and a new earth was a dream that was deep in Jewish thought. Isaiah spoke of the new heaven and the new earth which God will make, wherein life will be one continual act of worship to God (Isaiah 66:22). This idea is also strong between the Testaments.

"And the sea was no more" is one of the most famous phrases in the Revelation. The ancient peoples hated the sea. One who took a sea voyage faced disaster. People were afraid of it. In the new age, there would be no fear. In Jewish dreams, the end of the sea is the end of a power hostile to God and man. In God's new world, everything that terrifies man would be removed.

279

"And I saw the holy city, new Jerusalem, coming down out of heaven from God, prepared as a bride adorned for her husband." (Verse 2)

The "holy city" would have a heavenly origin. It would come down from God out of heaven.

When we read John's version of the new Jerusalem, we find that it uses and amplifies many of the dreams of the new Jerusalem which the prophets already had. Even when Jerusalem was battered and broken, the Jews never lost their faith that God would restore it. The term "new Jerusalem" is used figuratively for the divine society redeemed in glory.

The new Jerusalem is compared to a bride—the perfect symbol of happiness. It is a happy place because God is to be in the midst of His people forever.

"And I heard a great voice from the throne saying, 'Behold, the dwelling of God is with men. He will dwell with them, and they shall be His people, and God himself will be with them." (Verse 3)

A voice is now heard from the throne summarizing the blessings that the inhabitants of the eternal city will enjoy.

Here is the promise of fellowship with God. The supremely important truth about the new Jerusalem is the presence of God. God is to give His presence to men forever and ever. Life in heaven will be life permanently in the presence of God.

"He will wipe away every tear from their eyes, and death shall be no more, neither shall there be mourning nor crying nor pain any more, for the former things have passed away." (Verse 4)

The result of God's presence with His people is that there will be no more tears or death or mourning or crying or pain to distract men. This is a promise for the future. Death is swallowed up in victory for those who know Christ.

The Presence of God

Revelation 21:22–27

"And I saw no temple in the city, for its temple is the Lord God the Almighty and the Lamb." (Verse 22)

The new Jerusalem has no temple, for the whole city is full of the presence of "the Lord God, the Almighty and the Lamb." The reason why the city needs no temple is that the presence of both God and the Lamb is continually there.

The absence of the temple is in keeping with the Christian view expressed in Hebrews 9:23–28, that the sacrifice of Christ made once and for all has done away with all other sacrifice.

"And the city has no need of sun or moon to shine upon it, for the glory of God is its light, and its lamp is the lamb." (Verse 23)

There will be no sun or moon in the new Jerusalem, for "the glory of God is its light, and its lamp is the lamb." The lamb is one of John's favorite descriptions for Christ. In Revelation, Christ is spoken of as the slain Passover Lamb by whose sacrificed blood the martyrs are redeemed.

Only when we see things in the light of God do we see things as they are. Things which now seem important, such as ambition, money, prestige, pleasure and social position, lose their lure and importance when seen in the light of God.

"By its light shall the nations walk; and the kings of the earth shall bring their glory into it." (Verse 24)

The redeemed are from all nations of the earth. In the new Kingdom, the kings of the earth will bring glory to a King who is greater than all.

Isaiah has the picture of the day when all nations will go up to Mount Zion to be taught the Law, and to learn to walk in the ways of God (Isaiah 2:2–4).

"And nations shall come to your light, and kings to the brightness of your rising." (Isaiah 60:3)

Also, we read in Zechariah 14:9, "And the Lord will become king over all the earth; on that day the Lord will be one and his name one."

When John pictured the nations walking in the light of the city of God and the kings bringing their gifts to it, he was foretelling the consumation of a hope which was always in the heart of the greatest of his countrymen.

"And its gates shall never be shut by day—and there shall be no night there." (Revelation 21:25)

In ancient days, a city was surrounded by a protective wall.

This verse indicates there will be no need to safeguard the city, since all evil will have been destroyed.

More than once, John insists there will be no night in the city of God. The ancient people were afraid of the dark. In the new world, the frightening dark will be no more, for the presence of God will bring eternal light. With all the fears of today, we still need to remember that where God is, there is the light of God. In the new age, the darkness will be gone and there will be nothing but light.

"But nothing unclean shall enter it, nor any one who practices abomination or falsehood, but only those who are written in the Lamb's book of life." (Verse 27)

The Lamb's "Book of Life" is the book of one who loved men enough to die for them. Only those who say "No" to the love that speaks from the Cross are refused a place in the Lamb's Book of Life.

One can get in *Who's Who in America* by achievement. One can get in the social bluebook by birth or wealth. We can be sure of heaven, not by what we have done or who we are, but only by receiving Christ and what He has done for us.

LESSON IN LIFE

In these verses, we read the climax of the story of redemption. The ultimate and complete fulfillment of God's promise is revealed in the blessings and joys of the redeemed in the true holy city. The Christian's hope is realized. God's children have come home to be with the Father and there is peace, rejoicing and gladness.

This is God's answer to the longing of men to know about the future life.

Heaven is a place of perfect fellowship, perfect protection, perfect provision of needs and perfect service of God. There is a great contrast between the destiny of the wicked and the destiny of the redeemed.

Hope is the anchor of the soul. Hope is for both the living and the dying. Hope is for the hopeless. This is the Gospel.

"Whosoever believeth in him shall not perish but have everlasting life."

Brengle Memorial Library
DISCARD
The Salvation Army
School for Officer Training
Suffern, N.Y.